Envision It! | Visual Skills Handbook

Author's Purpose

Inform

Entertain

An author writes for many purposes, some of which are to inform, entertain, persuade, or express a mood or feeling. An author may have more than one purpose for writing. Sometimes the author's purpose is directly stated, but other times you have to figure it out on your own.

Persuade

Express

Categorize and Classify

When we categorize and classify, we look at how people or things are related based on their characteristics.

Cause and Effect

An effect can have more than one cause.

A cause is why something happened.

A cause can have more than one effect.

An effect is what happened.

Compare and Contrast

To compare and contrast is to look for similarities and differences in things.

Draw Conclusions

When we draw conclusions, we think about facts and details and then decide something about them.

Fact and Opinion

A statement of fact is something that can be proved true or false. A statement of opinion can't be proved.

Fact

Wow, you blew the tuba for 45 seconds straight!

Opinion

But I think it sounds HORRIBLE!

Generalize

To generalize is to make a broad statement or rule that applies to many examples.

Batteries never last very long.

Graphic Sources

Graphic sources show information in a way the reader can see.

Table/Chart

Tables and charts are boxes, squares, or rectangles that categorize information in rows and columns.

The Case of the Park Litterbugs

Detective on duty	Day	Garbage found
Jaime	Sunday	9
Jessica	Monday	11
Eric	Tuesday	2
Me	Wednesday	3
Ana Luz	Thursday	5
Milton	Friday	7
Libby	Saturday	15

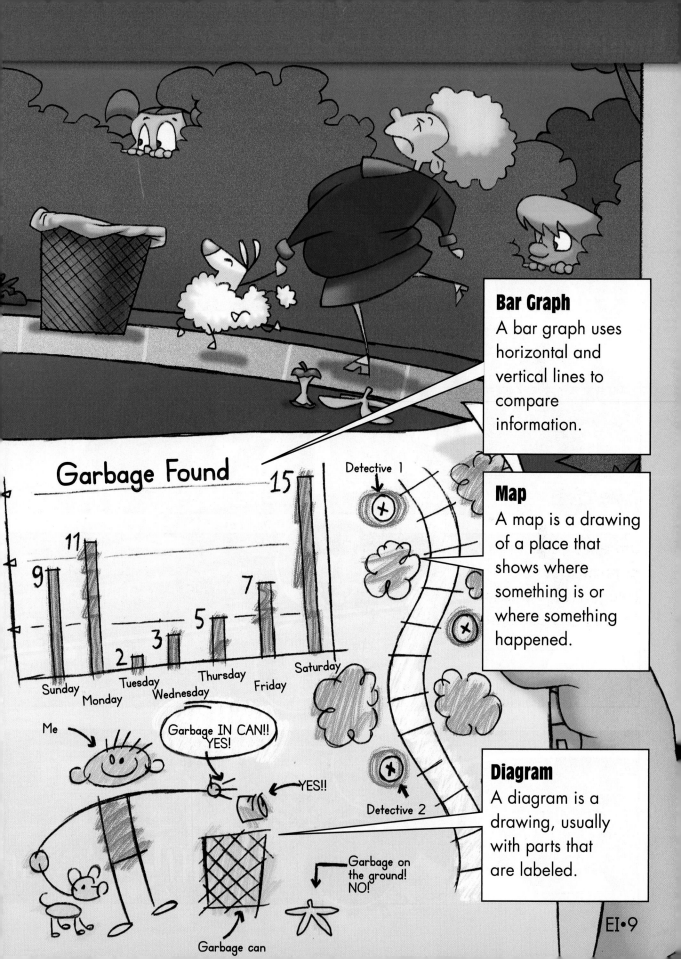

Bar Graph
A bar graph uses horizontal and vertical lines to compare information.

Map
A map is a drawing of a place that shows where something is or where something happened.

Diagram
A diagram is a drawing, usually with parts that are labeled.

Garbage Found

15
11
9
7
5
3
2

Sunday Monday Tuesday Wednesday Thursday Friday Saturday

Detective 1

Detective 2

Me

Garbage IN CAN!! YES!

YES!!

Garbage on the ground! NO!

Garbage can

EI•9

Room To Grow

Literary Elements

Stories are made up of four main elements: character, setting, plot, and theme. Each of these parts gives you an overall understanding of the story.

Characters

A character is a person or an animal in a story.

Setting

The setting is the time and place in which a story happens.

Plot

The plot is the pattern of events in a story.

The plot starts with a problem or goal and builds toward a climax. The plot ends with a resolution or outcome.

Theme

The theme is the big idea of a story. We look at the plot, setting, or characters to determine the theme of a story.

Main Idea and Details

Main idea is the most important idea about a topic. Details support the main idea.

Sequence

Sequence refers to the order of events in text. We also use sequence when we list the steps in a process.

Envision It! | Visual Strategies Handbook

Background Knowledge

Important Ideas

Inferring

Monitor and Clarify

Predict and Set Purpose

Questioning

Story Structure

Summarize

Text Structure

Visualize

Background Knowledge

Background knowledge is what you already know about a topic based on your reading and personal experience. Make connections to people, places, and things. Use background knowledge before, during, and after reading to monitor comprehension.

To use background knowledge
- with fiction, preview the title, author's name, and illustrations
- with nonfiction, preview chapter titles, headings, graphics, and other text features
- think about what you already know

Officer Lee and Freckles remind me of characters in a fantastic book I am reading about working dogs.

Let's Think About Reading!

When I use background knowledge, I ask myself
- Does this character remind me of someone?
- How is this story or text similar to others I have read?
- What else do I know about this topic from what I've read or seen?

Important Ideas

Important ideas are essential ideas in a nonfiction selection. Important ideas include information that provide clues to the author's purpose.

To identify important ideas
- read all titles, headings, and captions
- look for words in italics, boldface print, or bulleted lists
- look for signal words and phrases: *for example, most important,* and others
- use any photos, illustrations, diagrams, or maps
- note how the text is organized—cause and effect, problem and solution, or other ways

Wow! The lettering is in bold type.

It must be an important idea.

Types of Clouds

Let's Think About Reading!

When I identify important ideas, I ask myself
- What information is included in bold, italics, or other special lettering?
- What details support important ideas?
- Are there signal words and phrases?
- What do illustrations, photos, diagrams, and charts show?
- How is the text organized?
- Why did the author write this?

Inferring

When we **infer** we use background knowledge with clues in the text to come up with our own ideas about what the author is trying to present.

To infer

- identify what you already know
- combine what you know with text clues to come up with your own ideas

Brianna wore herself out before she reached the finish line.

Since you said Brianna wore herself out, that must mean you won the race!

Let's Think About Reading!

When I infer, I ask myself
- What do I already know?
- Which text clues are important?
- What is the author trying to present?

Monitor and Clarify

We **monitor comprehension** to check our understanding of what we've read. We **clarify** to find out why we haven't understood what we've read and to adjust comprehension.

To monitor and clarify

- use background knowledge as you read
- try different strategies: reread, ask questions, or use text features and illustrations

Aren't all deserts hot?

I think the caption will help clarify your understanding.

Antarctica: The Cold Desert!

Let's **Think** About **Reading!**

When I monitor and clarify, I ask myself
- Do I understand what I'm reading?
- What doesn't make sense?
- What fix-up strategies can I use?

Predict and Set Purpose

We **predict** to tell what might happen next in a story or article. The prediction is based on what has already happened. We **set a purpose** to guide our reading.

To predict and set a purpose

- preview the title, author's name, and illustrations or graphics
- identify why you're reading
- use what you already know to make predictions
- look back at your predictions to confirm them

> I predict you'll find out about Ellen Ochoa's space travels in this "Missions" section.

Let's Think About Reading!

When I predict and set a purpose, I ask myself
- What do I already know?
- What do I think will happen?
- What is my purpose for reading?

Questioning

Questioning is asking good questions about important text information. Questioning takes place before, during, and after reading.

To question
- read with a question in mind
- stop, think, and record your questions as you read
- make notes when you find information
- check your understanding and ask questions to clarify

Let's Think About Reading!

When I question, I ask myself
- Have I asked a good question with a question word?
- What questions help me make sense of my reading?
- What does the author mean?

Story Structure

Story structure is the arrangement of a story from beginning to end. You can use this information to summarize the plot.

To identify story structure
- note the conflict, or problem, at the beginning of a story
- track the rising action as conflict builds in the middle
- recognize the climax when the characters face the conflict
- identify how the conflict gets resolved and the story ends

Problem/Conflict

Rising Action

Resolution

Let's Think About Reading!

When I identify story structure, I ask myself
- What is the story's conflict or problem?
- How does the conflict build throughout the story?
- How is the conflict resolved in the end?
- How might this affect future events?

Summarize

We **summarize**, or retell, to check our understanding of what we've read. A summary is a brief statement—no more than a few sentences—and maintains a logical order.

To summarize fiction
- tell what happens in the story
- include the goals of the characters, how they try to reach them, and whether or not they succeed

To summarize nonfiction
- tell the main idea
- think about text structure and how the selection is organized

I swerved, and the squirrel ran off into the bushes!

You nearly hit a squirrel!

Let's Think About Reading!

When I summarize, I ask myself
- What is the story or selection mainly about?
- In fiction, what are the characters' goals? Are they successful?
- In nonfiction, how is the information organized?

Text Structure

We use **text structure** to look for the way the author has organized the text. For example, the author may have used cause and effect, problem and solution, sequence, or compare and contrast. Analyze text structure before, during, and after reading to locate information.

To identify text structure
- before reading: preview titles, headings, and illustrations
- during reading: notice the organization
- after reading: recall the organization and summarize the text

The Youth Baseball Guide uses compare and contrast organization as its text structure.

Introducing The Youth Baseball League

Comparing the Beginners' League and the Advanced League

Contrasting the Beginners' League and the Advanced League

Let's Think About Reading!

When I identify text structure, I ask myself
- What clues do titles, headings, and illustrations provide?
- How is information organized?
- How does the organization help my understanding?

Visualize

We **visualize** to create a picture or pictures in our mind as we read. This helps us monitor our comprehension.

To visualize

- combine what you already know with details from the text to make pictures in your mind
- use all your senses to put yourself in the story or text

TODAY:

Pineapple pizza with cheese: spicy sauce and sweet pineapple sprinkled on top

Let's **Think** About **Reading!**

When I visualize, I ask myself
- What do I already know?
- Which details create pictures in my mind?
- How can my senses put me in the story?

SCOTT FORESMAN
READING STREET

GRADE 4

COMMON CORE

Program Authors

Peter Afflerbach
Camille Blachowicz
Candy Dawson Boyd
Elena Izquierdo
Connie Juel
Edward Kame'enui
Donald Leu
Jeanne R. Paratore

P. David Pearson
Sam Sebesta
Deborah Simmons
Susan Watts Taffe
Alfred Tatum
Sharon Vaughn
Karen Kring Wixson

Glenview, Illinois

Boston, Massachusetts

Chandler, Arizona

Hoboken, New Jersey

ALWAYS LEARNING

PEARSON

We dedicate Reading Street to
Peter Jovanovich.

His wisdom, courage,
and passion for education
are an inspiration to us all.

Acknowledgments appear on pages 476–479, which constitute an extension of this copyright page.

PEARSON

ISBN-13: 978-0-328-72453-6
ISBN-10:   0-328-72453-X
13   16

Dear Reader,

A new school year is beginning. Are you ready? You are about to take a trip along a famous street—*Scott Foresman Reading Street.* During this trip you will meet exciting people, such as Lewis and Clark, a female astronaut who had to choose between music and science, a girl who understood the music of whales, and the man who gave clouds their names. You will visit spectacular places, such as the Grand Canyon, Yosemite, and Caprock Canyons State Park.

As you read selections about how to keep a weather journal, where whales migrate, and the lives of people who chase storms, you will gain new information that will help you in science and social studies.

While you're enjoying these exciting pieces of literature, you'll find that something else is going on—you are becoming a better reader, gaining new skills and polishing old ones.

Have a great trip—and send us a postcard!

Sincerely,
The Authors

Turning Points

What can we discover from new places and people?

Because of Winn-Dixie
by Kate DiCamillo

Week 2

Week 3

Unit 1 Contents

Week 6

Interactive Review

Unit 1

Envision It! A Comprehension Handbook

**Envision It! Visual Skills
Handbook EI•1–EI•13**

**Envision It! Visual Strategies
Handbook EI•15–EI•25**

Words! Vocabulary Handbook W•1–W•15

Unit 2 Contents

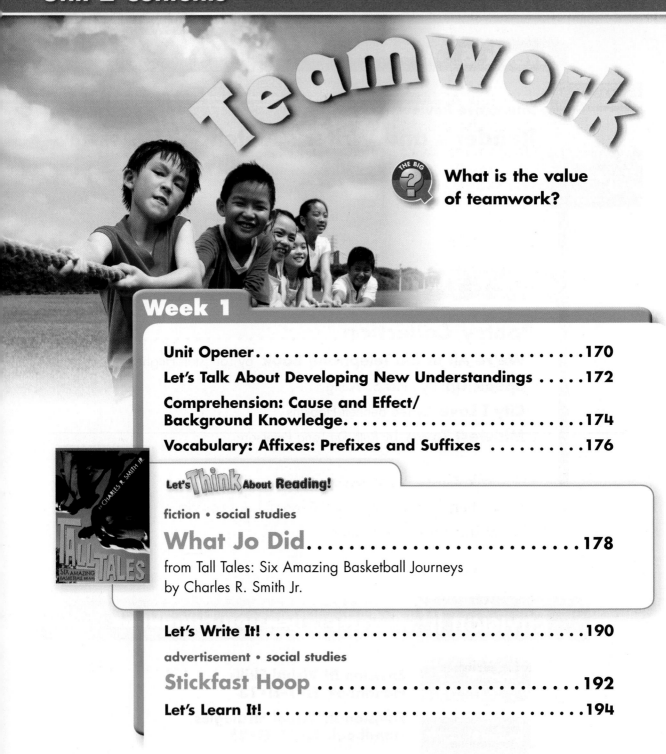

Teamwork

THE BIG ? **What is the value of teamwork?**

Week 1

Unit 2 Contents

Week 6

Unit 2

 **A Comprehension Handbook**

Unit 3 Contents

Patterns in Nature

THE BIG ? What are some patterns in nature?

Unit 3 Contents

Week 6

Unit 3

Envision It! A Comprehension Handbook

 **Envision It! Visual Skills Handbook** EI•1–EI•13

 **Envision It! Visual Strategies Handbook** EI•15–EI•25

Words! Vocabulary Handbook W•1–W•15

1

Don Leu
The Internet Guy

Right before our eyes, the nature of reading and learning is changing. The Internet and other technologies create new opportunities, new solutions, and new literacies. New reading comprehension skills are required online. They are increasingly important to our students and our society.

Those of us on the Reading Street team are here to help you on this new, and very exciting, journey.

See It!

- **Big Question Video**

- **Concept Talk Video**

- **Envision It! Animations**

- **eReaders**

Hear It!

- **eSelections**

- **Grammar Jammer**

I love my dog Thunder.

- **Vocabulary Activities**

Concept Talk Video

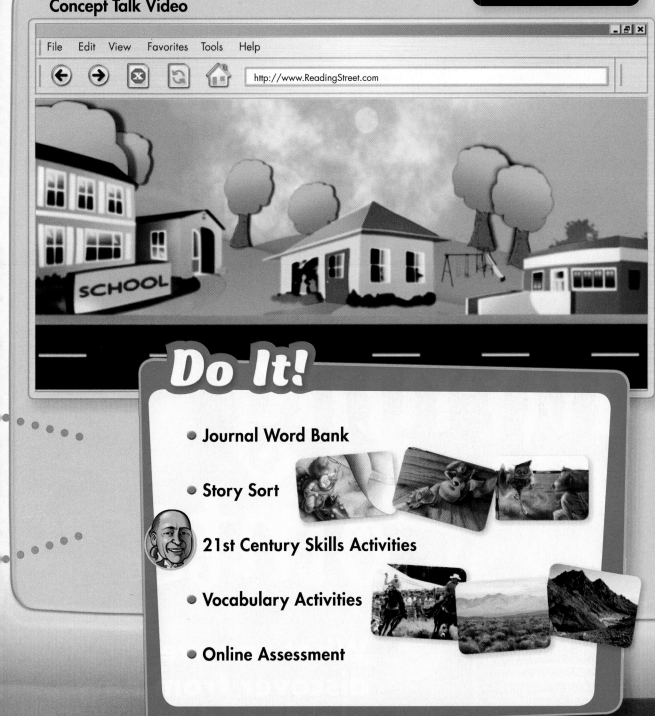

http://www.ReadingStreet.com

Do It!

- Journal Word Bank
- Story Sort
- 21st Century Skills Activities
- Vocabulary Activities
- Online Assessment

Turning Points

Reading Street Online

www.ReadingStreet.com
- Big Question Video
- eSelections
- Envision It! Animations
- Story Sort

THE BIG ?

What can we discover from new places and people?

Common Core State Standards

Speaking/Listening 1. Engage effectively in a range of collaborative discussions (one-on-one, in groups, and teacher-led) with diverse partners on grade 4 topics and texts, building on others' ideas and expressing their own clearly. **Also Language 6.**

Let's Talk About

Diversity

- Express opinions about what diversity means.

- Share ideas about the value of diversity in a community.

- Ask questions about what life would be like without diversity.

READING STREET ONLINE
CONCEPT TALK VIDEO
www.ReadingStreet.com

You will learn
3 0 0
Amazing Words
this year!

21

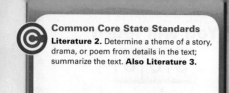

Common Core State Standards

Literature 2. Determine a theme of a story, drama, or poem from details in the text; summarize the text. **Also Literature 3.**

Envision It! Skill Strategy

Skill

Strategy

READING STREET ONLINE
ENVISION IT! ANIMATIONS
www.ReadingStreet.com

Comprehension Skill

Sequence

- Events in a story occur in a certain order, or sequence. The sequence of events can be important to understanding the story.

- Sometimes an author tells the events in a story out of sequence. When an author does this, an event that happened earlier in a story might be told *after* an event that happened later.

- It will help you figure out what is happening in a story if you stop and summarize the events that have taken place so far.

- Use the graphic organizer to sequence and summarize the plot of "Going Batty."

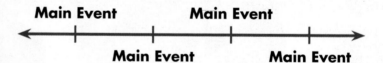

Main Event		**Main Event**	
	Main Event		**Main Event**

Comprehension Strategy

Summarize

Good readers summarize information as they read. When you read, identify the important ideas and briefly retell them in your own words. As you summarize, notice whether your thoughts about what you are reading change.

Going Batty

Mrs. Koch's fourth-grade class walked to the library, just as they did every afternoon. At the door, their mouths dropped open. Hanging everywhere were bats—upside-down, black bats. It took a few seconds before they realized the bats were paper. "Why all the bats?" they asked Mr. Egan, the librarian.

Mr. Egan laughed. "We had some excitement this morning." He went on to explain.

"The day started quietly. I checked in some books. Then a kindergarten class arrived for Story Hour. They sat in a circle while I began reading *Stellaluna*. Remember that story? It's about a little fruit bat. Well, suddenly the children yelled, 'Stellaluna! It's Stellaluna!' I love it when kids get excited about a story, but this was ridiculous! Then I saw they were pointing up. A bat had gotten into the library! I was able to trap it in a box and take it outside. The kids made paper bats to take its place."

The fourth graders looked around hopefully. But there were no bats—no real ones, anyway. They all sighed. Sometimes little kids have all the luck.

Skill Which grade is mentioned first in the story? Why do you suppose this should not be the first event on your graphic organizer?

Skill What time-word clues tell you that Mr. Egan is going to tell about events that happened earlier in the day?

Strategy Give a brief summary about the important events in paragraph three.

Your Turn!

Need a Review? See the *Envision It! Handbook* for help with sequencing and summarizing.

Let's Think About...

Ready to Try It? Use what you've learned about sequencing as you read *Because of Winn-Dixie*.

Common Core State Standards

Language 4. Determine or clarify the meaning of unknown and multiple-meaning words and phrases based on grade 4 reading and content, choosing flexibly from a range of strategies.

memorial

prideful

selecting

grand

peculiar

positive

recalls

Vocabulary Strategy for

🎯 Affixes: Suffixes

Word Structure Suppose you read an academic vocabulary word you don't know. You can use the suffix to help you figure out the word's meaning. Does the word have *-ful* or *-al* at the end? The Old English suffix *-ful* can make a word mean "full of," as in *tasteful*. The Old English suffix *-al* can make a word mean "of or like," as in *magical*.

Choose one of the *Words to Know* and follow these steps.

1. Put your finger over the *-ful* or *-al* suffix.

2. Look at the base word, the part of the word without the suffix. Put the base word in the phrase "full of _____" or "of or like _____."

3. Try that meaning in the sentence. Does it make sense?

As you read "The Storyteller," look for words that end in *-ful* or *-al*. Use the suffixes to help you figure out the meanings of academic vocabulary words.

Words to Write Reread "The Storyteller." Write a short essay about what you like best about the library. Use words from the *Words to Know* list in your essay.

The Storyteller

Thursday mornings at the James P. Guthrie Memorial Library are magical. That's because every Thursday morning Ms. Ada Landry tells historical fiction stories to anyone who wants to listen. But she does not just tell the stories. She acts them out. She makes them come alive.

When Ms. Ada describes what she calls "a prideful person," she puffs out her chest and looks down her nose. She talks in a loud, boastful, powerful voice. When she tells about a sly person, she narrows her eyes and pulls up her shoulders. She talks in a shady kind of voice. When she recalls things that happened long ago, she gets a faraway look in her eyes, and she talks in a quiet, dreamy, hopeful voice.

Ms. Ada's stories are entertaining, but they nearly always have a lesson in them too. A person who everyone thinks is a bit peculiar turns out to be kind or brave. A person who everyone thinks is grand proves to be cowardly or mean. A mistake or disaster ends up having a positive effect.

When it comes to selecting and telling stories, Ms. Ada is the best.

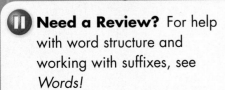

Your Turn!

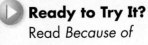

Need a Review? For help with word structure and working with suffixes, see *Words!*

Ready to Try It? Read *Because of Winn-Dixie* on pp. 26–37.

Because of Winn-Dixie

by Kate DiCamillo

 **Realistic fiction** has characters and events that are like people and events in real life. As you read, think about how the people and events in your life are similar to or different from the characters and events in this story.

Question of the Week

What experiences bring
diverse people together?

Let's
Think
About
Reading!

*I*ndia Opal Buloni, known best as Opal, has recently moved to Naomi, Florida, with her preacher father. Shortly after her arrival, Opal rescues a scrappy dog that she names Winn-Dixie, after the store in which she finds him.

She convinces her father, who often preaches about caring for the needy, that this dog is certainly in need. Thus a summer of adventures begins.

Let's **Think** About...

Who is telling the story? Why would the author tell the story through a first-person narrator?
Story Structure

I spent a lot of time that summer at the Herman W. Block Memorial Library. The Herman W. Block Memorial Library sounds like it would be a big fancy place, but it's not. It's just a little old house full of books, and Miss Franny Block is in charge of them all. She is a very small, very old woman with short gray hair, and she was the first friend I made in Naomi.

It all started with Winn-Dixie not liking it when I went into the library, because he couldn't go inside, too. But I showed him how he could stand up on his hind legs and look in the window and see me in there, selecting my books; and he was okay, as long as he could see me. But the thing was, the first time Miss Franny Block saw Winn-Dixie standing up on his hind legs like that, looking in the window, she didn't think he was a dog. She thought he was a bear.

29

Let's **Think** About...

Can you hear Miss Franny and Opal talking to each other? How does the author use the dialogue to create these characters?
Story Structure

This is what happened: I was picking out my books and kind of humming to myself, and all of a sudden, there was this loud and scary scream. I went running up to the front of the library, and there was Miss Franny Block, sitting on the floor behind her desk.

"Miss Franny?" I said. "Are you all right?"

"A bear," she said.

"A bear?" I asked.

"He has come back," she said.

"He has?" I asked. "Where is he?"

"Out there," she said and raised a finger and pointed at Winn-Dixie standing up on his hind legs, looking in the window for me.

"Miss Franny Block," I said, "that's not a bear. That's a dog. That's my dog. Winn-Dixie."

"Are you positive?" she asked.

"Yes ma'am," I told her. "I'm positive. He's my dog. I would know him anywhere."

Miss Franny sat there trembling and shaking.

"Come on," I said. "Let me help you up. It's okay." I stuck out my hand and Miss Franny took hold of it, and I pulled her up off the floor. She didn't weigh hardly anything at all. Once she was standing on her feet, she started acting all embarrassed, saying how I must think she was a silly old lady, mistaking a dog for a bear, but that she had a bad experience with a bear coming into the Herman W. Block Memorial Library a long time ago, and she never had quite gotten over it.

"When did that happen?" I asked her.

"Well," said Miss Franny, "it is a very long story."

"That's okay," I told her. "I am like my mama in that I like to be told stories. But before you start telling it, can Winn-Dixie come in and listen, too? He gets lonely without me."

"Well, I don't know," said Miss Franny. "Dogs are not allowed in the Herman W. Block Memorial Library."

"He'll be good," I told her. "He's a dog who goes to church." And before she could say yes or no, I went outside and got Winn-Dixie, and he came in and lay down with a *"huummmppff"* and a sigh, right at Miss Franny's feet.

She looked down at him and said, "He most certainly is a large dog."

"Yes ma'am," I told her. "He has a large heart, too."

Let's Think About...

Why does Miss Franny tell Opal the story?
Questioning

Let's **Think** About...

How does Miss Franny feel about Winn-Dixie now? What details tell you? **Inferring**

"Well," Miss Franny said. She bent over and gave Winn-Dixie a pat on the head, and Winn-Dixie wagged his tail back and forth and snuffled his nose on her little old-lady feet. "Let me get a chair and sit down so I can tell this story properly."

"Back when Florida was wild, when it consisted of nothing but palmetto trees and mosquitoes so big they could fly away with you," Miss Franny Block started in, "and I was just a little girl no bigger than you, my father, Herman W. Block, told me that I could have anything I wanted for my birthday. Anything at all."

Miss Franny looked around the library. She leaned in close to me. "I don't want to appear prideful," she said, "but my daddy was a very rich man. A very rich man." She nodded and then leaned back and said, "And I was a little girl who loved to read. So I told him, I said, 'Daddy, I would most certainly love to have a library for my birthday, a small little library would be wonderful.'"

"You asked for a whole library?"

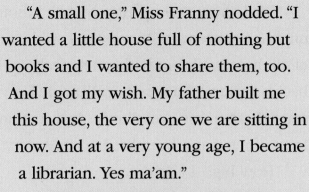

"A small one," Miss Franny nodded. "I wanted a little house full of nothing but books and I wanted to share them, too. And I got my wish. My father built me this house, the very one we are sitting in now. And at a very young age, I became a librarian. Yes ma'am."

"What about the bear?" I said.

"Did I mention that Florida was wild in those days?" Miss Franny Block said.

"Uh-huh, you did."

"It was wild. There were wild men and wild women and wild animals."

"Like bears!"

"Yes ma'am. That's right. Now, I have to tell you, I was a little-miss-know-it-all. I was a miss-smarty-pants with my library full of books. Oh, yes ma'am, I thought I knew the answers to everything. Well, one hot Thursday, I was sitting in my library with all the doors and windows open and my nose stuck in a book, when a shadow crossed the desk. And without looking up, yes ma'am, without even looking up, I said, 'Is there a book I can help you find?'"

Let's Think About...

What kind of person is Miss Franny? What details help you picture this setting?
Story Structure

"Well, there was no answer. And I thought it might have been a wild man or a wild woman, scared of all these books and afraid to speak up. But then I became aware of a very peculiar smell, a very strong smell. I raised my eyes slowly. And standing right in front of me was a bear. Yes ma'am. A very large bear."

"How big?" I asked.

"Oh, well," said Miss Franny, "perhaps three times the size of your dog."

"Then what happened?" I asked her.

"Well," said Miss Franny, "I looked at him and he looked at me. He put his big nose up in the air and sniffed and sniffed as if he was trying to decide if a little-miss-know-it-all librarian was what he was in the mood to eat. And I sat there. And then I thought, 'Well, if this bear intends to eat me, I am not going to let it happen without a fight. No ma'am.' So very slowly and very carefully, I raised up the book I was reading."

"What book was that?" I asked.

Let's Think About...

What details would you use to describe Miss Franny as a girl?

Summarize

"Why, it was *War and Peace,* a very large book. I raised it up slowly and then I aimed it carefully and I threw it right at that bear and screamed, 'Be gone!' And do you know what?"

"No ma'am," I said.

"He went. But this is what I will never forget. He took the book with him."

"Nuh-uh," I said.

"Yes ma'am," said Miss Franny. "He snatched it up and ran."

"Did he come back?" I asked.

"No, I never saw him again. Well, the men in town used to tease me about it. They used to say, 'Miss Franny, we saw that bear of yours out in the woods today. He was reading that book and

he said it sure was good and would it be all right if he kept it for just another week.' Yes ma'am. They did tease me about it." She sighed. "I imagine I'm the only one left from those days. I imagine I'm the only one that even recalls that bear. All my friends, everyone I knew when I was young, they are all dead and gone."

She sighed again. She looked sad and old and wrinkled. It was the same way I felt sometimes, being friendless in a new town and not having a mama to comfort me. I sighed, too.

Winn-Dixie raised his head off his paws and looked back and forth between me and Miss Franny. He sat up then and showed Miss Franny his teeth.

"Well now, look at that," she said. "That dog is smiling at me."

"It's a talent of his," I told her.

"It is a fine talent," Miss Franny said. "A very fine talent." And she smiled back at Winn-Dixie.

"We could be friends," I said to Miss Franny. "I mean you and me and Winn-Dixie, we could all be friends."

Miss Franny smiled even bigger. "Why, that would be grand," she said, "just grand."

Let's Think About...

How will friendship with Miss Franny help Opal? How will it help Miss Franny?
Questioning

And right at that minute, right when the three of us had decided to be friends, who should come marching into the Herman W. Block Memorial Library but old pinch-faced Amanda Wilkinson. She walked right up to Miss Franny's desk and said, "I finished *Johnny Tremain* and I enjoyed it very much. I would like something even more difficult to read now, because I am an advanced reader."

"Yes dear, I know," said Miss Franny. She got up out of her chair.

Amanda pretended like I wasn't there. She stared right past me. "Are dogs allowed in the library?" she asked Miss Franny as they walked away.

"Certain ones," said Miss Franny, "a select few." And then she turned around and winked at me. I smiled back. I had just made my first friend in Naomi, and nobody was going to mess that up for me, not even old pinch-faced Amanda Wilkinson.

Let's **Think** About...

Is Amanda's personality like Opal's or Miss Franny's? How does the author create a different kind of character?
Story Structure

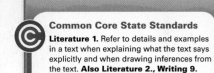

Common Core State Standards

Literature 1. Refer to details and examples in a text when explaining what the text says explicitly and when drawing inferences from the text. **Also Literature 2., Writing 9.**

Envision It! Retell

Think Critically

1. Do you or does someone you know own a pet? What is the relationship between a person and a pet like? Why do you think people bond so strongly with their pets? **Text to Self**

2. This author has won prizes for her books. Why? Find a part of this story you think could win a prize. **Think Like an Author**

3. Think about the events in the story. How does Miss Franny feel about Winn-Dixie at the beginning of the story? How does she feel at the end? **Sequence**

4. When summarizing a story, you only include important details. Which two of the following statements would you leave out of a summary of the story? Why?

   A. The Herman W. Block Memorial Library is a little old house full of books.

   B. Miss Franny Block is afraid of Winn-Dixie because she thinks he is a bear.

   C. Amanda Wilkinson returns a book to the library. **Summarize**

5. **Look Back and Write** Look back at pages 32–36. Do you think the story Miss Franny tells Opal about her encounter with a bear is factual or fanciful? Provide evidence from the text to support your answer.

   Key Ideas and Details • Text Evidence

Kate DiCamillo

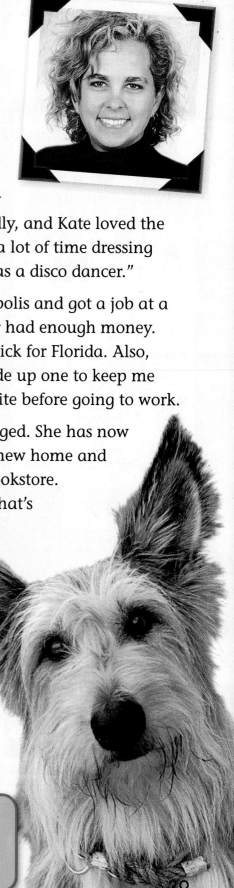

As a child, Kate DiCamillo was often sick. When Kate was five, a doctor said warm weather would be better for her health. She and her mother moved to a town in Florida. The people were friendly, and Kate loved the way they talked. "I also had a dog I loved. I spent a lot of time dressing Nanette up—in a green ballet tutu and then later as a disco dancer."

After college, Ms. DiCamillo moved to Minneapolis and got a job at a bookstore. She lived in a tiny apartment and never had enough money. "I wrote *Because of Winn-Dixie* because I was homesick for Florida. Also, my apartment building didn't allow dogs. So I made up one to keep me company." She got up at 4:00 every morning to write before going to work.

Since then, Ms. DiCamillo's life has really changed. She has now written three award-winning books. She bought a new home and a new car. And she no longer has to work at the bookstore. "I couldn't have imagined in my wildest dreams what's happened to me!"

Here are other books by Kate DiCamillo.

The Tiger Rising

The Tale of Despereaux

Reading Log

Choose a book from your library and read independently for 30 minutes. Record your reading by paraphrasing, or telling in your own words, in a logical order and meaningful way what you have read.

Common Core State Standards
Writing 3. Write narratives to develop real or imagined experiences or events using effective technique, descriptive details, and clear event sequences.
Also Writing 3.a., 3.d., Language 2.

Let's Write It!

Key Features of Realistic Fiction

- characters seem like real people

- plot events that could actually happen

- may be set in the past, the present, or the future

READING STREET ONLINE
GRAMMAR JAMMER
www.ReadingStreet.com

Realistic Fiction

Realistic fiction tells about made-up characters and events that seem believable. The student model on the next page is an example of realistic fiction.

Writing Prompt Write a realistic story about a character who reaches a turning point in his or her life.

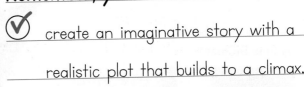

Writer's Checklist

Remember, you should . . .

✓ create an imaginative story with a realistic plot that builds to a climax.

✓ include believable details about the characters and setting.

✓ use vivid, descriptive words to make your story more interesting.

✓ write legibly using cursive script.

I Pick You!

"Could I see the Labrador retrievers?" Jack asked the animal shelter attendant.

"I'm sorry," she replied, "We don't have any Labs right now, but we have lots of great dogs you might like."

Jack was disappointed. He really wanted a Lab. For six months he'd been working hard to prove to his parents that he was responsible enough to have a dog.

Jack's excitement fizzled, but his dad urged him on. They trudged up and down the aisles, peering into the cages. They saw huge dogs, tiny dogs, and in-between dogs, but there wasn't one dog that was even part Lab.

Jack sat on a bench and put his head in his hands. Then something nudged Jack's knee. Jack looked up to see the most lively, friendly brown eyes he'd ever seen on a dog. The dog dropped a ball in his lap, gave him a broad smile, and bounced into a play-bow.

"You know," laughed Jack's dad, "they always say that you don't pick the dog, the dog picks you!"

Declarative and **interrogative sentences** are used correctly.

Genre Realistic fiction tells about believable characters and actions.

Writing Trait Word Choice Vivid words create a "word picture."

Conventions

Sentences

Remember A **declarative sentence** makes a statement and ends with a period. An **interrogative sentence** asks a question and ends with a question mark.

Common Core State Standards

Informational Text 1. Refer to details and examples in a text when explaining what the text says explicitly and when drawing inferences from the text. **Also Informational Text 8., Writing 1.**

Social Studies in Reading

Genre
Movie Review

- Persuasive text tries to influence the reader to think or to do something. A movie review is an example of persuasive text.

- In a movie review, the movie reviewer shares his or her opinion about a film.

- A movie review tells readers whether or not they should go see the movie being reviewed.

- Read "A Film with a Message of Hope." As you read, think about the elements that make this review a good example of persuasive text.

A Film with a Message of Hope

by Robert Sparks

Because of Winn-Dixie is a charming movie that will not disappoint. Directed by Wayne Wang, the film tells the story of a ten-year-old girl named Opal. She and her father have just moved to a small town in Florida. One day, while shopping in the Winn-Dixie grocery store, Opal finds a homeless dog. She takes the dog home and names him "Winn-Dixie," after the store where she found him. He is an ordinary-looking dog, yet he has an amazing smile.

The dog is Opal's first friend in her new town. Soon, Opal and Winn-Dixie make many other friends. These include Gloria Dump, who has a wildly overgrown backyard, a librarian named Miss Franny, and Otis, who runs the local pet store. These characters may not seem like typical friends for a ten-year-old girl, but they turn out to be good friends for Opal.

I enjoyed this movie very much. The character of Opal is played by the young actress, AnnaSophia Robb. She is absolutely perfect in the role. She portrays Opal as a thoughtful, friendly girl who is eager to surround herself with good friends. There is a sadness to the character of Opal because her mother left the family when she was a toddler. Opal misses her mother, but her love for Winn-Dixie and her new friends help her to find her place in the world. The film features outstanding performances by Jeff Daniels (Opal's father), Dave Matthews (Otis), Eva Marie Saint (Miss Franny), and Cicely Tyson (Gloria).

The movie is based on the award-winning children's book by Kate DiCamillo. Like the book, the movie *Because of Winn-Dixie* offers a message of hope and optimism. The movie seems to tell us that no matter what has happened in the past, we can all have a happy future. With a strong cast, a delightful story, and an adorable dog, this is a movie that you won't want to miss. This is a wonderful family film with a positive message.

Because of Winn-Dixie

Starring AnnaSophia Robb, Jeff Daniels, Cicely Tyson

Running Time: 1 hr. 37 min.

Directed by Wayne Wang

Let's **Think** About...

Does the author want his readers to see the movie? Identify the language he uses to convince readers. **Movie Review**

Let's **Think** About...

Reading Across Texts Look back at *Because of Winn-Dixie* and "A Film with a Message of Hope." Explain whether you agree with what the movie reviewer says is the story's message. Provide evidence for your opinion.

Writing Across Texts Use details from *Because of Winn-Dixie* and "A Film with a Message of Hope" to write your own review of the book or film. Would you recommend it? Why?

Common Core State Standards

Language 4. Determine or clarify the meaning of unknown and multiple-meaning words and phrases based on grade 4 reading and content, choosing flexibly from a range of strategies. **Also Literature 10., Foundational Skills 4.b.**

**READING STREET ONLINE
ONLINE STUDENT EDITION
www.ReadingStreet.com**

Vocabulary

Affixes: Suffixes

Word Structure A suffix at the end of a word can help you figure out the word's meaning. The suffix *-ful* means "full of." Knowing this helps you figure out that the word *careful* means "full of care." Similarly, knowing that the suffix *-less* means "without" helps you figure out that *fearless* means "without fear."

Practice It! Reread page 32 and look for words that end in *-ful*. Reread page 36 and find a word that ends in *-less*. Use the suffixes to help you figure out the meanings of the words.

Fluency

Expression

Reading with expression helps show the emotions of the characters in a story. Showing emotions makes the story more real. It also makes it easier to understand what is happening in the story.

Practice It! With a partner, practice reading aloud *Because of Winn-Dixie*, pages 32 and 33. First, read with a regular speaking voice. Then use what you know about Miss Franny and Opal to read with feeling. Express their emotions as you read the dialogue. Which way is more interesting?

Listening and Speaking

Dramatic Retelling

In a dramatic retelling, you choose a scene from a story and retell the scene from the point of view of one of the characters. The purpose of a dramatic retelling is to show the character's understanding of events.

Practice It! Choose a scene from *Because of Winn-Dixie*. Decide which character will retell the scene. Consider retelling a scene from Winn-Dixie's point of view or the bear's point of view. Include important details from the story in your retelling. Speak with expression. Retell the scene to the class.

Tips

Listening ...

- Listen attentively to the speaker.
- Make comments related to the action in the scene.

Speaking ...

- Retell events in the order they happened.
- Raise or lower your voice as you portray different characters in the scene.
- Look at the audience as you speak.

Teamwork ...

- Answer questions with detail.
- Offer suggestions to improve others' retellings.

Common Core State Standards

Speaking/Listening 1. Engage effectively in a range of collaborative discussions (one-on-one, in groups, and teacher-led) with diverse partners on grade 4 topics and texts, building on others' ideas and expressing their own clearly. **Also Language 6.**

Oral Vocabulary

Let's Talk About

Opportunity

- Share opinions about why people want to explore new lands.

- Speak clearly when explaining what opportunities await those who explore new places.

- Describe what opportunities you would pursue in a new place.

**READING STREET ONLINE
CONCEPT TALK VIDEO
www.ReadingStreet.com**

46

CLAIM·NO·96
—OWNER—
LAFE CANTILLON

Envision It! | Skill Strategy

Skill

Strategy

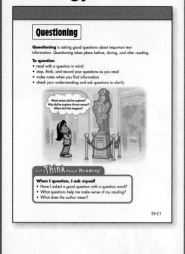

Comprehension Skill

Author's Purpose

- The author's purpose is the reason or reasons an author has for writing.

- An author may write to persuade, to inform, to entertain, or to express ideas and feelings.

- Use the graphic organizer below to identify author's purpose as you read "Jefferson's Bargain."

	Author's Purpose	Why do you think so?
Before you read: What do you think it will be?		
As you read: What do you think it is?		

Comprehension Strategy

Questioning

As you read, ask questions. Think of a question before you read and make notes as you find the answer. You can stop while reading, think of a question, and record the answer. These answers will help you recall and understand what you read.

48

Jefferson's BARGAIN

About 200 years ago, when the United States was still new, our third President, Thomas Jefferson, had a big idea. He wanted to discover what lay west of the Mississippi River. This land was known as Louisiana.

Today one of our southern states is called Louisiana. But at that time, "Louisiana" was all of the land between the Mississippi River in the east and the Rocky Mountains in the west. This was an area of more than 800,000 square miles!

France said it owned this land. However, it was at war with England. It didn't want to fight another war with the United States over Louisiana. So France agreed to sell the land. President Jefferson got it for—are you ready?—less than 3 cents an acre!

The land became known as the Louisiana Purchase. In time it would become all or part of thirteen states. But when Jefferson sent Lewis and Clark to explore this area in May of 1804, the two men and their group would enter a far-reaching wilderness.

Skill Look at the title and skim the text. Why do you think the author wrote this article?

Strategy Ask questions as you read. Is the area of Louisiana 800,000 square miles today?

Strategy Record answers as you read. The 800,000 square miles of land today is split into thirteen states.

Your Turn!

⏸ **Need a Review?** See the *Envision It! Handbook* for help with author's purpose and questioning.

▶ **Ready to Try It?** Use what you've learned about author's purpose as you read *Lewis and Clark and Me: A Dog's Tale*.

Common Core State Standards

Language 4. Determine or clarify the meaning of unknown and multiple-meaning words and phrases based on grade 4 reading and content, choosing flexibly from a range of strategies.

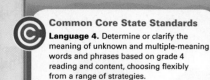

docks

migrating

scent

scan

wharf

yearned

Vocabulary Strategy for

🔊 Affixes: Word Endings

Word Structure When you read an academic vocabulary word you don't know, you may be able to use the ending to figure out its meaning. Is *-ed* or *-ing* at the end of the word? The ending *-ed* is Old English and is added to a verb to make it past tense, or tell about past actions. The ending *-ing* is added to a verb to make it tell about present or ongoing actions.

1. Find a word that ends in *-ed* or *-ing*. Put your finger over the *-ed* or *-ing*.

2. Look at the base word. Do you know what the base word means?

3. Try your meaning in the sentence.

4. If it makes sense, add the ending and read the sentence again.

Read "Westward Ho!" Use what you know about endings to help you figure out this week's *Words to Know*.

Words to Write Reread "Westward Ho!" Imagine you are exploring an unknown river. Describe your first day on the water. Include details on what you see, hear, smell, and feel to help the reader experience your trip. Use words from the *Words to Know* list.

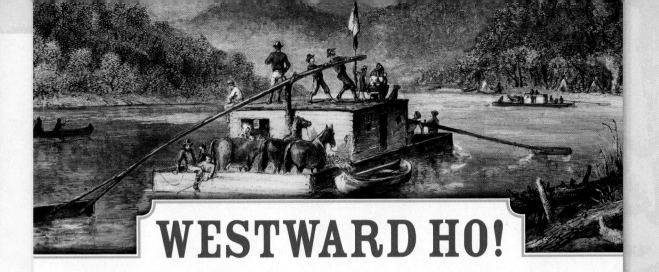

WESTWARD HO!

In the 1800s, America grew ever larger as land in the West was bought. As it grew, men and women of a certain kind yearned to travel west into the unknown. They had pioneer spirit.

There were no roads, of course. However, rivers made good highways for boats. In my mind I can see the pioneers with all their goods, waiting on the wharf in St. Louis. Sailors are busy loading and unloading ships. The pioneers load their belongings onto flatboats tied to the docks.

As they traveled, pioneers would scan the country for food and Indians. There were no grocery stores. And they never knew how the Indians would receive them. If the Indians were friendly, they might talk and trade. If a trapper was present, they were lucky. Trappers knew the country and the Indians well.

It must have been exciting to see this country for the first time. Pioneers saw endless herds and flocks of animals migrating. They breathed pure air full of the scent of tall grasses and wildflowers.

Your Turn!

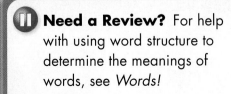

Need a Review? For help with using word structure to determine the meanings of words, see *Words!*

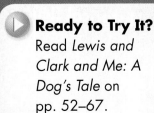

Ready to Try It? Read *Lewis and Clark and Me: A Dog's Tale* on pp. 52–67.

Lewis and Clark and Me

• A DOG'S TALE •

by Laurie Myers   illustrations by Michael Dooling

Genre

Historical fiction is based on real events in history, but it is a story that could never really happen—in this case, because a dog can't write. As you read, look for the facts on which this story is based.

Note to readers: The extracts from Meriwether Lewis's journal published in this excerpt retain their original spelling.

The year is 1803. Lewis and Clark are planning their expedition to explore the territory west of the Mississippi River. Lewis is looking for a dog to accompany the expedition, and as the story opens, he meets a 150-pound Newfoundland dog named Seaman, who goes on to tell of their adventures.

"Seaman!"

I glance at the man beside me.

"Look alive. Here's buyers."

Something caught my attention beyond him, down the wharf—a group of men, but I saw only one. It was Lewis. He was a full head taller than the other men I had known on the docks. And he was dressed in a different way—white breeches and a short blue coat with buttons that shone in the sun. A tall pointed hat with a feather made him look even taller.

Lewis walked along the dock with a large stride. There was a purpose about him. My life on the wharves was good, but I was a young dog and yearned for more. At the time I didn't know exactly what. I sensed that this man was part of what I wanted. I sat straighter as he approached. The man who owned me stood straighter, too. Lewis slowed.

"Need a dog, sir?" my man asked.

"I'm lookin'," Lewis replied. He stooped down and looked me right in the eye. I wagged my tail and stepped forward. I wanted to sniff this strange man. He extended his hand for me. He didn't smell like any I had ever smelled, and it made me want to sniff him all over.

Lewis scratched the back of my neck, where I liked to be scratched.

"I'm headed out west, up the Missouri River," Lewis said. My man's face brightened.

"This dog be perfect, sir. These dogs can swim. Newfoundlands, they call them. Rescue a drowning man in rough water or in a storm. Look at these paws. You won't find another dog with paws like that. They's webbed." He spread my toes to show the webbing.

"So they are," Lewis replied. Lewis began feeling my chest and hindquarters. His hands were large and muscular.

"Water rolls off this coat," my man added. He pulled up a handful of my thick, dense double coat.

Lewis examined my coat and nodded.

"I know the Mississippi, sir, but I don't know the Meesori," my man said.

"It's off the Mississippi, headin' northwest."

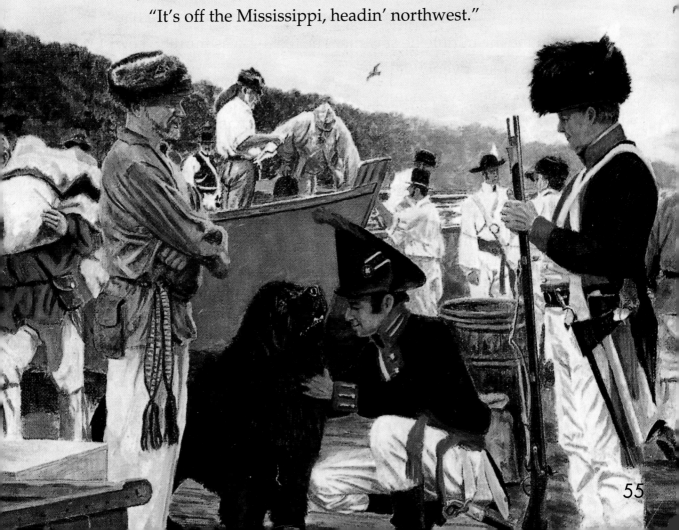

"North, you say. Ah. It'll be cold up that river. Won't bother this one, though." He patted me firmly on the back.

Lewis stood and looked around. He found a piece of wood that had broken off a crate. He showed it to me, then threw it.

"Go," he said.

I wanted to go. I wanted to do whatever this man asked. But I belonged to another. I looked at my man.

"Go on," he said.

I ran for the stick and returned it to Lewis.

"How much?" Lewis asked.

"Twenty dollars. And a bargain at that."

Lewis looked down at me. I lifted my head proudly.

"Won't find a better dog than this. Perfect for your trip," my man said, trying to convince Lewis.

It wasn't necessary. Lewis wanted me. I could tell. He had liked me the minute he saw me. The feeling was mutual. Lewis paid my man twenty dollars.

"Does he have a name?" Lewis asked.

"I been callin' him Seaman, but you can name him anything you like."

"Come, Seaman," Lewis called.

As we walked away, my rope in his hand, he put his other hand on my head. After that, he didn't need a rope. I would follow this man to the ends of the Earth.

...the dog was of the newfoundland breed one that I prised much for his docility and qualifications generally for my journey....

Meriwether Lewis November 16, 1803

Squirrels

I caught fish off the docks. I chased animals in the woods.
But hunting came alive for me on the river—the Ohio, Lewis
called it.

I have always loved the water, so the day we boarded the
boat and pushed out onto the Ohio River was just about the
happiest day of my life. Lewis was excited, too. I could tell by
the way he walked. And his voice was louder than usual.

The men were also excited. I could hear it in their voices.
They didn't complain when they loaded the boat. Lewis was
telling them what to load and how to load it. Anyway, that
afternoon, Lewis and I and some men started down the river.

I rode in the back of the boat. It was the highest place and
gave me the best view. From there I could scan both banks and
the water with just a glance. The first two weeks I couldn't
get enough of it. There were animals I had not seen before.
Smells I had not smelled. My skin tingled with excitement.

The river was low, and the men had to pole much
of the way. When they weren't poling, they were digging
channels for our boat or hiring oxen to pull the boat from
the shore.

We were only a couple of weeks down the river when
I had my first great day of hunting. The river wasn't quite
as shallow and the current not too strong, so the crew
rowed along leisurely.

I was lying on the back deck of the boat. I had just
scanned the shore—nothing of interest, just a few beaver
and a deer. I decided to close my eyes for a nap. I blinked
a few times and was ready to lay my head on my paws
when something on the water up ahead caught my eye.

I stuck my nose in the air and sniffed. I recognized the scent immediately. Squirrel.

A squirrel on water? That was unusual. I had seen plenty of squirrels, but I had never seen one swim. There was something else strange. The smell of squirrel was especially strong. I had never known one squirrel to project so powerful a scent.

I stood to take a look. Right away I spotted a squirrel off the starboard side. He was swimming across the river. Another squirrel followed close behind. Without a second thought, I leaned over the side of the boat to get a better look.

I saw another squirrel. And another. I could not believe my eyes; hundreds of squirrels were crossing the river. The water up ahead was almost black with them. Every muscle in my body tightened to full alert.

Lewis was on the other side of the boat, talking to two of the men. I turned to him and barked.

"What is it?" he asked.

It is impossible to describe the urge I felt. It was as strong as anything I had ever known. I had to get those squirrels.

I barked again. Lewis scanned the water ahead.

"Look at that," he said to the men. "Squirrels crossing the river. Now why would they do that?"

"Food?" one man suggested.

Lewis paused for a moment. "There are hickory nuts on both banks."

"Migrating?" suggested the other.

Lewis nodded. "Maybe. Or perhaps they're—"

I barked again. They were wasting time wondering why the squirrels were crossing. It didn't matter. The squirrels were there. Hundreds of them, right in front of us. Sometimes men spend too much time thinking. They miss the fun of life.

"They'd make a fine supper," the first man suggested
with a smile.

Lewis nodded. He looked at me. "Let's see what you can do,
Seaman. Go on. Fetch us a squirrel."

That's what I was waiting for. I sprang off the boat and hit
the water swimming. I was going to get every squirrel in that
river for Lewis. My webbed feet made it easy. I reached the first
squirrel in just minutes.

When it saw me, its eyes bulged with fear. It tried to steer its
sleek, fat body away. In one swift move I grabbed it by the neck
and killed it. I carried it back to the boat. Lewis leaned over the
side and took it from me.

"Good dog. Fetch another," he said.

The crew had stopped rowing, and the boat drifted slowly toward the mass of squirrels.

"Look at Captain Lewis's dog!" yelled one of the rowers.

I turned and started swimming again. I could hear the men cheering me on. In two strokes I was on another squirrel.

"Good dog!" Lewis yelled. "Go!"

"Go," the crew echoed. "Go, Seaman, go!"

I went. And went. Over and over, I went. I went until I was exhausted. I don't know how long it lasted. Maybe one hour. Maybe four.

All I know is that when I finished, there was a pile of squirrels in the boat. Lewis and the crew were laughing and cheering. All the rest of the day the men were patting me and saying, "Good dog" and "Good boy" and "We'll be eatin' good tonight." The admiration of the crew was great, but the look of pride on Lewis's face was better than all the men's praise added together.

That night the men fried the squirrels, and we ate well.

In the three years that followed, I hunted almost every day. But the squirrels on the Ohio were my favorite.

...observed a number of squirrels swiming the Ohio... they appear to be making to the south;... I made my dog take as many each day as I had occasion for, they wer fat and I thought them when fryed a pleasent food... he would take the squirel in the water kill them and swiming bring them in his mouth to the boat....

Meriwether Lewis September 11, 1803

Bear-Dog

"Indians."

We had not been on the shore very long before I heard Lewis say the word.

Lewis and Clark and I had crossed the river to make some observations. That's when these Indians appeared. They were different from other people I had known—the boatmen and city folk.

I didn't sense that Lewis or Clark were concerned, so I wasn't. The Indians seemed friendly enough. Lewis talked to them. It wasn't until later that I realized Lewis gave the same talk to every group of Indians we met. He talked about the "great white father" in Washington.

The Indians listened patiently as one of the English-speaking Indians translated. Lewis used hand motions to help. As he talked on, it became obvious to me that the Indians were not interested in Lewis or what he was saying. They were staring at me. Finally, Lewis realized what was going on, and he invited the Indians to take a closer look.

They gathered around. They touched me. They whispered about me. They acted like they had never seen a dog before. Then I noticed an Indian dog standing to the side. I took one look at that animal and realized why they were so interested in me.

That dog could not have been more than twenty pounds. Newfoundlands can weigh up to 150 pounds, and I'm a large Newfoundland. If that scrawny dog was the only dog they had seen, then I was a strange sight indeed.

"Bear," one of the English-speaking Indians said.

I looked up. He was pointing at me.

"Dog," Lewis replied patiently.

The Indian looked at his own dog. He looked back at me.

"Bear," he said again.

Lewis looked at me and smiled. Clark was smiling, too.

I lifted my head.

"I guess he does look like a bear," Lewis said.

Lewis picked up a stick and threw it.

"Fetch," he said.

I fetched.

"Stay," he said.

I stayed.

"Sit," he said.

I sat.

The Indians were impressed.

"Dog," Lewis said politely. Lewis was always nice.

The Indian who had called me "bear" turned to consult with his friends.

Finally, he turned.

"Bear-dog," he said with satisfaction.

Lewis smiled.

"Yes, I guess you could call him bear-dog."

Later, George Drouillard explained to us that the Indians don't have a separate word for *horse*. They call a horse "elk-dog." I guess it made sense for them to call me a bear-dog.

The Indian suddenly turned and walked through the crowd to his horse. He pulled out three beaver skins. He held them out to Lewis.

"For bear-dog," he said.

It wasn't often that I saw Lewis surprised. He was then.

I took a step closer to Lewis.

Lewis looked the Indian square in the eye and said, "No trade. Bear-dog special."

As we rode back to camp in the boat, Lewis said to me, "Three beaver skins! Can you believe that?"

No, I could not. The idea that Lewis and I would ever separate was unthinkable. Not many dogs and men fit together like Lewis and I. If you have ever experienced it, then you know what I'm talking about. And if you haven't, well, it's hard to explain. All I can tell you is that when a dog and a man fit like Lewis and I did, nothing can separate them. Lewis said it best.

"No trade."

...one of the Shawnees a respectable looking Indian offered me three beverskins for my dog with which he appeared much pleased... of course there was no bargan, I had given 20$ for this dogg myself—

Meriwether Lewis   November 16, 1803

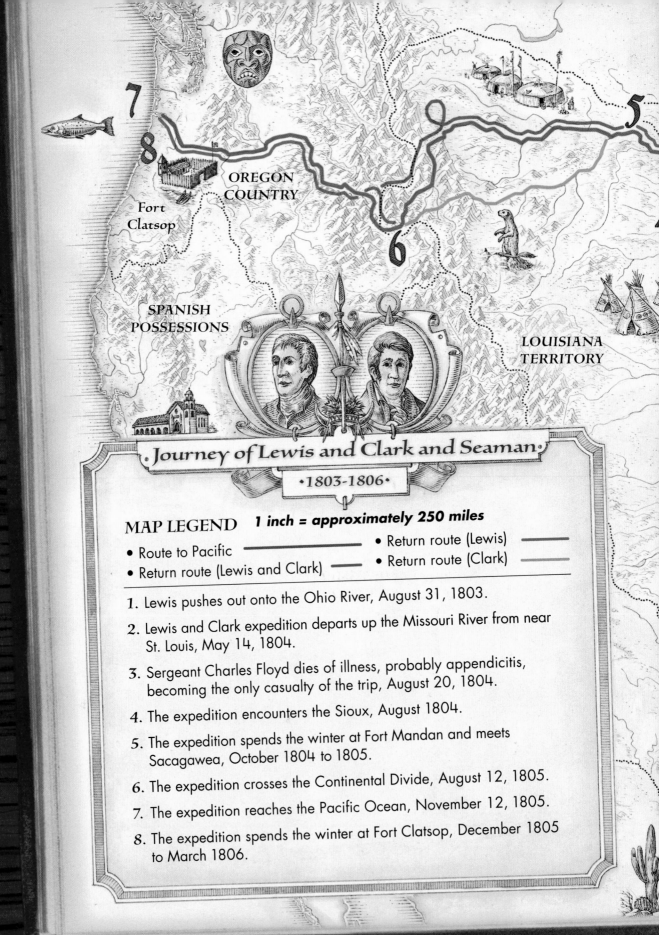

Journey of Lewis and Clark and Seaman

•1803-1806•

OREGON COUNTRY

Fort Clatsop

SPANISH POSSESSIONS

LOUISIANA TERRITORY

MAP LEGEND — 1 inch = approximately 250 miles

- Route to Pacific ———————
- Return route (Lewis and Clark) ——
- Return route (Lewis) ——————
- Return route (Clark) ——————

1. Lewis pushes out onto the Ohio River, August 31, 1803.

2. Lewis and Clark expedition departs up the Missouri River from near St. Louis, May 14, 1804.

3. Sergeant Charles Floyd dies of illness, probably appendicitis, becoming the only casualty of the trip, August 20, 1804.

4. The expedition encounters the Sioux, August 1804.

5. The expedition spends the winter at Fort Mandan and meets Sacagawea, October 1804 to 1805.

6. The expedition crosses the Continental Divide, August 12, 1805.

7. The expedition reaches the Pacific Ocean, November 12, 1805.

8. The expedition spends the winter at Fort Clatsop, December 1805 to March 1806.

BRITISH
POSSESSIONS

N

INDIANA
TERRITORY

3

2

St. Louis

1

MISSISSIPPI
TERRITORY

Common Core State Standards

Literature 1. Refer to details and examples in a text when explaining what the text says explicitly and when drawing inferences from the text. **Also Writing 9.**

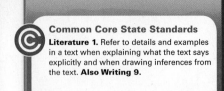

Envision It! | Retell

Think Critically

1. Both Opal Buloni and Meriwether Lewis adopt dogs. How does Opal's relationship with Winn-Dixie compare with Meriwether Lewis's relationship with Seaman? **Text to Text**

2. Reread the parts from Meriwether Lewis's journal. Some of the words are misspelled. Why didn't the author correct them? **Think Like an Author**

3. An author's purpose can be to help readers visualize a scene. Do you think this might have been one of Laurie Myers's purposes? Explain. **Author's Purpose**

4. Read pages 55–56. Seaman's owner tells Lewis, "Won't find a better dog than this. Perfect for your trip." Why does the owner say this? Do you agree with the statement? Why? **Questioning**

5. **Look Back and Write** Look back at the last section of the story, titled "Bear-Dog," on pages 62–64. Do you think this was a good name for Seaman? Why? Provide evidence from the story to support your answer.

Key Ideas and Details • Text Evidence

Meet the Author and the Illustrator

Laurie Myers and Michael Dooling

Laurie Myers says she got the idea for *Lewis and Clark and Me* after reading about Meriwether Lewis and his dog. "I've had many dogs over the years and I've been closer to some than others. I saw in Seaman and Lewis a unique closeness that I wanted to express."

To prepare, Ms. Myers read a lot of books about the expedition. "I most enjoyed reading the actual journals by Lewis and Clark. They're filled with great descriptions of wildlife and the adventures they had."

Michael Dooling also helped research the book before doing the pictures. He often asks family and friends to pose in historical costumes while he draws or paints. "Every day at my house is like Halloween!" he says. He also visits schools to teach children about history and art. He comes dressed in a colonial costume and takes children through the steps of making picture books.

Here are other books by Laurie Myers.

Surviving Brick Johnson

My Dog, My Hero

Reading Log

Use the *Reader's and Writer's Notebook* to record your independent reading.

Common Core State Standards

Writing 2.a. Introduce a topic clearly and group related information in paragraphs and sections; include formatting (e.g., headings), illustrations, and multimedia when useful to aiding comprehension. **Also Writing 2., 4., Language 2.**

Let's Write It!

Key Features of Expository Composition

- tells of real people and events

- presents factual information

- includes a topic sentence, a body, and a closing sentence

- may include text features such as photos, subheadings, and maps

READING STREET ONLINE
GRAMMAR JAMMER
www.ReadingStreet.com

Expository Composition

An expository composition gives factual information about a topic. The student model on the next page is an example of an expository composition.

Writing Prompt Think about another time in history when people found opportunity in a new place. Now write an expository composition about it.

Writer's Checklist

Remember, you should . . .

☑ have a central idea in your topic sentence.

☑ use facts, details, and explanations for support.

☑ end with a concluding statement.

☑ capitalize historical events, documents, languages, races, and nationalities.

The California Gold Rush

Golden Opportunities

The accidental discovery of gold by a worker at Sutter's Mill in 1848 drew thousands of people to California in search of opportunity. The news spread quickly: "Gold has been found on the American River!" People began to flock to California from all over the country. "Go West, young man," was the advice offered by a famous writer. People moved, hoping to get rich by finding gold. They went to California in covered wagons and on sailing ships. Nearly 100,000 people arrived in California in 1849.

Business Opportunities

Some people found gold, but most people did not. Instead, they found other opportunities. They started farms, opened stores, and built hotels and restaurants. San Francisco grew from a tiny, shabby town into a bustling boomtown. People found many opportunities in California because of the gold rush, even though very few people actually found gold.

Writing Trait Organization The composition is organized around a main idea.

Imperative and exclamatory sentences are used correctly.

Genre An **expository composition** discusses real events.

Conventions

Sentences

Remember An **imperative sentence** gives a command and usually ends with a period. An **exclamatory sentence** expresses strong feeling and ends with an exclamation mark.

71

Common Core State Standards

Informational Text 3. Explain events, procedures, ideas, or concepts in a historical, scientific, or technical text, including what happened and why, based on specific information in the text. **Also Informational Text 5., 9.**

Social Studies in Reading

Genre
Biography

- A biography tells the story of a person's life.

- Biographies usually organize a person's life events in the order, or sequence, in which they happened.

- Some biographies may include examples of cause-and-effect relationships. Ask yourself: What events caused that person to make a specific choice?

- Read "Ellen Ochoa: Space Pioneer." As you read, look for elements in the text that make this a biography. What events caused Ellen to become an astronaut?

Ellen Ochoa: Space Pioneer
by David Arroyo

In 1958, a baby girl was born in Los Angeles, California. Little did her parents know that she would grow up to become the world's first female astronaut of Hispanic American heritage. Her name was Ellen Ochoa, and this is her story.

Born and raised in California, Ellen was an excellent student. At school, she loved math and music. She went to college at San Diego State University. There, she earned a degree in physics. After college, she had a decision to make. Would she become a scientist or a musician? She was so good at the flute that she could have become a professional flutist.

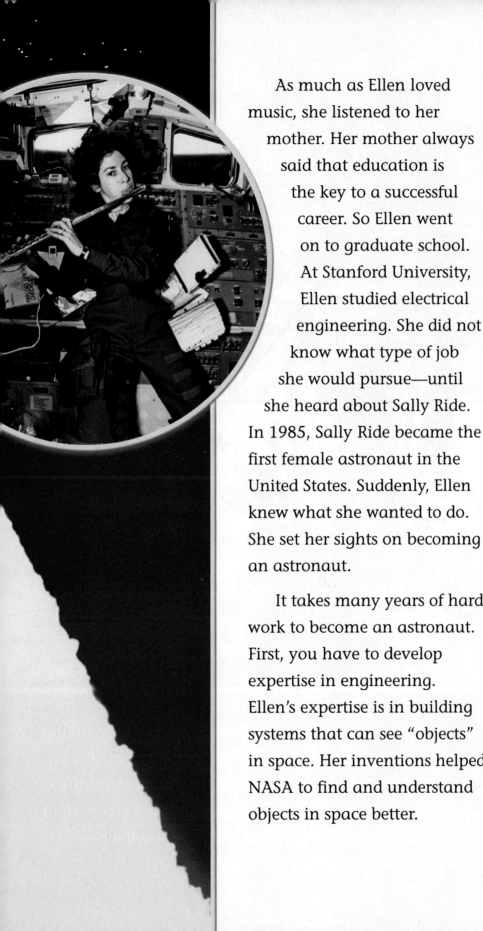

As much as Ellen loved music, she listened to her mother. Her mother always said that education is the key to a successful career. So Ellen went on to graduate school. At Stanford University, Ellen studied electrical engineering. She did not know what type of job she would pursue—until she heard about Sally Ride. In 1985, Sally Ride became the first female astronaut in the United States. Suddenly, Ellen knew what she wanted to do. She set her sights on becoming an astronaut.

It takes many years of hard work to become an astronaut. First, you have to develop expertise in engineering. Ellen's expertise is in building systems that can see "objects" in space. Her inventions helped NASA to find and understand objects in space better.

Let's **Think** About...

How does the sequence of life events on this page help you understand Ellen Ochoa's life? **Biography**

73

NASA was impressed with Ellen's engineering talent. In 1990, NASA accepted Ellen into its astronaut training program. She became an official astronaut in 1991. In 1993, Ellen took her first flight into space. She spent nine days on the space shuttle *Discovery* as a mission specialist. The next year, she traveled on another space shuttle mission.

There is a lot more to being an astronaut than taking a trip on a space shuttle. While on her shuttle missions, Ellen studied the sun's effect on the Earth's climate and atmosphere. She examined the Earth's ozone layer. All of her years of school and her scientific knowledge helped her to do this important research.

Today, Ellen Ochoa is still working for NASA. This remarkable woman is a pioneer in spacecraft technology, an inventor, an astronaut, and a scientist. Out of respect for her accomplishments, two schools have been named after her. The students and staff at one of the schools said they wanted her name because Ellen Ochoa was an inspiration to them. Without a doubt, Ellen Ochoa will continue to inspire people for a long time to come.

Let's Think About...

What similarities and differences are there between the events and experiences told in Ellen Ochoa's biography and the events and characters' experiences in *Lewis and Clark and Me*? **Biography**

Let's Think About...

Reading Across Texts Look back at *Lewis and Clark and Me* and "Ellen Ochoa: Space Pioneer." What characteristics do Lewis, Clark, and Ellen Ochoa all share? Make a list.

Writing Across Texts Use your list to write a paragraph about what makes a good explorer.

Common Core State Standards

Language 4. Determine or clarify the meaning of unknown and multiple-meaning words and phrases based on grade 4 reading and content, choosing flexibly from a range of strategies. **Also Foundational Skills 4., Speaking/Listening 1.c.**

Let's **Learn It!**

Vocabulary

Word Endings

Word Structure Looking at the endings of words can help you figure out their meanings. For example, the ending *-s* on a noun tells that the noun is plural. The ending *-ed* on a verb tells that the action happened in the past. The ending *-ing* on a verb tells that the action is still continuing.

Practice It! Reread page 55 of *Lewis and Clark and Me*. Look for words with the endings *-s*, *-ed*, and *-ing*. Cover each ending with your finger. Read the word. Think about its meaning without the ending. Then use the ending to help you figure out the meaning of the word.

Fluency

Appropriate Phrasing

As you read, use punctuation cues to help you know when to slow down, pause, or change the pitch of your voice. Commas, periods, question marks, dashes, and exclamation points help guide your voice while you read.

Practice It! With a partner, practice reading *Lewis and Clark and Me*, page 64. Slow down for commas and stop for periods. Make your voice higher when you see a question mark at the end of a sentence. Pause after a dash. When each of you has read the paragraphs once, give each other suggestions on ways to improve.

Listening and Speaking

Introduction

In an introduction, a speaker formally presents one person to another person or group of people. One purpose of an introduction is to tell the audience something that the person being introduced has done or hopes to do.

Practice It! Prepare an introduction for the dog Seaman from *Lewis and Clark and Me*. Imagine that there is an American Dogs Hall of Fame and that Seaman is its newest member. Explain who Seaman was and why he is a good choice for the Hall of Fame. Describe what Seaman looked like, his talents, and his personality. Present your introduction to the class.

Tips

Listening ...

• Listen attentively to the speaker.

• Ask questions related to the subject.

Speaking ...

• Use accurate information to communicate your ideas.

• Choose a formal or informal tone and keep that tone throughout the introduction.

• Make eye contact with the audience as you speak.

Teamwork ...

• Answer questions with detail.

• Offer suggestions to improve others' introductions.

Oral Vocabulary

Let's Talk About

New Homes

- Share experiences about moving to a new home.

- Ask questions about what is hard and what is fun about moving.

- Express opinions with appropriate volume.

READING STREET ONLINE
CONCEPT TALK VIDEO
www.ReadingStreet.com

Common Core State Standards

Literature 3. Describe in depth a character, setting, or event in a story or drama, drawing on specific details in the text (e.g., a character's thoughts, words, or actions). **Also Literature 1.**

Skill

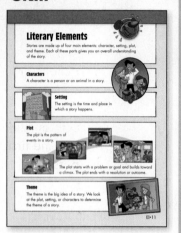

Strategy

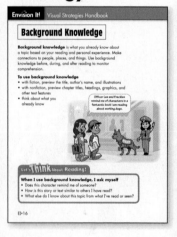

Comprehension Skill

Literary Elements: Character, Setting, and Plot

- Characters are the people in a story. We learn what characters are like by noticing how they act and what they say in the story.

- When a character tells the story using *I*, *me*, and *my*, the author is writing in the first person. If events are told by a narrator who is not in the story, using *he, him, his, she,* and *her*, the author is writing in the third person.

- The setting of a story is where it takes place and when it happens.

- The plot is the sequence of events in a story.

- Use the chart to identify characters, setting, and plot as you read "The 'Broken' Arm."

Characters	Setting	Plot

Comprehension Strategy

Background Knowledge

Good readers use what they know to help them understand a story. Before reading, look at the title and pictures. If you know something about the subject matter of the story, it will help you understand what you are reading.

The "Broken" Arm

Eliza and her sister Harriet took turns washing the dishes. When Harriet did the dishes, Eliza played the fiddle or did her homework. When Eliza did the dishes, Harriet would sit with her father and watch the stars.

One night Eliza was limping when she came in from doing her chores. It was her night to do the dishes.

"My ankle! It hurts!" she cried. Pa looked at it.

"Don't worry," Pa said. "It's not broken. But you need to stay off it. Harriet can do the dishes tonight."

Pa sat with Eliza for the rest of the night, soothing her and bandaging her ankle.

Skill Describe the interactions of Eliza and Harriet. Describe their relationship. Is this story told in the first or third person?

Harriet scowled every time she placed a dish in the rack—she just boiled up inside. Then she got an idea.

The next night, Harriet came into the house crying.

"Ow, Pa. My arm hurts!"

"What's wrong?" Pa asked.

"My arm! I think it's broken!"

Pa looked at the arm. He knew he wouldn't find any broken bones because Harriet had just spent the last hour lying in the grass looking at the clouds.

"Does it really hurt, Harriet?" Pa said, with a doubtful smile on his face. Harriet knew her father well. She knew she couldn't fool him. "Well," she said as her arm dropped to her side. "I guess I'd rather do the dishes than really have a broken arm!"

Strategy Does knowing that Harriet and Eliza switched off every night to do the dishes help you understand how Harriet felt?

Skill Describe how Harriet feels at the end of this story. Explain how she has changed.

Your Turn!

 Need a Review? See *Envision It! Handbook* for help with character, setting, and plot and background knowledge.

▷ **Ready to Try It?** Use what you've learned about character, setting, and plot as you read *On the Banks of Plum Creek*.

On the Banks of Plum Creek

Common Core State Standards

Language 4.c. Consult reference materials (e.g., dictionaries, glossaries, thesauruses), both print and digital, to find the pronunciation and determine or clarify the precise meaning of key words and phrases. **Also Language 4.**

Envision It! | Words to Know

badger

jointed

rushes

bank

bristled

patched

ruffled

Vocabulary Strategy for

🎯 Multiple-Meaning Words

Dictionary/Glossary You may read a word whose meaning you know, but the word doesn't make sense in the sentence. The word may have more than one meaning, or multiple meanings. Use a dictionary or glossary to find the meaning that fits.

1. Try the meaning that you know. Does it make sense in the sentence?

2. If it doesn't, look up the word to see what other meanings it has.

3. Read all the meanings given for the word. Try each meaning in the sentence.

4. Choose the one that makes the most sense.

Read "Foggy River Schoolhouse." Stop at any words that have multiple meanings, such as *bank* or *ruffled*. Look them up in a dictionary or glossary to see what other meanings they could have.

Words to Write Reread "Foggy River Schoolhouse." Imagine that you live in the nineteenth century and go to school in a one-room schoolhouse. Write a journal entry describing a typical day. Use words from the *Words to Know* list.

FOGGY RIVER SCHOOLHOUSE

My older brother, Edward, got me in trouble today. He wanted to make me laugh, so he threw sticky burrs at me during Miss Osgood's arithmetic lesson. Some of the burrs landed on my desk and were easy to throw right back at Edward, but a few of those bristled burrs got caught in the folds of my ruffled petticoat. I had such trouble getting them unstuck from the cloth that Edward couldn't hold in his laughter. Miss Osgood was not happy, and she sent both of us to the corner to face the wall.

My teacher, Miss Osgood, calls me a "country girl" because I'd rather play outside in the rushes than sit inside and learn arithmetic. Who would blame me! That schoolroom can get pretty cramped. All of the students from Foggy River learn in the same room. I do love to practice drawing the jointed letters of the alphabet, but I'd much rather do it on the soft bank of the open creek where I might catch a glimpse of a badger or a beaver.

Maybe when I get older I'll like being at school more. Then I'll be able to chop wood for the stove and fetch water, which means I'll get to go outside! Edward is older, so he gets to do these chores. My school chore is to clap the erasers.

Even at home, my chores keep me inside. Tonight I have to mend the hole in Edward's patched flannel shirt. Maybe I'll choose a mismatched color for his patch!

Your Turn!

⏸ Need a Review? For additional help with using a dictionary or glossary to determine the meaning of multiple-meaning words, see *Words!*

▶ Ready to Try It? Read *On the Banks of Plum Creek* on pp. 84–99.

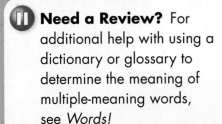

83

On the Banks of Plum Creek

by Laura Ingalls Wilder
illustrated by Garth Williams

Question of the Week
**Why do we want to
explore new places?**

Rushes and Flags

Every morning after Mary and Laura had done the dishes, made their bed and swept the floor, they could go out to play.

All around the door the morning-glory flowers were fresh and new, springing with all their might out of the green leaves. All along Plum Creek the birds were talking. Sometimes a bird sang, but mostly they talked. "Tweet, tweet, oh twitter twee twit!" one said. Then another said, "Chee, Chee, Chee," and another laughed, "Ha ha ha, tiraloo!"

Laura and Mary went over the top of their house and down along the path where Pa led the oxen to water.

There along the creek rushes were growing, and blue flags. Every morning the blue flags were new. They stood up dark blue and proud among the green rushes.

Each blue flag had three velvet petals that curved down like a lady's dress over hoops. From its waist three ruffled silky petals stood up and curved together. When Laura looked down inside them, she saw three narrow pale tongues, and each tongue had a strip of golden fur on it.

Sometimes a fat bumble-bee, all black velvet and gold, was bumbling and butting there.

The flat creek bank was warm, soft mud. Little pale-yellow and pale-blue butterflies hovered there, and alighted and sipped. Bright dragonflies flew on blurry wings. The mud squeezed up between Laura's toes. Where she stepped, and where Mary stepped, and where the oxen had walked, there were tiny pools of water in their footprints.

Where they waded in the shallow water a footprint would not stay. First a swirl like smoke came up from it and wavered away in the clear water. Then the footprint slowly melted. The toes smoothed out and the heel was only a small hollow.

There were tiny fishes in the water. They were so small that you could hardly see them. Only when they went swiftly sometimes a silvery belly flashed. When Laura and Mary stood still these little fishes swarmed around their feet and nibbled. It was a tickly feeling.

On top of the water the water-bugs skated. They had tall legs, and each of their feet made a wee dent in the water. It was hard to see a water-bug; he skated so fast that before you saw him he was somewhere else.

The rushes in the wind made a wild, lonely sound. They were not soft and flat like grass; they were hard and round and sleek and jointed. One day when Laura was wading in a deep place by the rushes, she took hold of a big one to pull herself up on the bank. It squeaked.

For a minute Laura could hardly breathe. Then she pulled another. It squeaked, and came in two.

The rushes were little hollow tubes, fitted together at the joints. The tubes squeaked when you pulled them apart. They squeaked when you pushed them together again.

Laura and Mary pulled them apart to hear them squeak. Then they put little ones together to make necklaces. They put big ones together to make long tubes. They blew through the tubes into the creek and made it bubble. They blew at the little fishes and scared them. Whenever they were thirsty, they could draw up long drinks of water through those tubes.

Ma laughed when Laura and Mary came to dinner and supper, all splashed and muddy, with green necklaces around their necks and the long green tubes in their hands. They brought her bouquets of the blue flags and she put them on the table to make it pretty.

"I declare," she said, "you two play in the creek so much, you'll be turning to water-bugs!"

Pa and Ma did not care how much they played in the creek. Only they must never go upstream beyond the little willow valley. The creek came around a curve there. It came out of a hole full of deep, dark water. They must never go near enough to that hole, even to see it.

"Some day I'll take you there," Pa promised them. And one Sunday afternoon he told them that this was the day.

Deep Water

In the dugout Laura and Mary took off all their clothes and over their bare skins they put on old patched dresses. Ma tied on her sunbonnet, Pa took Carrie on his arm, and they all set out.

They went past the cattle path and the rushes, past the willow valley and the plum thickets. They went down a steep, grassy bank, and then across a level place where the grass was tall and coarse. They passed a high, almost straight-up wall of earth where no grass grew.

"What is that, Pa?" Laura asked; and Pa said, "That is a tableland, Laura."

He pushed on through the thick, tall grass, making a path for Ma and Mary and Laura. Suddenly they came out of the high grass and the creek was there.

It ran twinkling over white gravel into a wide pool, curved against a low bank where the grass was short. Tall willows stood up on the other side of the pool. Flat on the water lay a shimmery picture of those willows, with every green leaf fluttering.

Ma sat on the grassy bank and kept Carrie with her, while Laura and Mary waded into the pool.

"Stay near the edge, girls!" Ma told them. "Don't go in where it's deep."

The water came up under their skirts and made them float. Then the calico got wet and stuck to their legs. Laura went in deeper and deeper. The water came up and up, almost to her waist. She squatted down, and it came to her chin.

Everything was watery, cool, and unsteady. Laura felt very light. Her feet were so light that they almost lifted off the creek bottom. She hopped, and splashed with her arms.

"Oo, Laura, don't!" Mary cried.

"Don't go in any farther, Laura," said Ma.

Laura kept on splashing. One big splash lifted both feet. Her feet came up, her arms did as they pleased, her head went under the water. She was scared. There was nothing to hold on to, nothing solid anywhere. Then she was standing up, streaming water all over. But her feet were solid.

Nobody had seen that. Mary was tucking up her skirts, Ma was playing with Carrie. Pa was out of sight among the willows. Laura walked as fast as she could in the water. She stepped down deeper and deeper. The water came up past her middle, up to her arms.

Suddenly, deep down in the water, something grabbed her foot.

The thing jerked, and down she went into the deep water. She couldn't breathe, she couldn't see. She grabbed and could not get hold of anything. Water filled her ears and her eyes and her mouth.

Then her head came out of the water close to Pa's head. Pa was holding her.

"Well, young lady," Pa said, "you went out too far, and how did you like it?"

Laura could not speak; she had to breathe.

"You heard Ma tell you to stay close to the bank," said Pa. "Why didn't you obey her? You deserved a ducking, and I ducked you. Next time you'll do as you're told."

"Y-yes, Pa!" Laura spluttered. "Oh, Pa, p-please do it again!"

Pa said, "Well, I'll—!" Then his great laughter rang among the willows.

"Why didn't you holler when I ducked you?" he asked Laura. "Weren't you scared?"

"I w-was—awful scared!" Laura gasped. "But p-please do it again!" Then she asked him, "How did you get down there, Pa?"

Pa told her he had swum under water from the willows. But they could not stay in the deep water; they must go near the bank and play with Mary.

All that afternoon Pa and Laura and Mary played in the water. They waded and they fought water fights, and whenever Laura or Mary went near the deep water, Pa ducked them. Mary was a good girl after one ducking, but Laura was ducked many times.

Then it was almost chore time and they had to go home. They went dripping along the path through the tall grass, and when they came to the tableland Laura wanted to climb it.

Pa climbed part way up, and Laura and Mary climbed, holding to his hands. The dry dirt slipped and slid. Tangled grass roots hung down from the bulging edge overhead. Then Pa lifted Laura up and set her on the tableland.

It really was like a table. That ground rose up high above the tall grasses, and it was round, and flat on top. The grass there was short and soft.

Pa and Laura and Mary stood up on top of that tableland, and looked over the grass tops and the pool to the prairie beyond. They looked all around at prairies stretching to the rim of the sky.

Then they had to slide down again to the lowland and go on home. That had been a wonderful afternoon.

"It's been lots of fun," Pa said. "But you girls remember what I tell you. Don't you ever go near that swimming-hole unless I am with you."

Strange Animal

All the next day Laura remembered. She remembered the cool, deep water in the shade of the tall willows. She remembered that she must not go near it.

Pa was away. Mary stayed with Ma in the dugout. Laura played all alone in the hot sunshine. The blue flags were withering among the dull rushes. She went past the willow valley and played in the prairie grasses among the black-eyed Susans and goldenrod. The sunshine was very hot and the wind was scorching.

Then Laura thought of the tableland. She wanted to climb it again. She wondered if she could climb it all by herself. Pa had not said that she could not go to the tableland.

She ran down the steep bank and went across the lowland, through the tall, coarse grasses. The tableland stood up straight and high. It was very hard to climb. The dry earth slid under Laura's feet, her dress was dirty where her knees dug in while she held on to the grasses and pulled herself up. Dust itched on her sweaty skin. But at last she got her stomach on the edge; she heaved and rolled and she was on top of the tableland.

She jumped up, and she could see the deep, shady pool under the willows. It was cool and wet, and her whole skin felt thirsty. But she remembered that she must not go there.

The tableland seemed big and empty and not interesting. It had been exciting when Pa was there, but now it was just flat land, and Laura thought she would go home and get a drink. She was very thirsty.

She slid down the side of the tableland and slowly started back along the way she had come. Down among the tall grasses the air was smothery and very hot. The dugout was far away and Laura was terribly thirsty.

She remembered with all her might that she must not go near that deep, shady swimming-pool, and suddenly she turned around and hurried toward it. She thought she would only look at it. Just looking at it would make her feel better. Then she thought she might wade in the edge of it but she would not go into the deep water.

She came into the path that Pa had made, and she trotted faster.

Right in the middle of the path before her stood an animal.

Laura jumped back, and stood and stared at it. She had never seen such an animal. It was almost as long as Jack, but its legs were very short. Long gray fur bristled all over it. It had a flat head and small ears. Its flat head slowly tilted up and it stared at Laura.

She stared back at its funny face. And while they stood still and staring, that animal widened and shortened and spread flat on the ground. It grew flatter and flatter, till it was a gray fur laid there. It was not like a whole animal at all. Only it had eyes staring up.

Slowly and carefully Laura stooped and reached and picked up a willow stick. She felt better then. She stayed bent over, looking at that flat gray fur.

It did not move and neither did Laura. She wondered what would happen if she poked it. It might change to some other shape. She poked it gently with the short stick.

A frightful snarl came out of it. Its eyes sparkled mad, and fierce white teeth snapped almost on Laura's nose.

Laura ran with all her might. She could run fast. She did not stop running until she was in the dugout.

"Goodness, Laura!" Ma said. "You'll make yourself sick, tearing around so in this heat."

All that time, Mary had been sitting like a little lady, spelling out words in the book that Ma was teaching her to read. Mary was a good little girl.

Laura had been bad and she knew it. She had broken her promise to Pa. But no one had seen her. No one knew that she had started to go to the swimming-hole. If she did not tell, no one would ever know. Only that strange animal knew, and it could not tell on her. But she felt worse and worse inside.

That night she lay awake beside Mary. Pa and Ma sat in the starlight outside the door and Pa was playing his fiddle.

"Go to sleep, Laura," Ma said, softly, and softly the fiddle sang to her. Pa was a shadow against the sky and his bow danced among the great stars.

Everything was beautiful and good, except Laura. She had broken her promise to Pa. Breaking a promise was as bad as telling a lie. Laura wished she had not done it. But she had done it, and if Pa knew, he would punish her.

Pa went on playing softly in the starlight. His fiddle sang to her sweetly and happily. He thought she was a good little girl. At last Laura could bear it no longer.

She slid out of bed and her bare feet stole across the cool earthen floor. In her nightgown and nightcap she stood beside Pa. He drew the last notes from the strings with his bow and she could feel him smiling down at her.

"What is it, little half-pint?" he asked her. "You look like a little ghost, all white in the dark."

"Pa," Laura said, in a quivery small voice, "I—I—started to go to the swimming-hole."

"You did!" Pa exclaimed. Then he asked, "Well, what stopped you?"

"I don't know," Laura whispered. "It had gray fur and it— it flattened out flat. It snarled."

"How big was it?" Pa asked.

Laura told him all about that strange animal.

Pa said, "It must have been a badger."

Then for a long time he did not say anything and Laura waited. Laura could not see his face in the dark, but she leaned against his knee and she could feel how strong and kind he was.

"Well," he said at last, "I hardly know what to do, Laura. You see, I trusted you. It is hard to know what to do with a person you can't trust. But do you know what people have to do to anyone they can't trust?"

"Wh—at?" Laura quavered.

"They have to watch him," said Pa. "So I guess you must be watched. Your Ma will have to do it because I must work at Nelson's. So tomorrow you stay where Ma can watch you. You are not to go out of her sight all day. If you are good all day, then we will let you try again to be a little girl we can trust."

"How about it, Caroline?" he asked Ma.

"Very well, Charles," Ma said out of the dark. "I will watch her tomorrow. But I am sure she will be good. Now back to bed, Laura, and go to sleep."

The next day was a dreadful day.

Ma was mending, and Laura had to stay in the dugout. She could not even fetch water from the spring, for that was going out of Ma's sight. Mary fetched the water. Mary took Carrie to walk on the prairie. Laura had to stay in.

Jack laid his nose on his paws and waggled, he jumped out on the path and looked back at her, smiling with his ears, begging her to come out. He could not understand why she did not.

Laura helped Ma. She washed the dishes and made both beds and swept the floor and set the table. At dinner she sat bowed on her bench and ate what Ma set before her. Then she wiped the dishes. After that she ripped a sheet that was worn in the middle. Ma turned the strips of muslin and pinned them together, and Laura whipped the new seam, over and over with tiny stitches.

She thought that seam and that day would never end.

But at last Ma rolled up her mending and it was time to get supper.

"You have been a good girl, Laura," Ma said.

"We will tell Pa so. And tomorrow morning you and I are going to look for that badger. I am sure he saved you from drowning, for if you had gone to that deep water you would have gone into it. Once you begin being naughty, it is easier to go on and on, and sooner or later something dreadful happens."

"Yes, Ma," Laura said. She knew that now.

The whole day was gone. Laura had not seen that sunrise, nor the shadows of clouds on the prairie. The morning-glories were withered and that day's blue flags were dead. All day Laura had not seen the water running in the creek, the little fishes in it, and the water-bugs skating over it. She was sure that being good could never be as hard as being watched.

Next day she went with Ma to look for the badger. In the path she showed Ma the place where he had flattened himself on the grass. Ma found the hole where he lived. It was a round hole under a clump of grass on the prairie bank. Laura called to him and she poked a stick into the hole.

If the badger was at home, he would not come out. Laura never saw that old gray badger again.

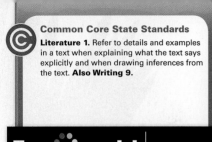

Envision It! | Retell

Think Critically

1. Laura Ingalls Wilder's stories have been read and watched worldwide by both adults and children. Why do you think people find her books so appealing? **Text to World**

2. Is this story told in the first person or the third person? Explain how you know. How would the story have been different if Laura had been the narrator of the events? **Think Like an Author**

3. Think about Pa's relationship with his family. What are some words you might use to describe his character? Use examples from the story to support your word choices.
   Literary Elements: Character, Setting, and Plot

4. Before reading this story, what did you know about families who moved west to settle our country? Did this information help you to understand Laura's life on the prairie? Why?
   Background Knowledge

5. **Look Back and Write** Look back at page 97. Describe Pa's feelings when Laura tells him that she has broken her promise to him. Provide evidence to support your answer.
   Key Ideas and Details • Text Evidence

Meet the Author and the Illustrator

Laura Ingalls Wilder

Laura Ingalls Wilder was born in a log cabin in 1867 near the village of Pepin, in Wisconsin. Her family moved often, always looking for a better homestead site. When she was a grown woman, with a child of her own, she would tell stories of life on the frontier and the fun she had.

"I was a regular little tomboy, and it was fun to walk the two miles to school," she said much later in life during an interview.

It was her daughter, Rose, who encouraged her to write about her adventures growing up on the prairie. Laura re-created for readers the life-threatening blizzards, swarms of locusts, prairie fires, and the rollicking good times with Pa, Ma, Mary, Carrie, Grace, and, of course, with Jack, the faithful family dog.

Here is another book by Laura Ingalls Wilder.

Little House in the Big Woods

Garth Williams

Garth Williams was born in New York State in 1912. He was a painter, sculptor, and an architect before he became a children's book illustrator. Garth Williams illustrated more than 100 children's books, including *Stuart Little, Charlotte's Web,* and the *Little House* books.

Use the *Reader's and Writer's Notebook* to record your independent reading.

Common Core State Standards

Writing 3.a. Orient the reader by establishing a situation and introducing a narrator and/or characters; organize an event sequence that unfolds naturally. **Also Writing 3.d., 4., Language 1.f.**

Parody

A **parody** is a written work that imitates the style of another author or written work using humor or exaggeration. The student model on the next page is an example of the beginning of a parody.

Writing Prompt Write a parody of *On the Banks of Plum Creek*.

Let's Write It!

Key Features of Parody

- imitates another work, usually with humor
- follows the form of the original
- changes or exaggerates parts of the original work

READING STREET ONLINE
GRAMMAR JAMMER
www.ReadingStreet.com

Writer's Checklist

Remember, you should . . .

☑ show a clear connection to the original story using details about the characters and setting.

☑ use humor or exaggeration to express your ideas.

☑ imitate the original author's voice and style.

☑ use a complete subject and complete predicate in sentences.

Life on Plum Creek

Every morning after Mary and Laura had washed the dishes, cleaned their rooms, swept every room in the house, hung out the laundry, walked the dog, and cleaned out the wood stove, they could finally go out to play.

All around the front door, Virginia creeper vines twined. They seemed to be waiting, ready to spring at anyone who tried to pass through the doorway. **The grasping green tentacles clutched at the girls as they passed.** Mary wished she had a hatchet so she could get rid of the vines once and for all! Outside the birds were screeching, "Caw, Caw, Caw." "Ack-Ack-Ackka-Ack-Ack!" another cackled.

"Noisy crows!" said Laura, ducking as a large black bird skimmed her head. "What about the robins and sparrows that sing pretty songs on the other side of the creek? Why can't they sing for us instead of the squawking crows?"

"Maybe they can if we can get Pa to leave the oxen and take us to the other side of the creek. Let's go!" Mary said as they darted down the path.

Genre A **parody** follows the form and style of the original.

Complete subjects and predicates are used correctly.

Writing Trait Voice The language gives a sense of flavor to the story.

Conventions

Complete Subjects and Predicates

Remember The **complete subject** of a sentence contains the topic and the words that modify it. The **complete predicate** of a sentence tells about the subject and includes the verb.

Next, you decide to find out more about *On the Banks of Plum Creek* by Laura Ingalls Wilder. You find these results in an encyclopedia search.

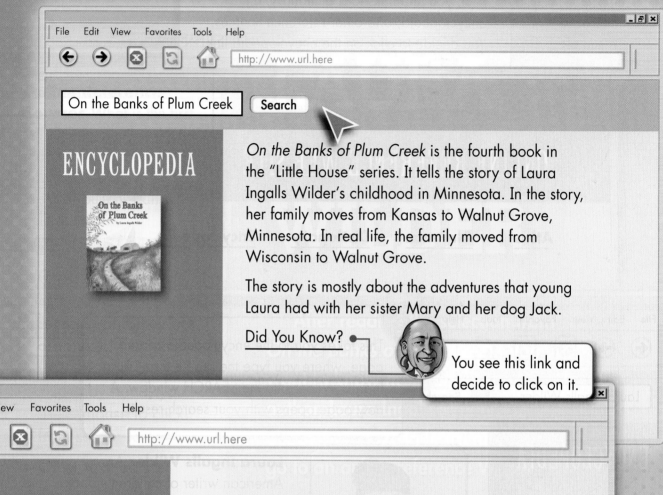

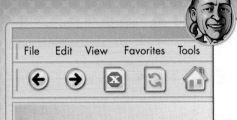

On another Web site, you find these photographs of Laura Ingalls Wilder, her family, and life on the prairie. Now you are getting a better picture of what Laura's life must have been like when she was young.

Common Core State Standards

Language 4.c. Consult reference materials (e.g., dictionaries, glossaries, thesauruses), both print and digital, to find the pronunciation and determine or clarify the precise meaning of key words and phrases. **Also Foundational Skills 4.b., Writing 7., Speaking/Listening 1.b., Language 4.**

Let's Learn It!

READING STREET ONLINE
ONLINE STUDENT EDITION
www.ReadingStreet.com

Vocabulary

Multiple-Meaning Words

Dictionary/Glossary Some familiar words may have multiple meanings, or more than one meaning. When a word you know doesn't make sense in a sentence, try to use context clues to figure it out. You can also use a dictionary or glossary to find other meanings of the word.

Practice It! Look at the title *On the Banks of Plum Creek* and the heading "Rushes and Flags" on page 86. Write as many meanings as you know for the words *banks, rushes,* and *flags.* Check your definitions in a dictionary or the glossary. Then look at how the word *tearing* is used on page 95 and how the word *whipped* is used on page 98. Use a dictionary to decide which meaning of each word is used in the story.

Fluency

Rate and Accuracy

Reading too quickly can make it difficult to understand what you read. Matching the pace of your reading to the mood of the story can help you make sense of the story.

Practice It! With a partner, practice reading aloud *On the Banks of Plum Creek,* page 87, paragraphs 1–4. Match your reading pace to the mood of the writing. Read the descriptive paragraphs at a pace that allows you to make a picture in your mind of what you are reading. Does this help you make better sense of what you read?

108

Listening and Speaking

When you give a presentation, speak clearly and directly to the audience.

Advertisement

The purpose of most ads is to inform people about a product, service, or place. An ad can be in a newspaper, on television, on the radio, or on the Internet. Some advertisements create a negative impact on consumers. Some advertisers want to convince people to buy their products so much that they make unrealistic, even dishonest, claims.

Practice It! With a partner, create a positive magazine ad that will convince people to visit a town, a city, or another area in the United States. Use the library or Internet to find information about the area. Choose details, such as interesting landforms, wildlife, tourist attractions, and events, to include in your ad. Present your ad to the class. Acknowledge reactions and interest.

Tips

Listening ...

- Listen attentively to the speaker.
- Make comments related to the subject of the ad.

Speaking ...

- Correctly use the complete subject and complete predicate in a sentence.
- Speak clearly to communicate your ideas.

Teamwork ...

- Offer suggestions to improve others' advertisements.

Common Core State Standards

Speaking/Listening 1.c. Pose and respond to specific questions to clarify or follow up on information, and make comments that contribute to the discussion and link to the remarks of others. **Also Language 6.**

Oral Vocabulary

Let's Talk About

The Southwest

- Ask questions about which states make up the Southwest.

- Share opinions about what is interesting about the Southwest.

- Describe a place in the Southwest to visit.

READING STREET ONLINE
CONCEPT TALK VIDEO
www.ReadingStreet.com

111

Common Core State Standards
Literature 1. Refer to details and examples in a text when explaining what the text says explicitly and when drawing inferences from the text. **Also Literature 2.**

Envision It! | Skill Strategy

Skill

Strategy

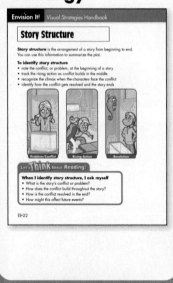

READING STREET ONLINE
ENVISION IT! ANIMATIONS
www.ReadingStreet.com

Comprehension Skill

🔄 Author's Purpose

- An author may write to persuade, inform, entertain, or express ideas or feelings.

- An author can have more than one purpose. The theme of a story can teach a moral or lesson as well as entertain.

- Use this chart to identify the author's purpose as you read "The Fox and the Grapes."

Ideas	Author's Purpose	Text
what they are how they are expressed	persuade inform entertain express	title and any heads facts and information fictional characters and plot pattern of ideas

Comprehension Strategy

🔄 Story Structure

Readers note the structure of fiction: the problem or goal, rising action (building up to the climax), climax (where the conflict is confronted), and outcome (where the conflict is resolved). Readers also know when a story is told by a character involved in the action (first person) or by one not involved in the action (third person).

The FOX and the Grapes

Adapted from Aesop

Skill What do you think the author's purpose will be? Look at the title, the byline, and the illustrations for clues.

There once was a hungry fox who came upon a grapevine wound around a high trellis. Hanging from the vine was a bunch of grapes.

"What DEE-LISH-US – looking grapes," the fox said to himself. "I think I'll just step up and grab a few." So he stood up on his hind legs under the trellis, but the grapes were out of reach.

"Hmmm," said the fox. "Those DEE-licious grapes are higher up than I thought." So the fox jumped up as high as he could, but the grapes were still out of reach.

Strategy What is the rising action, the climax, and the resolution of the story? Who is describing the action?

"This is ridiculous," said the fox. "How hard can it be to grab some dee-licious grapes?" So the fox stepped back, took a running leap—and missed. The grapes were still out of reach.

"Humph!" said the fox, walking away with a toss of his tail. "I thought at first those grapes looked delicious, but now I see they are sour."

Skill Summarize the lesson about life this Aesop fable teaches us. Explain the message it gives the reader.

Your Turn!

⏸ Need a Review? See the *Envision It! Handbook* for help with author's purpose and story structure.

▶ Ready to Try It? Use what you've learned about author's purpose as you read *The Horned Toad Prince*.

113

Envision It! | Words to Know

lassoed

prairie

riverbed

bargain

favor

offended

shrieked

Vocabulary Strategy for

🎯 Synonyms and Antonyms

Context Clues Synonyms and antonyms can be clues to the meaning of an unfamiliar word. Synonyms are words with almost the same meaning. In the analogy *boy* is to *man* as *girl* is to *woman, boy* and *man* are synonyms. Antonyms are words with opposite meanings. Use an antonym to complete this analogy: *girl* is to *boy* as *man* is to _____.

1. Complete this analogy using a word from the *Words to Know*: *laughed* is to *cried* as *whispered* is to _____.

2. Look at the sentence in which an unfamiliar word appears. The author may give a synonym or antonym in the same sentence.

3. If there is not a synonym or an antonym in the same sentence, check the sentences around it. If you find a synonym or an antonym, try it in the sentence.

As you read "Tall Paul," look for synonyms or antonyms to give you context clues to the meaning of any unfamiliar word.

Words to Write Imagine you met Tall Paul. Write a tale about Tall Paul and a day you spent with him. Use *Words to Know* in the tale.

Tall Paul

Tall Paul was a cowboy who lived on the plains not so long ago. He was not just any cowboy, though. He was so long-legged he could cross a mile of prairie in just one step. And he was so big and strong he lassoed and caught a whole herd of cattle with a single toss of his rope.

Tall Paul did not eat any small meals. No, he had a mighty big appetite. He ate a mountain of flapjacks for breakfast. One time, out on the range, he got so thirsty he drank a river. The dry riverbed just lay there, gasping for water.

Tall Paul felt bad about that, so he struck a bargain with the sky. The sky would bring a flood of rain. In return, the sky asked this favor: "I will help you if you do me this service. My servant, Wind, can't blow the clouds over that mountain there. I need you to flatten it a little for me."

Tall Paul said to the mountain, "Now don't be offended. I'll just take a little off the top." The mountain shrieked and screamed, but the deed was done. Tall Paul jumped on that mountain and turned it into a nice little mesa. In an instant, the rains began to fall.

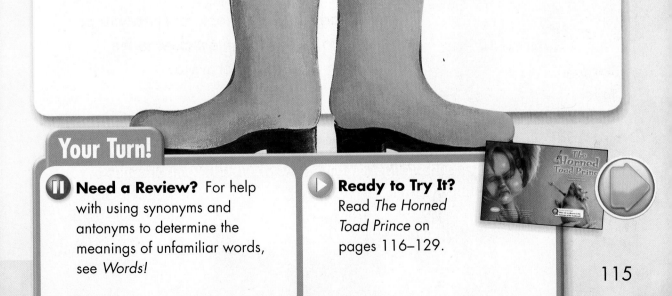

Your Turn!

⏸ **Need a Review?** For help with using synonyms and antonyms to determine the meanings of unfamiliar words, see *Words!*

▶ **Ready to Try It?** Read *The Horned Toad Prince* on pages 116–129.

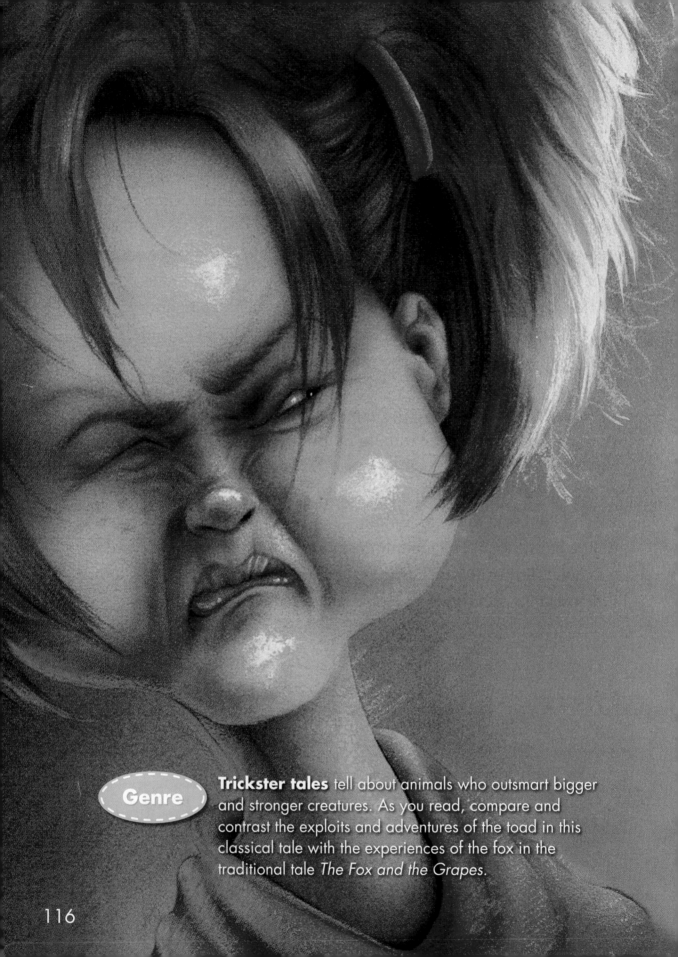

Genre

Trickster tales tell about animals who outsmart bigger and stronger creatures. As you read, compare and contrast the exploits and adventures of the toad in this classical tale with the experiences of the fox in the traditional tale *The Fox and the Grapes*.

116

The Horned Toad Prince

by Jackie Mims Hopkins
illustrated by Michael Austin

Question of the Week

What can we discover in the landscape of the Southwest?

Reba Jo loved to twang her guitar and sing while the prairie wind whistled through the thirsty sagebrush.

Singing with the wind was one of the ways Reba Jo entertained herself on the lonesome prairie. Sometimes she amused herself by racing her horse, Flash, against a tumbleweed cartwheeling across her daddy's land.

But her favorite pastime of all was roping. She lassoed cacti, water buckets, fence posts, and any unlucky critter that crossed her path.

One blustery morning, as she was riding the range looking for something to lasso, Reba Jo came upon a dry riverbed. Her daddy had warned her to stay away from these *arroyos*. He'd told her that a prairie storm could blow in quicker than a rattlesnake's strike, causing a flash flood to rip through the riverbed. The swift water would wash away anything or anyone in its way.

Reba Jo knew she should turn back. But right at the edge of this gully she spied a vulture, all fat and sassy, sitting on top of a dried-up old well, just daring her to toss her spinning rope around his long ugly neck.

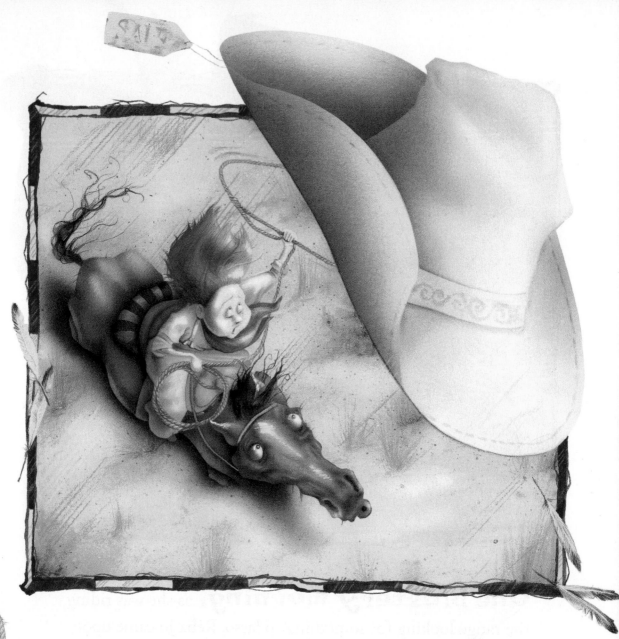

As Reba Jo's lasso whirled into the air, a great gust of wind came whipping through the *arroyo* and blew her new cowgirl hat right off her head and down to the bottom of the dusty old well.

Reba Jo scrambled to the edge of the well. She peered down into the darkness and commenced to crying. Suddenly she heard a small voice say, "*¿Qué pasa, señorita?*"

She looked around and wondered if the wind blowing through the *arroyo* was fooling her ears.

But then, there in the sand, she spotted a big fat horned toad looking up at her. "What's the matter, *señorita?*" he asked again.

"Oh," she cried, "the brand-new hat my daddy bought for me just blew down into this stinkin' old well. I'll never be able to get it out, and I'll be in a peck of trouble when he finds out I've been playin' down here near the *arroyo.*"

121

The horned toad looked at her slyly and said, "I'll fetch your *sombrero* for you if you will do *tres pequeños* favors for me."

She sniffed and asked, "Three small favors? Like what?"

"All you have to do is feed me some chili, play your *guitarra* for me, and let me take a *siesta* in your *sombrero*."

"Some chili, a song, and a nap in my hat? I don't think so, *amigo*," replied Reba Jo.

"Okay, *señorita*, but do you mind if I follow you home and listen as you explain to your *padre* where your new *sombrero* is, and how it got there?"

"Good point, toad," Reba Jo said. "You've got yourself a deal."

Reba Jo placed the little critter in a splintered wooden bucket and carefully lowered him down the dry well, where he retrieved Reba Jo's hat.

Then, without so much as a *muchas gracias*, Reba Jo
snatched her hat from the horned toad and galloped home.
As she rode out of sight, she ignored the horned toad's cries
of "*¡Espérate!* Wait up, *señorita,* wait up!"

'Long about midday, when Reba Jo had sat down to eat,
she heard a tap, tap, tapping at the ranch house door.

Reba Jo opened the door, but when she saw it was the fat
horned toad, she slammed the door in his face.

His small voice called, "*Señorita, señorita, por favor.* Please
let me come in."

The horned toad rapped on the door again. This time Reba
Jo's father opened it and spotted the little fella on the porch.

"*Hola, señor,*" said the horned toad.

"Well howdy, mister toad. What brings you here?"

"A little deal that I made with your daughter, *señor.*"

"What's this all about, Reba Jo?" her father asked her.

Reba Jo admitted that the horned toad had done her a
favor and in return she had promised to feed him some chili,
play her guitar for him, and let him take a nap in her hat.

124

"Now, Reba Jo," said her daddy, "if you strike a bargain in these parts, a deal's a deal. Come on in, pardner, you look mighty hungry."

"I am indeed. *Yo tengo mucha hambre*," said the horned toad. "I hope that is chili I smell." He peeked at Reba Jo's meal.

"Dadburn it!" Reba Jo muttered. She pushed her bowl of chili toward him.

Soon the horned toad's belly was bulging. "Now, for a little *serenata*," he said.

Reba Jo stomped over, grabbed her guitar, and belted out a lullaby for her guest.

Then the drowsy little horned toad eyed Reba Jo's hat and yawned, saying, "That lovely music has made me *muy soñoliento*. I'm ready for my *siesta*."

"Forget it, Bucko," Reba Jo snapped. "You're not gettin' near my hat. No lizard cooties allowed!"

"**Now, señorita,** remember what your wise *padre* said about striking a bargain in these parts," said the clever little horned toad.

"I know, I know," grumbled Reba Jo, "a deal's a deal." And with that, she flipped him into her hat.

"Before I take my *siesta*, I have just one more favor to ask," said the horned toad.

"Now what?" asked Reba Jo.

"Would you give me a kiss, *por favor?*" asked the horned toad.

"You've gotta be kiddin'!" shrieked Reba Jo. "You know dang well a kiss wasn't part of this deal, you low-life reptile."

"If you do this one last thing for me, we'll call it even, and I'll be on my way *pronto*," the horned toad said.

"You'll leave right away?" Reba Jo asked suspiciously. "You promise?"

"*Sí, te prometo,*" agreed the horned toad.

Reba Jo thought hard for a minute. She glared at the horned toad. "I can't believe I'm even considerin' this," she said, "but if it means you'll leave right now . . . pucker up, Lizard Lips."

Before Reba Jo could wipe the toad spit off her lips, a fierce dust devil spun into the yard, swept the horned toad off his feet, and whirled him around in a dizzying cloud of prairie dust.

When the dust cleared, there before Reba Jo stood a handsome young *caballero*.

"Who are you?" Reba Jo demanded, staring at the gentleman.

"I am Prince Maximillian José Diego López de España."

"Whoa, how did this happen?" Reba Jo asked in amazement.

"**Many, many years ago** when I came to this country, I offended the great spirit of the *arroyo*. The spirit put a spell on me and turned me into a horned toad. For many years I've been waiting for a cowgirl like you to break the spell. *Muchas gracias* for my freedom, *señorita*. Now I'll be leaving as I promised."

"Now hold on for just a dadburn minute," said Reba Jo, stepping in front of the nobleman. "I recollect my daddy readin' me a story where somethin' like this happened. Aren't we supposed to get hitched and ride off into the sunset?"

With a twinkle in his eye, the *caballero* replied, "*Lo siento*. So sorry, Reba Jo, when you strike a bargain in these parts, a deal's a deal. *Adiós, señorita!*"

Common Core State Standards

Writing 9. Draw evidence from literary or informational texts to support analysis, reflection, and research. **Also Literature 1.**

Envision It! Retell

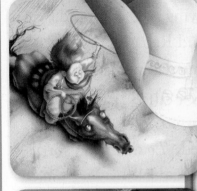

Think Critically

1. On page 129, Reba Jo says, "I recollect my daddy readin' me a story where somethin' like this happened." Does Reba Jo's tale remind you of another tale? Which one? Why? **Text to Text**

2. This story is fit for a storyteller. Find a part of the tale that would be especially good if read aloud by a storyteller. Why is that such a good part to read? **Think Like an Author**

3. An author's purpose can be to teach the reader an important lesson. What lesson do you think the author teaches in this story? **Author's Purpose**

4. What was the most important event in the story? Why do you think this? **Story Structure**

5. **Look Back and Write** Look back at pages 123–128. What do you think of Reba Jo's behavior toward the horned toad? Explain. Provide evidence to support your answer.

   Key Ideas and Details • Text Evidence

Meet the Author and the Illustrator
Jackie Mims Hopkins and Michael Austin

Jackie Mims Hopkins wasn't much of a reader as a young girl. "I didn't enjoy reading any book of length. I couldn't sit still long enough to read." Now she is an author and a librarian!

Ms. Hopkins got the idea for *The Horned Toad Prince* when she was researching horned toads for another book. "I realized there weren't many stories about them. I decided it was time to write a story about the little critters," she says. "I started thinking about which fairy tale could be used with a horned toad as the main character. 'The Frog Prince' was a perfect match."

Michael Austin created the art for this story. "*The Horned Toad Prince* stood out to me right away because of its personality and energy," he says. As an artist, Mr. Austin has always had a "strange point of view." He enjoys drawing because it gives him a chance to "draw things my own way, strange or not."

Here are other books by Jackie Mims Hopkins.

Use the *Reader's and Writer's Notebook* to record your independent reading.

131

Common Core State Standards

Writing 4. Produce clear and coherent writing in which the development and organization are appropriate to task, purpose, and audience. **Also Language 1., 2.c.**

Friendly Letter

A **friendly letter** is a letter in which the writer's thoughts are expressed in an informal way. The student model on the next page is an example of a friendly letter.

Writing Prompt Imagine you are Reba Jo. Write a letter to a friend explaining what happened when you met up with a horned toad.

Let's Write It!

Key Features of a Friendly Letter

- usually includes five parts: heading, salutation, body, closing, and signature

- heading may include only the date

- written in a friendly voice, often to someone you know well

READING STREET ONLINE
GRAMMAR JAMMER
www.ReadingStreet.com

Writer's Checklist

Remember, you should . . .

☑ include a heading, salutation, body, closing, and signature.

☑ use language that is appropriate to your audience and purpose.

☑ use simple and compound sentences with subject-verb agreement.

☑ use commas correctly in compound sentences.

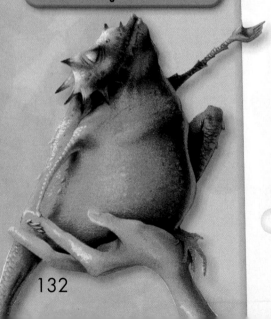

August 25, 20__

Dear Juanita,

Guess what! Today I was riding Flash out on the prairie, wearing my brand new cowgirl hat, when the wind blew my hat into a well. Then an ugly old toad spoke to me!

The toad said he would get my sombrero, but first I had to agree to do three favors for him. The third favor was ridiculous. Can you believe that old toad wanted to sleep in my brand new hat? I agreed, but I took off for home as soon as I got my hat.

Well, that old toad followed me home! Daddy said I had to do the three favors. In order to keep the toad out of my hat, I agreed to kiss him. Then, just like in a fairy tale, my kiss turned that old toad into a handsome young prince! But fairy tales aren't all they're cracked up to be. He wasn't a nice prince at all. He's gone now, and I'm well rid of him. Don't kiss any toads!

Your friend,

Reba Jo

Writing Trait Conventions Commas are used correctly.

Compound sentences use commas and conjunctions.

Genre A **friendly letter** includes a closing and a signature.

Conventions

Compound Sentences

Remember A **compound sentence** is a sentence that contains two or more simple sentences, which are often connected by a comma and a conjunction such as *and, or,* or *but.* Each part of a compound sentence has a subject and a predicate.

133

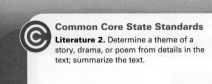

Social Studies in Reading

Genre
Fable

- A fable is a fictional story that presents a lesson (or moral) about life. Most fables are traditional stories that were passed down from generation to generation.

- Many fables use animals as their main characters.

- Some fables also contain trickster characters. Tricksters try to trick other characters in order to get something they want or to escape a dangerous situation.

- Read "The Fox and the Tiger." Look for elements that make this story a fable. What do you think the lesson of the fable is?

The Fox and the Tiger

**a fable from China
retold by Susan McCloskey**

One morning, Tiger said, "I'm hungry! I'd better find something to eat!"

Tiger set out across the forest, and after a while he came across Fox.

"This is my lucky day!" Tiger said to Fox. "I'm very hungry, and you will make a fabulous breakfast!"

Fox stretched and yawned. "Oh," Fox said, "I was just thinking the same thing about you! If I weren't enjoying the sun so much, I'd gobble you up!"

"Hah!" Tiger laughed. "That's silly! I'm bigger and stronger. If I want to eat you for breakfast, I will!"

"Don't you know me?" Fox asked. "I'm King of the Forest. I will eat whomever I please. Sit beside me. You'll see that the animals are afraid to approach the waterhole when I'm here!"

"This I have to see," said Tiger, and he sat next to Fox.

Before long, Monkey came by to drink.

"I'm the King of the Forest!" cried Fox.

Monkey turned, saw Fox with Tiger, and scurried away.

The same thing happened again when Elephant approached the waterhole. Fox called out, "I'm the King of the Forest!" Elephant saw Fox with Tiger, and she thundered away.

When Tiger saw how fearful the animals were, he became afraid too. "Oh, my," he said to Fox. "Look how late it is. I mustn't delay you from your. . . ."

"Breakfast?" said Fox, gazing hungrily at Tiger.

Tiger ran, and he never went near Fox's waterhole again.

MORAL *It is possible to borrow power when you have none of your own.*

Let's **Think** About...

Summarize and explain in your own words the lesson or moral as the theme of this fable. **Fable**

Let's **Think** About...

Reading Across Texts Are the characters in *The Horned Toad Prince* and "The Fox and the Tiger" alike or different? Make a chart to compare and contrast them.

Writing Across Texts Use your chart. Write a paragraph explaining how Reba Jo and the horned toad are like Fox and Tiger.

Common Core State Standards

Language 5.c. Demonstrate understanding of words by relating them to their opposites (antonyms) and to words with similar but not identical meanings (synonyms). **Also Foundational Skills 4.b., Speaking/Listening 4., Language 4.a.**

Let's Learn It!

READING STREET ONLINE
ONLINE STUDENT EDITION
www.ReadingStreet.com

Vocabulary

Synonyms and Antonyms

Context Clues When you read a word whose meaning you don't know, look at the sentence or a nearby sentence. You may find a synonym, or a word with almost the same meaning as the unfamiliar word, to use as a clue to figure out the meaning of the word.

Practice It! With a partner, find the word *arroyos* in *The Horned Toad Prince* on page 119, paragraph 1. Use a synonym in the sentence before it as a clue to help you figure out the meaning of *arroyos*. Tell its meaning to your partner. Then find the synonyms in nearby sentences that help you figure out meanings for the words *sombrero*, *guitarra*, and *siesta* on page 122. Discuss the words' meanings with your partner.

Fluency

Expression

Changing the volume of your voice as you read makes a story more interesting. Reading the character's dialogue louder or softer than the third-person narrator's voice will make the characters come alive.

Practice It! With a partner, practice reading aloud *The Horned Toad Prince*, pages 120–121. Use story cues to adjust the volume of your voice. When you read that Reba Jo hears a "small voice," whisper as you read the toad's dialogue. How loudly or softly do you read Reba Jo's response to the toad?

Listening and Speaking

When you give a presentation, make eye contact with the audience.

Oral Presentation/ Report

In an oral presentation, a speaker talks about a topic in front of an audience. The purpose of an oral presentation is to inform people about the topic.

Practice It! Prepare an oral presentation about a feature of the American Southwest. Choose an animal, plant, or landform as your topic. Think about questions you have about your topic. For example, *What does the animal look like?* or *Who are its enemies?* Research the answers and use them to prepare your presentation. Use photographs, drawings, or maps. Give your presentation to the class.

Tips

Listening ...

- Listen attentively to the speaker.

- Be ready to ask questions related to the topic.

Speaking ...

- Use complete compound sentences correctly.

- Make eye contact as you speak.

Teamwork ...

- Ask questions related to the topic.

- Answer questions with detail.

Common Core State Standards

Speaking/Listening 1. Engage effectively in a range of collaborative discussions (one-on-one, in groups, and teacher-led) with diverse partners on grade 4 topics and texts, building on others' ideas and expressing their own clearly. **Also Language 6.**

Oral Vocabulary

Let's Talk About

The West

- Express opinions about which states make up the West.

- Share ideas about favorite western states.

- Speak clearly when sharing opinions.

READING STREET ONLINE
CONCEPT TALK VIDEO
www.ReadingStreet.com

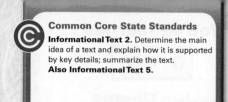

Common Core State Standards

Informational Text 2. Determine the main idea of a text and explain how it is supported by key details; summarize the text. **Also Informational Text 5.**

Envision It! | Skill Strategy

Skill

Strategy

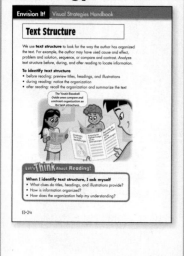

READING STREET ONLINE
ENVISION IT! ANIMATIONS
www.ReadingStreet.com

Comprehension Skill

Main Idea and Details

- The topic is what a paragraph, part of an article, or a whole article is about.

- The most important thing an author has to say about the topic is the main idea.

- The pieces of information that tell more about the main idea are the supporting details.

- Use the graphic organizer to summarize main idea and supporting details as you read "Send a Ranger!"

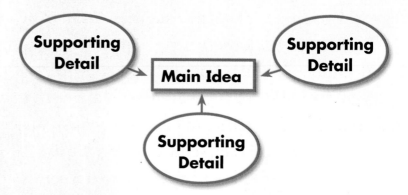

Comprehension Strategy

Text Structure

Understanding the way a text is organized can help you understand what you are reading. Before you read, preview the text and look for text features such as titles, headings, underlined words, and clue words (words that show cause and effect, sequence, or compare and contrast) to help you know what to expect.

SEND A RANGER!

The job of a ranger is made up of many different jobs. Park rangers are like police officers—they make sure people obey the rules of the park. Park rangers are like teachers—they take people on nature walks and tell them about important places in our history. Park rangers are like scientists—they keep track of information about plants and animals. Park rangers are like firefighters—they keep close watch to help put a stop to forest fires. Park rangers are like rescue workers—they hunt for people who are lost or hurt.

Skill Summarize the details you learned about a ranger's job. Summarize the main idea of this paragraph.

Yes, the job of a park ranger is made up of many different jobs. In fact, Stephen Mather, the first director of the National Parks Service, has said: "If a trail is to be blazed, send a ranger; if an animal is floundering in the snow, send a ranger; if a bear is in a hotel, send a ranger; if a fire threatens a forest, send a ranger; and if someone is to be saved, send a ranger."

Skill Why do you think the author restated a sentence used earlier? Is this a clue about what the main idea is?

Strategy Can you find a comparison the author used to describe the job of a ranger?

Does this sound like fun to you? Maybe you would like to be a park ranger.

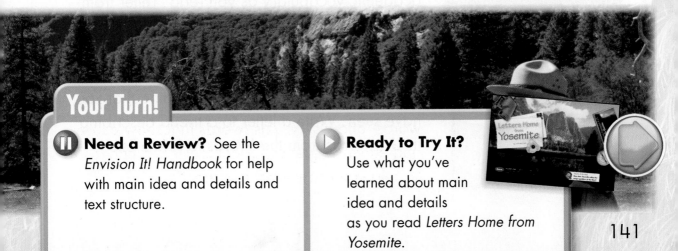

Your Turn!

⏸ **Need a Review?** See the *Envision It! Handbook* for help with main idea and details and text structure.

▶ **Ready to Try It?** Use what you've learned about main idea and details as you read *Letters Home from Yosemite.*

Envision It! | Words to Know

glacier

slopes

wilderness

impressive

naturalist

preserve

species

Vocabulary Strategy for

◎ Affixes: Suffixes -ist, -ive, -ness

Word Structure Suppose you come to an academic word that has the suffix -ist, -ive, or -ness at the end. You can use the suffix to figure out the word's meaning. The Latin suffix -ist makes a word mean "one who is an expert," as in biologist, an expert in biology. The Greek suffix -ive can make a word mean "tending or inclined to" as in active, which means "tending to act." The Old English -ness means "the quality of," as in goodness.

1. Find a word with the suffix -ist, -ive, or -ness. Put your finger over the suffix.

2. Look at the base word. Put the base word in the phrase "one who is an expert in ____" or "tending or inclined to ____" or "the quality of ____."

3. Does that meaning make sense in the sentence?

Use what you know about suffixes to figure out academic vocabulary as you read "Letter from Denali."

Words to Write Reread "Letter from Denali." Think of a park or other natural setting that you have seen. Write a letter to a friend describing it. Use words from the Words to Know list.

Letter from Denali

Dear Kevin,

Here we are in Denali National Park in Alaska. Denali is a gigantic park. The emptiness is overwhelming. It has more than 6 million acres of wilderness, so we certainly won't be seeing the whole park!

Denali was established to preserve the land, the animals, and plants that live here. More than 650 species of flowering plants and 217 species of animals live in Denali! That's what the naturalist on the guided walk told us yesterday. Our group was very attentive when a botanist who was with us said that to live in Denali year-round, a plant or animal species has to be able to survive long, cold winters.

Today we hiked up the lower slopes of Mt. McKinley. It is the highest mountain in North America, and it is part of Denali. We could see a giant glacier looking like a huge field of ice farther up on the mountain. It was a very impressive sight. Mt. McKinley has several glaciers, and some are more than 30 miles long!

I have taken a zillion pictures, but I really think this is a place you have to see in person.

Love,

Lisa

Your Turn!

 Need a Review? For help with using word structure and suffixes to determine the meanings of unfamiliar words, see *Words!*

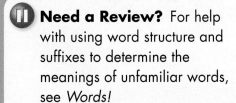 **Ready to Try It?** Read *Letters Home from Yosemite* on pp. 144–155.

Letters Home from Yosemite

by Lisa Halvorsen

Yosemite National Park
Visitor's Guide

Question of the Week
How does Yosemite reflect the unique qualities of the West?

145

Arrival in . . .
San Francisco

As our plane touched down in San Francisco, I knew we were in for an exciting vacation. I'd been reading about Yosemite on the plane. I learned that it is America's third national park. Yosemite is known throughout the world for its amazing scenery. It has incredible waterfalls, rock formations, alpine lakes and meadows, and giant sequoia trees. It's located in the east central part of California and covers 1,170 square miles. That's an area about the size of Rhode Island!

Efforts to protect the wilderness around Yosemite began in 1864. That's when President Abraham Lincoln signed the Yosemite Grant deeding the land to California. Yosemite was finally established as a national park on Oct. 1, 1890, by an act of Congress.

Views of **Yosemite**

Yosemite Valley

Topography

Our tour guide said that one of the first people to visit this area was John Muir, a Scottish naturalist. He fought hard to convince the U.S. government to preserve Yosemite as a national park. The name supposedly comes from the Indian name "yo'hem-iteh." That means grizzly bear.

Yosemite is right in the middle of the Sierra Nevada Mountains. These mountains stretch for 430 miles along California's eastern border. The area covers 15.5 million acres, which is about the size of Vermont, New Hampshire, and Connecticut combined! This is the highest and longest single continuous range of mountains in the lower 48 states (not including Alaska and Hawaii).

Native Americans were the first people to live in Yosemite, about 7,000 to 10,000 years ago. When explorers arrived at Yosemite Valley in the 1830s and 1840s, Southern Sierra Miwok Indians were living there. They called the Yosemite Valley "Ahwahnee" (Place of the Gaping Mouth).

Sierra Nevadas from east of Tioga Pass

Merced River

Badger Pass

The first tourists arrived in 1855. They traveled on horseback. I wonder if they were as amazed as I am by the first glimpse of this scenic park.

Today, more than 3.5 million people visit the park every year. Most come in the summer months. That's a lot of visitors! And a lot of cars! But what's nice is that 94% of the park has been designated as wilderness. These areas can only be reached by foot or on horseback.

After a four-hour drive from San Francisco, we arrived at the Arch Rock entrance station. This is on the western side of the park, just north of Badger Pass. Badger is a popular ski spot. It opened in 1935 and was California's first ski area. Seven years earlier, the first ski school in the state was started in Yosemite Valley. That's where we'll begin exploring the park.

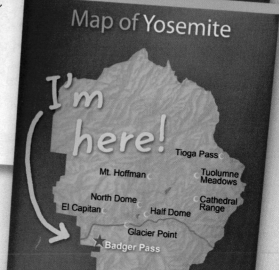

Map of Yosemite

I'm here!

Tioga Pass

Mt. Hoffman

Tuolumne Meadows

North Dome

Cathedral Range

El Capitan

Half Dome

Glacier Point

Badger Pass

Rafting on the Merced River

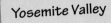

Yosemite Valley

Yosemite Valley is only seven miles long and one mile wide, but it's where the most services are. Our campground is here, and so are many of the park's best natural attractions. It's the most heavily visited part of the park.

Today, we learned about the Miwok and Paiute people, and about the natural history of the park. Then we hopped on the shuttle bus to see famous sights like Yosemite Falls, El Capitan, and Happy Isles. One of my favorite places was Mirror Lake, where we saw Tenaya Canyon reflected in the water.

Bridalveil Creek/Fall

It seems that wherever we look, there's something bigger, higher, or more impressive than before. More than half of America's highest waterfalls are found in Yosemite. One of the prettiest is Bridalveil Fall. It is located near the entrance to Yosemite Valley.

The Ahwahneechee called Bridalveil Fall "Pohono." It means "spirit of the puffing wind." Sometimes hard winds actually blow the falls sideways! I'm glad I brought my raincoat because we got soaked by the spray on the way up! This waterfall is 620 feet high. That's as tall as a 62-story building!

Bridalveil Fall

Giant Sequoias

I saw a Grizzly Giant! No, it's not a huge person. It's an enormous sequoia tree! It's the largest species of tree in the world and it is found only on the western slopes of the Sierra Nevada Mountains. A sequoia tree can grow to over 300 feet tall and 40 feet around, and can live more than 3,000 years!

At about 2,700 years old, the Grizzly Giant is the oldest tree in the park and the fifth oldest in the world. Many of the sequoias have nicknames, like the Clothespin Tree, Siamese Twins, and the Dead Giant. You can even walk through some of them!

Mariposa Grove of sequoia trees

Bobcat

Yosemite Wildlife

I'm so excited! This morning on our way to Glacier Point we saw a black bear and her two cubs. The young ones were as cute as teddy bears. The ranger reminded us how dangerous these bears really are. They have a very strong sense of smell and will rip open a tent or even break into a car to get food! That's why we put all our food—and even our toothpaste—in the bear-proof metal box at the campground.

An adult black bear can weigh as much as 500 pounds. The average size is about 300 pounds. Not all of them are black. They may be brown, cinnamon, or sometimes tan. Between 300 and 500 bears live in the park.

We have seen a ton of mule deer since we arrived. They like to graze along the roadsides and in the meadows in the early morning and late afternoon. They can be just as aggressive as bears when approached. Mule deer have long ears like mules. They can run up to 35 miles an hour and can jump 24 feet in a single leap. You'd never know it from looking at them!

The park is also home to mountain lions, bobcats, coyotes, black-tailed jackrabbits, yellow-bellied marmots, rattlesnakes, and California bighorn sheep. Thousands of sheep once roamed the slopes of the Sierra Nevada Mountains. They were nearly wiped out by hunters, disease,

Mule deer

Black bear

Steller's jay

and lack of food. A ranger said they were successfully reintroduced to the park in 1986.

More than 240 species of birds have been spotted in Yosemite. Some of them are endangered, like the willow flycatcher and the great gray owl. Some—like the bald eagle—just spend the winter in the park. My favorite is the Steller's jay, a noisy blue bird with a black crest. It will steal food off your plate if you don't watch out!

I also like to watch bats swooping through the air to catch insects. Did you know that one bat can eat up to 600 mosquito-sized insects in an hour? Yosemite has 15 species of bats. These include the rare spotted bat, which has big ears and three white spots on its back.

Glacier Point

The view from Glacier Point was totally awesome. It made me dizzy to look over the edge. It's 3,200 feet—a little more than 1/2 mile—straight down to the floor of Yosemite Valley! In the distance I could see Yosemite Falls. I could also see El Capitan and Half Dome. I like the way light reflected off the bare rock surfaces at sunrise and sunset, "painting" them pink, purple, and gold.

The ranger told us that this is a good place to see peregrine falcons in flight. They can dive at speeds up to 200 miles per hour and catch their prey in mid-air. They nest in high places on very narrow rock ledges.

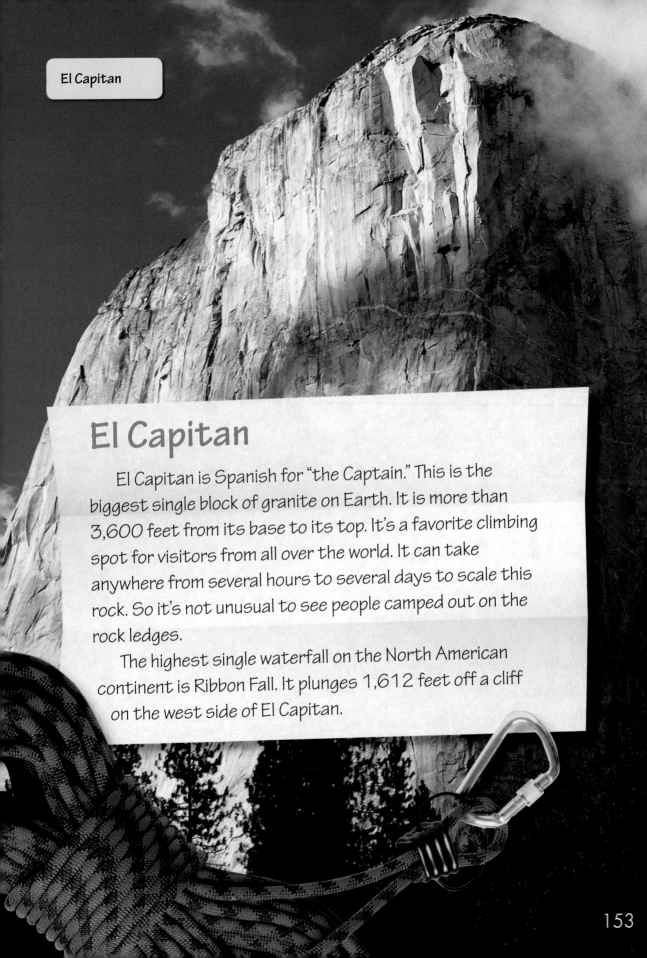

El Capitan

El Capitan

El Capitan is Spanish for "the Captain." This is the biggest single block of granite on Earth. It is more than 3,600 feet from its base to its top. It's a favorite climbing spot for visitors from all over the world. It can take anywhere from several hours to several days to scale this rock. So it's not unusual to see people camped out on the rock ledges.

The highest single waterfall on the North American continent is Ribbon Fall. It plunges 1,612 feet off a cliff on the west side of El Capitan.

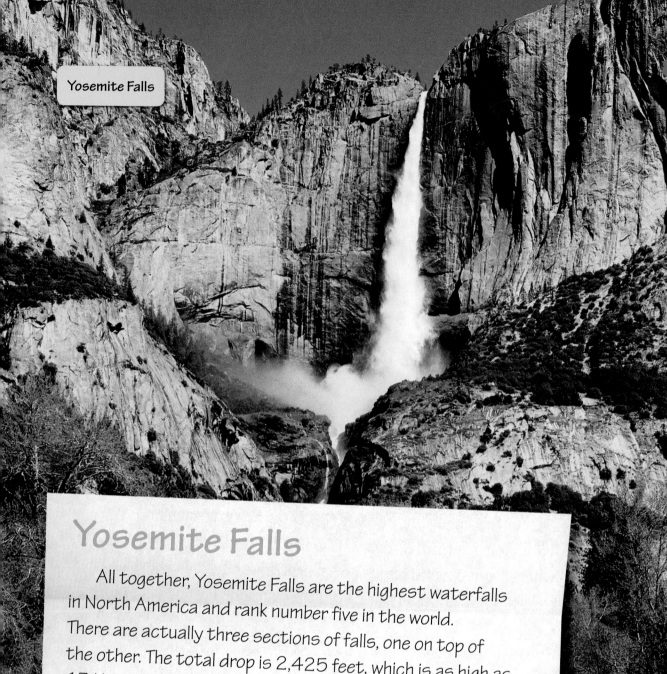

Yosemite Falls

Yosemite Falls

All together, Yosemite Falls are the highest waterfalls in North America and rank number five in the world. There are actually three sections of falls, one on top of the other. The total drop is 2,425 feet, which is as high as 13 Niagara Falls!

In late spring and early summer, so much water goes over the falls that you can feel the ground shake! By the end of the summer, the falls may be no more than a trickle. And some years they dry up altogether.

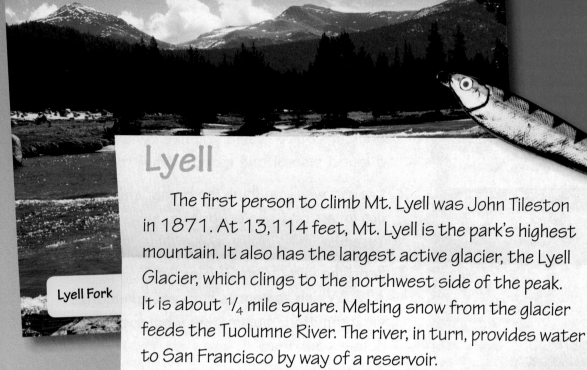

Lyell Fork

Lyell

The first person to climb Mt. Lyell was John Tileston in 1871. At 13,114 feet, Mt. Lyell is the park's highest mountain. It also has the largest active glacier, the Lyell Glacier, which clings to the northwest side of the peak. It is about $\frac{1}{4}$ mile square. Melting snow from the glacier feeds the Tuolumne River. The river, in turn, provides water to San Francisco by way of a reservoir.

Today the rivers and streams of Yosemite provide places to fish, wade, or raft. But in the past, people flocked to the water to pan for gold! While some gold was found, the area did not yield as much of this precious metal as the foothills to the west of the park did.

Tioga Pass

On our last day we drove over Tioga Pass. It's 9,945 feet above sea level. It's the highest highway pass in the Sierra Nevada range and in all of California.

Because it's so high, many flowers and plants that grow here differ from those in lower elevations such as the Yosemite Valley. The trees are also small and stunted, because it's difficult for them to grow at such high altitudes.

Wherever you go—high in the mountains or low in the valleys—Yosemite is truly one of the most awesome places on Earth!

Tioga Pass

155

Common Core State Standards

Informational Text 1. Refer to details and examples in a text when explaining what the text says explicitly and when drawing inferences from the text. **Also Informational Text 2., 5., Writing 9.**

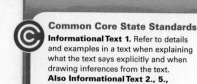

Envision It! Retell

Yosemite Valley

Merced River

Mariposa Grove of sequoia trees

READING STREET ONLINE
STORY SORT
www.ReadingStreet.com

Think Critically

1. The first tourists arrived in Yosemite on horseback in 1855. Would you like to have been a tourist then or one today? Why? **Text to Self**

2. Explain why you think the author chose to use letters and photographs to tell about Yosemite. **Think Like an Author**

3. Read the letter from Glacier Point on page 152. Which sentences help you summarize the main idea? Summarize what supporting details you found.
   Main Idea and Details

4. Look at the selection and notice the author's use of headings. How do the headings help you gain an overview of the contents of the text? **Text Structure**

5. **Look Back and Write** Look back at the letter titled "Yosemite Wildlife" on pages 151–152. Of the animals mentioned, which do you find most interesting? Why? Provide evidence to support your answer.
   Key Ideas and Details • Text Evidence

Meet the Author

Lisa Halvorsen

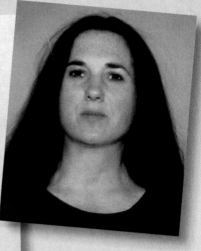

Lisa Halvorsen has traveled all over the world in her work as a travel writer. She has visited more than 40 countries on six continents. Her favorite trips have been to the Galapagos Islands, Turkey, Ecuador, Kenya, and New Zealand.

Ms. Halvorsen started traveling at an early age. She moved seven times before she started kindergarten! Today, she lives in northern Vermont with her two cats, Dusty Miller and Gina. Her pastimes include hiking, canoeing, sailing, and gardening.

"Writing opens up a lot of doors," says Ms. Halvorsen. "It gives me a chance to travel and meet people I might not meet if I weren't a writer."

What is her advice to young writers? "Be curious, be adventurous, and read as much as you can. Write about what you love. Don't be afraid to ask questions and look for answers to what interests you."

Here are other books by Lisa Halvorsen.

Letters Home from Grand Canyon

Letters Home from Yellowstone

Reading Log

Use the *Reader's and Writer's Notebook* to record your independent reading.

Common Core State Standards

Writing 3.a. Orient the reader by establishing a situation and introducing a narrator and/or characters; organize an event sequence that unfolds naturally. **Also Writing 3., 4., Language 1.**

Let's Write It!

Key Features of a Personal Narrative

- tells about a personal experience
- written in the first person
- usually organized in the order in which the events occurred

READING STREET ONLINE
GRAMMAR JAMMER
www.ReadingStreet.com

Personal Narrative

A **personal narrative** is a true story about a personal memory or other experience. The student model on the next page is an example of a personal narrative.

Writing Prompt Write about a time you went on vacation or spent time at a place you had never been to before.

Writer's Checklist

Remember, you should . . .

☑ choose a real personal experience.

☑ describe your thoughts and feelings.

☑ add details that will appeal to your audience.

☑ choose whether you want to use cursive or manuscript printing.

"I can smell the ocean!" exclaimed Sam, my little brother. He was right—the air did smell different. It smelled salty, fresh, and maybe even a little fishy. We'd been driving for a long time, and we were getting close to our vacation destination in Cape May, New Jersey. Sam and I were excited.

As soon as we got settled at our rented cottage, we headed for the beach. I kicked off my sandals so I could feel the soft white sand between my toes.

Sam and I wanted to rush straight into the water, but first we had to spread out our blanket, and then we had to slather sunscreen all over ourselves. Finally, we were allowed to go wading in the icy water. The waves rolled in steadily toward the shore, making a soothing, rhythmic sound.

As each wave hit the beach, it left seaweed, shells, and smooth stones. Tiny bubbles erupted from the wet sand when the water went back out. "Sand crabs," explained my Dad. "If you dig down quickly, you might catch one."

Writing Trait Voice establishes the speaker and engages the audience.

Independent clauses and complex sentences are used correctly.

Genre A **personal narrative** includes details to appeal to the audience.

Conventions

Clauses and Complex Sentences

Remember A **complex sentence** has one **independent clause** and at least one **dependent clause**.

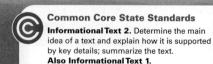

Common Core State Standards
Informational Text 2. Determine the main idea of a text and explain how it is supported by key details; summarize the text. **Also Informational Text 1.**

Science in Reading

Genre
Magazine Article

- A magazine article is an example of expository text. Expository text contains information about a subject.

- Expository texts will include a main idea, or the topic of the text. Details in the text will support that idea.

- Some expository texts may also organize ideas using cause-and-effect relationships.

- Read "The Bison of Caprock Canyons." Look at elements that make this selection an expository text. What is the article's main idea? What details support the main idea?

The Bison of Caprock Canyons

by Joseph Walters

Deep inside Caprock Canyons State Park and Trailway in Quitaque, Texas, a herd of bison grazes on the short grass growing across the prairie. Long ago, giant herds of these creatures roamed the region. Today, this small herd is all that remains.

How did these animals almost disappear from this area of Texas?

Let's **Think** About...

Summarize the main idea of this magazine article. Summarize the details that support this idea.
Magazine Article

In the 1800s, settlers and ranchers hunted the bison. Millions were used for food and clothing. As the number of bison decreased dramatically, a successful cattle rancher named Charles Goodnight and his wife, Mary Ann, who lived in the area near Caprock Canyons, decided to do something about it.

They began by saving a few bison calves whose mothers had been killed. Soon, the number of bison grew to two hundred.

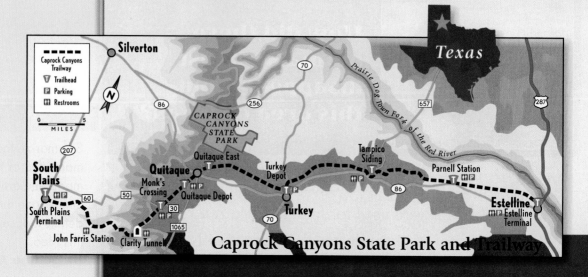

Caprock Canyons State Park and Trailway

Now, Caprock Canyons State Park and Trailway boasts the largest herd of bison in the Texas state park program. Once a year, park officials will keep track of the bison population. First, they corral the bison into pens. The bison are then weighed and checked for disease or illness. Finally, the bison are tagged. Officials keep a close eye on newborn calves to make sure they are healthy and eating properly.

Officials need to be very careful when working around the bison. Although gentle by nature, some bison can weigh almost 2,000 pounds. They can easily knock over an adult with just a nudge. During feeding time, officials throw food from the back of a truck to the bison. Then they will stay inside the truck while the bison eat. That way, the officials won't get hurt. Some bison are known to push against the truck with their horns.

Let's Think About...

Describe the effects of the Goodnights' work saving baby bison. **Magazine Article**

There are many other forms of wildlife in Caprock Canyons State Park, as well. If you are lucky, you might see one of the Aoudad sheep that roam the park. These animals, which look like mountain goats, were brought over from Africa years ago. They can be found grazing on desert grass and bushes located inside the park's more than 15,000 acres of land. Other animals you might see include possums, golden eagles, and bobcats.

However, the bison are one of the park's biggest attractions. Thousands of hikers and children visit Caprock Canyons every year to see these creatures. Visitors walk onto an observation deck and observe the large, shaggy animals through telescopes. From there they can watch the bison graze, sleep, or amble across the prairie.

Let's Think About...

Reading Across Texts The two selections you just read are connected by theme. Think of reasons why these two parks exist. List your reasons.

Writing Across Texts What if the author of "Letters from Yosemite" visited Caprock Canyons? Write a letter describing the experience from the author's point of view.

163

Poetry

- **Lyrical poetry** rhymes, uses meter, and is made up of stanzas. It has the form and musical quality of a song.

- Poems that **rhyme** have lines that end in the same sounds.

- **Free verse** poems may not rhyme or have regular meter. In some, the lines do not begin with capital letters. Some have line breaks that don't look like stanzas.

- Read "We're All in the Telephone Book" and "Speak Up." Find the lines that rhyme.

We're All in the Telephone Book

by Langston Hughes

We're all in the telephone book,
Folks from everywhere on earth—
Anderson to Zabowski,
It's a record of America's worth.

We're all in the telephone book.
There's no priority—
A millionaire like Rockefeller
Is likely to be behind me.

For generations men have dreamed
Of nations united as one.
Just look in your telephone book
To see where that dream's begun.

When Washington crossed the Delaware
And the pillars of tyranny shook,
He started the list of democracy
That's America's telephone book.

Speak Up

by Janet S. Wong

You're Korean, aren't you?

Why don't you speak Korean?

Say something Korean.

C'mon. Say something.

Say some other stuff.
Sounds funny.
Sounds strange.

Listen to me?

But I'm American,
can't you see?

But I was born here.

Yes.

Just don't, I guess.

I don't speak it.
I can't.

Halmoni. Grandmother.
Haraboji. Grandfather.
Imo. Aunt.

Hey, let's listen to you
for a change.

Say some foreign words.

Your family came from
somewhere else.
Sometime.

So was I.

Let's **Think** About...

Does "We're All in the Telephone Book" rhyme? Is this a free verse or a lyrical poem? Explain how you know.

Let's **Think** About...

How is the structure of "Speak Up" different from "We're All in the Telephone Book?" Do you think it is free verse or a lyrical poem? Explain how you know.

167

CITY I LOVE

by Lee Bennett Hopkins

In the city
I live in—
city I love—
mornings wake
to
swishes, swashes,
sputters
of sweepers
swooshing litter
from gutters.

In the city
I live in—
city I love—
afternoons pulse
with
people hurrying,
scurrying—
races of faces
pacing to
must-get-there
places.

In the city
I live in—
I live in—
city I love—
nights shimmer
with lights
competing
with stars
above
unknown
heights.

In the city
I live in—
city I love—
as dreams
start to creep
my city
of senses
lulls
me
to
sleep.

Midwest Town

by Ruth De Long Peterson

Farther east it wouldn't be on the map—
Too small—but here it rates a dot and a name.
In Europe it would wear a castle cap
Or have a cathedral rising like a flame.

But here it stands where the section roadways meet.
Its houses dignified with trees and lawn;
The stores hold *tête-à-tête* across Main Street;
The red brick school, a church—the town is gone.

America is not all traffic lights,
And beehive homes and shops and factories;
No, there are wide green days and starry nights,
And a great pulse beating strong in towns like these.

Teamwork

Reading Street Online

www.ReadingStreet.com
• Big Question Video
• eSelections
• Envision It! Animations
• Story Sort

THE BIG
?

What is the value of teamwork?

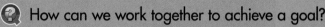

Common Core State Standards

Speaking/Listening 1. Engage effectively in a range of collaborative discussions (one-on-one, in groups, and teacher-led) with diverse partners on grade 4 topics and texts, building on others' ideas and expressing their own clearly. **Also Language 6.**

Let's Talk About

Developing New Understandings

- Ask what understandings can you gain from learning something new.

- Describe a new skill you would like to learn.

- Offer suggestions to others about how to learn a new skill.

READING STREET ONLINE
CONCEPT TALK VIDEO
www.ReadingStreet.com

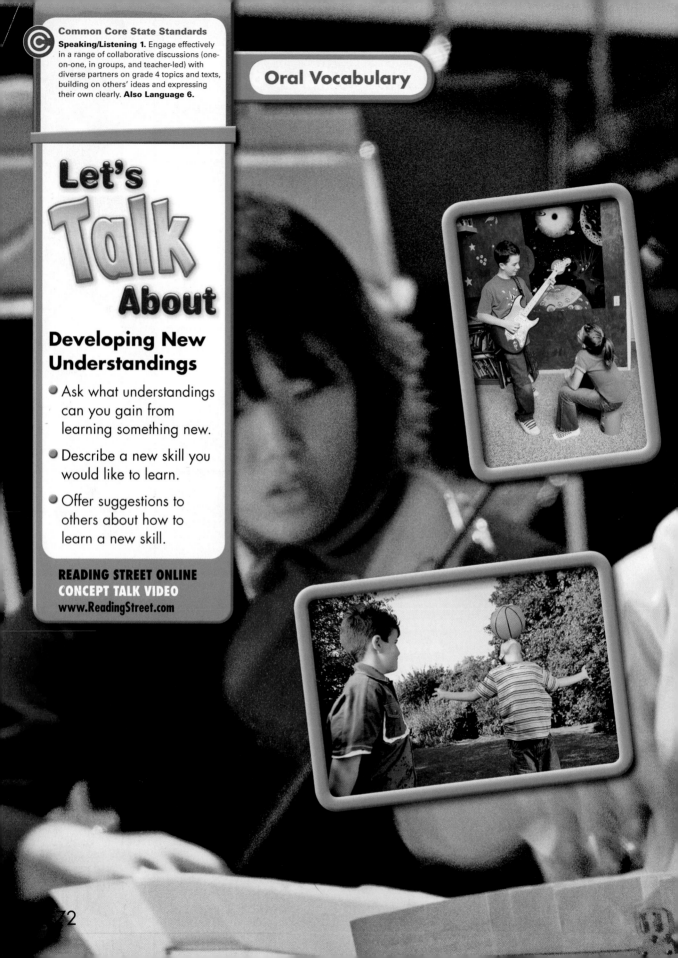

Common Core State Standards

Informational Text 5. Describe the overall structure (e.g., chronology, comparison, cause/effect, problem/solution) of events, ideas, concepts, or information in a text or part of a text. **Also Informational Text 1.**

Envision It! | Skill Strategy

Skill

Strategy

READING STREET ONLINE
ENVISION IT! ANIMATIONS
www.ReadingStreet.com

Comprehension Skill

Cause and Effect

- The *cause* is why something happened. The *effect* is what happened.

- Clue words such as *because, so,* and *cause* sometimes signal an explicit cause-and-effect relationship. For example, *It started to snow so the girl put on her hat.* This sentence shows an explicit relationship between a cause and an effect.

- Sometimes there are no clue words. The relationship is implicit. You have to figure out for yourself that one thing causes another.

- A cause can have more than one effect.

- Use the graphic organizer to identify causes and their effects as you read "Up, Up, and Down."

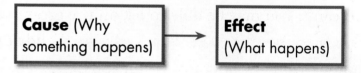

Cause (Why something happens)   →   **Effect** (What happens)

Comprehension Strategy

Background Knowledge

Good readers use their background knowledge to help them understand what they read. As you read new information, think about whether you have ever seen or experienced what you are reading about.

Up, Up, and Down

Did you ever see basketball players leap high into the air to shoot a ball into a basket? Or even higher still to block a shot? How do they jump so high?

The trick is to beat Earth's gravity. Because of this force, a person is pulled to the ground. To move away from this force, you need energy.

Think of a spring, or better yet, think of a spring in a pogo stick. Your weight on the stick presses the spring down. That stores energy in the spring. When that energy is released, it is enough to lift the stick and you off the ground.

In a similar way, you can build up energy in your legs. If you stand straight and then try to jump up, you can't. You may be able to lift off the ground an inch or so, but that's all. That's why you bend at the knees before jumping up. When you bend, it's as if you are putting a "spring" in your legs. Release that spring, and up you go.

Of course, the energy is not nearly enough to overcome Earth's gravity. That's why Earth will always pull you back down again.

Skill Look for a clue word in this paragraph to help find the cause-and-effect relationship. Is the relationship explicit or implicit?

Skill Look for causes and their effects in this paragraph. What causes energy to be stored? What effect does releasing it have?

Strategy Think of what you know about jumping off the ground as you read this paragraph. Explain what that "spring" feels like.

Your Turn!

⏸ **Need a Review?** See *Envision It! Handbook* for help with cause and effect and background knowledge.

Let's Think About...

▶ **Ready to Try It?** Use what you've learned about cause and effect as you read *What Jo Did*.

Envision It! | Words to Know

hoop

jersey

rim

fouled

marveled

speechless

swatted

unbelievable

Vocabulary Strategy for

Affixes: Prefixes and Suffixes

Word Structure Prefixes and suffixes have their own meanings. When they are added to words, they change the meaning of the original word, or the base word. The Middle English prefix *un-* means "the opposite of " or "not," as in *undefeated*. The suffix *-able* means "able to be," as in *unbeatable*. The Middle English suffix *-less* means "without," as in *scoreless*. You can use affixes to help you figure out the meanings of words.

1. Look at an unfamiliar word to see if it has a base word you know.

2. Has the prefix *un-* or the suffix *-able* or *-less* been added to the base word?

3. Think about how the prefix or suffix changes the meaning of the base word.

4. Try the meaning in the sentence to see if it makes sense.

Read "At the Game." Look for prefixes and suffixes to help you figure out the meanings of unfamiliar words.

Words to Write Reread "At the Game." Imagine that you just played a game of basketball. Write a paragraph describing the game. Use words from the *Words to Know* list.

At the Game

"Hello again, sports fans. This is Bud Sherman, WXXT Channel 6, coming to you from the Grandview Center, where the third-place Tigers are battling the second-place Lions in the first round of the HSBA playoffs. Tiger forward Matt Roberts has had a flawless game, scoring 28 points so far. Lion center Darren Jones has been unbelievable under the basket.

"Now Roberts moves in and shoots the ball. He's looking for another three-pointer. The ball hits the rim. Maxwell tries a shot, but it's swatted away by Jones.

Grundig has the ball and he's heading for the Tigers' hoop. Oh, my, he's been fouled by Lee, who grabbed Grundig's jersey and arm. I imagine Coach Simmons is unhappy. That's Lee's fourth foul in this half. Grundig, a reliable free-thrower, makes both points. Pfizer throws in to Barton, who passes to—Roberts!

"You know, I have always marveled at the way Roberts moves around the court, but his performance tonight just leaves me speechless. Roberts shoots from 30 feet out, and he scores! The Tigers win, 87-84."

Your Turn!

 **Need a Review?** For additional help with prefixes and suffixes, see *Words!*

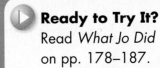 **Ready to Try It?** Read *What Jo Did* on pp. 178–187.

What Jo Did

text and images by Charles R. Smith Jr.

Let's
Think
About
Reading!

Little Joanna Marie loved to play basketball.
She especially loved the sound the ball made as it
fell through the net. She would practice every day,
touching the backboard as often as she could. Since
Joanna's parents had no idea how high a basketball
rim should be, they hung it on the side of their roof,
which was a whopping sixteen feet high.

Joanna saw rims on TV and figured they looked
about the same height as her own—**she had no
idea they were only ten feet high.**

Joanna also didn't realize that most people
couldn't jump up and touch the backboard because
she hadn't ever played with anyone else. But her
parents marveled at how high she jumped, and how
she could run up to the backboard with the ball and
lay it up and in. Her father was especially proud
because he couldn't even touch the bottom of the
net. Not even with the help of a broom.

Let's **Think** About...

What do you know
about basketball
that makes you
think that Jo will
be a really good
player?

**Background
Knowledge**

One day Joanna, her hair bundled up under her baseball cap, was dribbling her basketball on the way to the store to get some sugar for her mother. Her mother said that she didn't have to hurry home, as long as she was in by dark. As Joanna moved down the street, a basketball came rolling out of nowhere and bumped her high-tops.

"I'm sorry, man, I didn't mean to hit you with the ball like that," said a young boy dressed in sneakers, shorts, and a Bulls tank top as he picked up the ball.

"Oh, that's okay. I wasn't even paying attention," Joanna said.

"Hey, we need one more to play a game. You in?" he asked her.

"Sure, why not?" she responded.

As Joanna approached the other boys, she remembered that she had her hat on.

They probably think I'm a boy, she thought. *Might as well enjoy the ride.*

The boys picked teams, and since Joanna was smaller than everyone else, she got picked last. It didn't bother her, though, because she had never played with anyone before and was just happy to be there.

"Hey, kid, what's your name?" asked a freckle-faced kid with red hair.

"Ahhh . . . Jo. My name is Jo," Joanna said nervously.

"All right, Joe, you pick up T.J. over there, see. Make sure he doesn't score a basket. He can jump pretty high, ya know!"

Let's **Think** About...

What do you think the boys expect from Jo?
Inferring

181

Let's **Think** About...

The sequence of events are important to understanding the conflict between T.J. and Jo. How will T.J. react to Jo's blocking his shot?
Story Structure

Jo moved around, not really touching the ball at first, just trying to get a feel for playing with other people. She had never even passed the ball or received a pass herself. Playing with others took getting used to, but in no time she was passing the ball. The only thing that puzzled her was why the hoop was so low.

Even though the boys passed the ball around a lot, T.J. didn't really touch it much, and when he did, he didn't take a shot. Finally, he was wide open for a jump shot when Jo came out of nowhere, jumped high into the air, **and swatted his shot into the next court.**

182

"Wow, did you see that?

Did you see how high he jumped?" the freckle-faced kid said, his mouth wide open.

"I've never seen anybody jump that high. Not even Michael Jordan," said the kid with the Bulls jersey on.

"Unbelievable."

"Where'd you learn to do that?"

"Oh, my goodness!!!"

"Poor T.J."

"Hey—I got fouled, and besides, it wasn't that high," said T.J., but his face was so red that he couldn't hide his embarrassment.

"Uh, uh . . . it's just something I picked up. I practice a lot with my dad," Jo added, surprised at how big a deal the boys made of her block.

"Man! You must have some dad," one of the boys said.

The game continued, and Jo was passed the ball more often. Her teammates encouraged her to shoot more, and when she did, they were amazed how the ball arced in the air like a rainbow before falling straight through the hoop, without touching the rim. As the game progressed, Jo felt hot, but she knew she couldn't take her hat off, or else she'd be found out.

Whenever a boy got the ball and Jo came over to play defense, he quickly passed the ball away. Jo blocked a few more shots, which created more *ooooohs* and *aaaaaaahs*, and one of the boys on her team asked her if she could dunk the ball.

"Dunk? What's that?" Jo asked. This was a word she had never heard before.

Let's Think About...

Why are the other players passing the ball to Jo now?
Story Structure

"A dunk. You know—a slam, a jam, to throw it down. You jump up and put the ball in the rim while holding on to it."

"Ohhhh . . . that," she said, trying to hide the fact that she had never heard of it before.

"See, what you do is, you dribble the ball, jump up, and put the ball in the rim with your hand," said a kid with a Lakers jersey on, trying to demonstrate on the ground as best he could.

"You guys, can we finish this game? It's getting dark and my mom wants me home soon," T.J. said, still upset that Jo was getting all the attention and that his shot was blocked.

"Hold your horses, T.J.," said the freckle-faced kid. "I wanna see Joe dunk. I'll bet that he can dunk it better than Michael can."

"Well, I'll give it a shot," Jo said, curious herself to see if she could "dunk."

She started at half-court, dribbling the ball quickly, and headed straight for the rim. As she approached, she remembered how high her basket was and realized that this one was much lower. Maybe she *could* jump a little farther out and dunk the ball through. As she got to the free throw line, she lifted her left leg up and went **flying into the air, till she was so high** she was looking down on the hoop. Now all she had to do was put the ball in the rim with both hands.

Let's **Think** About...

How do you think T.J. feels as he waits to see if Jo can dunk?
Story Structure

184

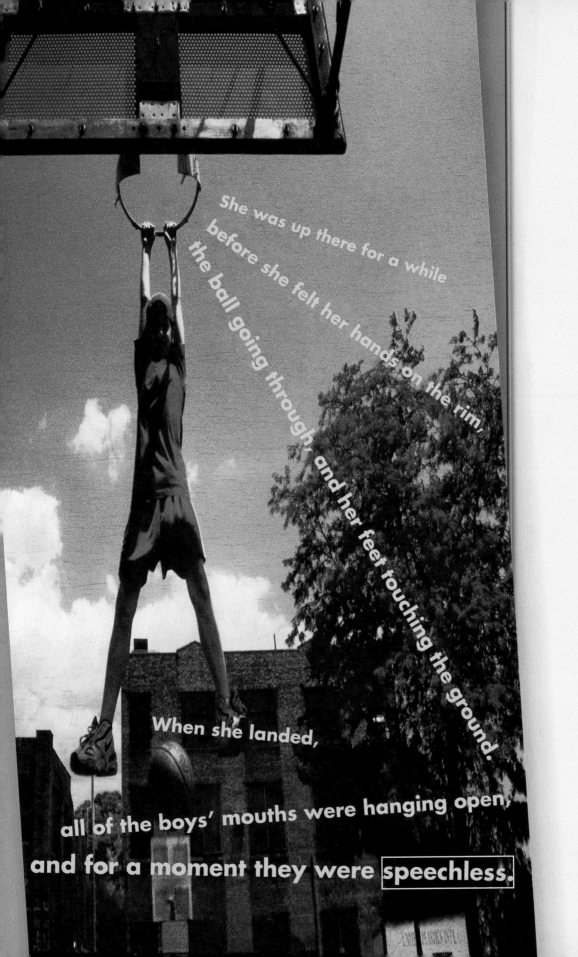

She was up there for a while before she felt her hands on the rim, the ball going through, and her feet touching the ground.

When she landed, all of the boys' mouths were hanging open, and for a moment they were speechless.

185

Then: "No way."

"It can't be!"

"Am I seeing right?"

"That's impossible."

"How did she . . . ?"

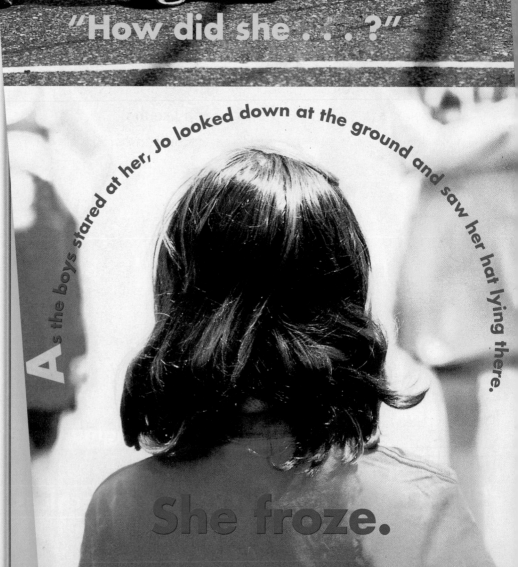

As the boys stared at her, Jo looked down at the ground and saw her hat lying there.

She froze.

"So, like . . . you're a girl?" said the kid with the Lakers jersey.

"Ahhhh . . . yeah . . . you could say that," Jo answered slowly.

"I can't believe it, you guys, we've been playing basketball with a girl," T.J. said with disgust.

"Hey, she may be a girl, but I'd play on her team anytime." The kid with the Bulls jersey approached Jo and gave her a high five.

After that, they congratulated Jo and introduced themselves. They even came up with a nickname for her: Jumpin' Jo. In the end, T.J. walked up to her and apologized.

"Sorry, Jo," he whispered. "I just never played against a girl before. Especially a girl as good as you. I've never seen anyone who can jump like that! You should come and play with us again sometime.

But next time, leave the hat at home."

Let's **Think** About...

Why do you think players give each other nicknames? What does this tell you about how the boys feel about Jo? **Questioning**

Common Core State Standards

Literature 1. Refer to details and examples in a text when explaining what the text says explicitly and when drawing inferences from the text. Also Writing 9.

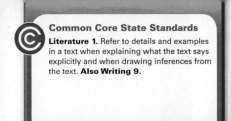

Envision It! Retell

READING STREET ONLINE
STORY SORT
www.ReadingStreet.com

Think Critically

1. Basketball is just one of many team sports that has fans in all parts of the world. Why do you think team sports are so popular around the world? Explain. **Text to World**

2. Is this story told in the first person or third person? Explain how you know. How would the story have been different if it were told from Joanna's point of view?
   Think Like an Author

3. What does Joanna do to T.J.'s jump shot? Why does he react the way he does?
   Cause and Effect

4. Recall a time you watched a basketball game or played in one. Was there one player who stood out from the other members of the team? What were your thoughts as you watched this player?
   Background Knowledge

5. **Look Back and Write** Look back at pages 186–187. When the boys discovered that Jo was really Joanna, were they pleased? Describe how the boys reacted.
   Key Ideas and Details • Text Evidence

Meet the Author and Photographer

Charles R. Smith Jr.

Here are other books by Charles R. Smith Jr.

Tall Tales: Six Amazing Basketball Dreams

Loki & Alex: The Adventures of a Dog & His Best Friend

Charles R. Smith Jr. loves photography, writing, and basketball. These three interests all came together for his book *Tall Tales: Six Amazing Basketball Dreams*. The story "What Jo Did" is just one of the stories in this book.

Before he began writing books, Mr. Smith worked as a photographer in New York City. "The jobs paid the bills but were boring for me. So I decided to begin a series of photos called Street Basketball in New York." A children's book editor saw the photos and suggested Mr. Smith use them for a book. The result was *Rim Shots*, a book of photos, poems, and thoughts about basketball.

For his next book, he decided to use infrared film. The film responds to heat and makes unusual colors. "In my story 'What Jo Did,' you can see the effect in the way the trees look and the colors of the players' clothes."

Mr. Smith knows his stories are "a bit unbelievable." He says that good storytelling begins with some truth. "But realizing you don't have to stick to the truth is even better."

Reading Log

Use the *Reader's and Writer's Notebook* to record your independent writing.

Common Core State Standards

Writing 4. Produce clear and coherent writing in which the development and organization are appropriate to task, purpose, and audience. **Also Language 2., 2.a., 3.a., 5.**

Let's Write It!

Key Features of a Poem

- often arranged in lines
- sometimes has a regular rhythm
- may have rhyming lines
- takes many forms

READING STREET ONLINE
GRAMMAR JAMMER
www.ReadingStreet.com

Descriptive

Poem

A **poem** is a piece of writing that often has a particular rhythm and rhyme scheme. Poetry can take many forms, such as shape poetry or limericks. The student model on the next page is an example of a limerick.

Writing Prompt Write a poem about teamwork.

Writer's Checklist

Remember, you should . . .

☑ choose a poetic form in which to write.

☑ use figurative language to show sensory details.

☑ use rhythm and rhyme in your poem.

☑ use common and proper nouns correctly.

The Sprinter

There once was a **sprinter** named Babbit,

who ran like he was a **jack rabbit**.

His **team** always won,

and had lots of fun,

for first place with them was a habit.

Common and proper nouns are used correctly.

Writing Trait Word Choice Figurative language creates a visual image.

Genre A limerick is a humorous form of **poetry** that uses the rhyme scheme a-a-b-b-a.

Conventions

Common and Proper Nouns

Remember A **common noun** names any person (principal), place (foreign country), or thing (holiday). A **proper noun** names a specific person (Mr. Collins), place (France), or thing (Independence Day) and begins with a capital letter.

191

Common Core State Standards

Informational Text 7. Interpret information presented visually, orally, or quantitatively (e.g., in charts, graphs, diagrams, time lines, animations, or interactive elements on Web pages) and explain how the information contributes to an understanding of the text in which it appears. **Also Informational Text 8.**

Social Studies in Reading

Genre
Advertisement

- An advertisement is a kind of persuasive text. An ad tries to influence the reader to buy or do something.

- In an advertisement, a writer uses language and pictures to persuade viewers.

- When you read an advertisement, be aware of the difference between the ad's positive impact and its negative impact.

- Read the ad for a Stickfast Hoop. As you read, think about how the advertisement tries to influence you. What does the author want you to think or do?

STICKFAST HOOP

You love basketball. If you had your chance, you'd play it all the time.

Well, now you can. Introducing the amazing Stickfast Hoop!

A Stickfast Hoop can stick to any surface: a wall, a door, a tree, a refrigerator. That means that you can play basketball anywhere you want, any time you want.

With a Stickfast Hoop, you can put a hoop up in any room in your house. Want to move the game out of the family room and into the basement? It's easy. A Stickfast Hoop contains a restickable gluing agent. You can stick and unstick it to any surface. And no matter how many times you stick it to something new, the hoop never loses its grip.

Dunk All Over Your House!

No other hoop comes close to a Stickfast Hoop. That's because it's made of an amazingly strong and smooth plastic. It is guaranteed never to decay or break. Ten years from now, your hoop will be as solid and shiny as it was the day you bought it.

Set it up in seconds! Have fun!

The Stickfast Hoop lets *you* call the shots. A standard hoop is regulation height. That's way too high when you're a kid! A Stickfast Hoop lets you decide on the height you want. As you get taller, you can stick the hoop higher and higher. In no time, you'll be reaching for the stars!

Our advice? Grab a Stickfast Hoop.

You'll be glad you did. You'll play basketball all the time. You'll dunk all over your house! There is nothing more important than that!

Let's **Think** About...

What are the positive impacts of this advertisement? What are its negative impacts? **Advertisement**

Let's **Think** About...

Reading Across Texts If Joanna from the story *What Jo Did* had a Stickfast Hoop, do you think she would use it? Would using it help or hurt her basketball playing?

Writing Across Texts Write a journal entry for Joanna describing why she would or would not use a Stickfast Hoop. Make sure you include details from the advertisement.

Common Core State Standards
Language 4.b. Use common, grade-appropriate Greek and Latin affixes and roots as clues to the meaning of a word (e.g., *telegraph, photograph, autograph*). **Also Foundational Skills 4.b., Speaking/Listening 4., 6.**

Let's Learn It!

READING STREET ONLINE
ONLINE STUDENT EDITION
www.ReadingStreet.com

Vocabulary

Affixes: Prefixes and Suffixes

Word Structure Prefixes are added to the beginning of words. They change the meanings of words. The prefixes *dis-*, *non-*, and *un-* mean "not." Suffixes are added to the end of words. They also change words' meanings. The suffixes *-er* and *-or* mean "one who."

Practice It! Make a prefix and suffix chart. Label each column with one of the prefixes and suffixes shown above. In each column, list as many words with the prefix or suffix that you know.

Fluency

Appropriate Phrasing

Partner Reading When you read, notice the different lengths of sentences. Paying attention to the rhythm of sentences makes the story flow more smoothly.

Practice It! With a partner, read aloud *What Jo Did*, page 183, paragraphs 1–9. Notice the different lengths of the sentences in the characters' dialogue. Read with rhythm to give meaning to the action in the story.

Media Literacy

 Get Ready For Middle School

When you give a presentation, speak clearly and loudly.

Sportscast

A sports announcer describes the action of a sports event. Expression is important when reporting. Using different camera shots makes viewers feel as if they were at the game.

Practice It! With a partner, create a TV sportscast of an action sequence from a sporting event. Write a script about the play. Rehearse with your partner, with one of you as the sportscaster and the other as the director. The sportscaster must follow the oral directions of the director. Deliver your report to the class.

Tips

- TV sports directors use different camera angles to show a sporting event. Wide-angle views show the entire action. Close-ups center on one player or on one play.

- A sports announcer speaks with a lot of expression to increase the viewers' sense of excitement. Think about the difference between a sports announcer's tone of voice and the tone of someone reading the news.

- Even though you are speaking quickly, speak correctly. Use common and proper nouns correctly.

195

Common Core State Standards

Language 1. Demonstrate command of the conventions of standard English grammar and usage when writing or speaking. **Also Language 6.**

Oral Vocabulary

Let's Talk About

Working Together

- Discuss the benefits of working together.

- Speak with appropriate rate to express ideas.

- Use proper language conventions.

READING STREET ONLINE
CONCEPT TALK VIDEO
www.ReadingStreet.com

127

Common Core State Standards
Literature 1. Refer to details and examples in a text when explaining what the text says explicitly and when drawing inferences from the text. **Also Literature 3.**

Envision It! | Skill Strategy

Skill

Strategy

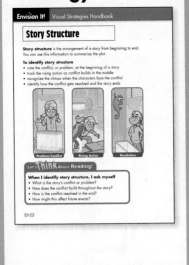

READING STREET ONLINE
ENVISION IT! ANIMATIONS
www.ReadingStreet.com

Comprehension Skill

🎯 Draw Conclusions

- Draw conclusions to form an opinion based on your background knowledge or on the facts and details stated in a text.

- You can draw a conclusion while you read or after you read.

- Check an author's conclusions or your own conclusions by asking: *Is this the only logical choice? Are the facts accurate?*

- Use the graphic organizer below to help you draw conclusions about the kind of dog Tumbleweed is as you read "Chasing After Tumbleweed."

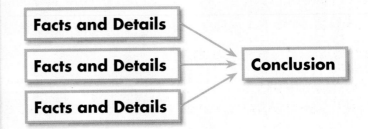

Comprehension Strategy

🎯 Story Structure

Good readers note the structure of a story they are reading in order to better understand the text. In fiction, most story events are arranged by sequence, or in time order.

CHASING AFTER TUMBLEWEED

Every morning Tumbleweed barks at the front door until we let him out to play. He loves to run all over the ranch. Some days I find him miles away at the southern border of our ranch. He knows that's where the prairie dogs hide. He loves to chase them. Getting him to come home every day is my job. It isn't an easy one!

Skill How can you use your background knowledge about dogs to draw a conclusion about Tumbleweed?

Sometimes I can convince my bus driver to stop on the way home to pick up Tumbleweed. "Make it quick!" the driver always says. "Everyone wants to get home!" That may be true. But no one seems to mind the wait as they pile to the side of the bus so they can laugh as they watch me chase Tumbleweed.

Skill Why does the bus driver stop for the narrator? Use details in the text to draw a conclusion about the bus driver.

Yesterday Dad helped me look for Tumbleweed in the helicopter. Dad uses the helicopter to drop hay to the cattle now that it's winter.

For hours we flew all over the ranch looking for Tumbleweed. But there was no sign of him. It was getting darker and colder by the minute. Where could he be?

Thankfully, my dad knows his cattle well. When he saw one cow flicking back snow with its hooves, he knew something was bothering it. He landed the helicopter and told me to go look under the cow. There he was. I'm going to have to teach Tumbleweed that it's warmer and safer underneath my bed!

Strategy Explain how the author's use of sequence helps you understand the story.

Your Turn!

⏸ **Need a Review?** See the *Envision It! Handbook* for help with drawing conclusions and story structure.

▶ **Ready to Try It?** Use what you've learned about drawing conclusions as you read *Coyote School News*.

199

Common Core State Standards

Language 4.c. Consult reference materials (e.g., dictionaries, glossaries, thesauruses), both print and digital, to find the pronunciation and determine or clarify the precise meaning of key words and phrases. **Also Language 4.**

Envision It! | Words to Know

coyote

roundup

spurs

bawling

dudes

Vocabulary Strategy for

🔊 Unknown Words

Dictionary/Glossary When you read, you may come across a word you don't know. If the author has not given any context clues in the words and sentences around the word, then you can use a dictionary or glossary to figure out the word's meaning.

1. Check the back of your book for a glossary. If there is no glossary, look up the word in a dictionary.

2. Find the entry for the word. The entries are listed in alphabetical order.

3. Each word is divided into syllables. Use the syllabication to help you pronounce the word. If you are still having difficulty, use the pronunciation key.

4. Read all the meanings given for the word.

5. Choose the meaning that makes sense in the sentence.

Use a dictionary or the glossary to help you determine the meanings, pronunciations, and syllabication of unknown words as you read "At a Guest Ranch."

Words to Write Reread "At a Guest Ranch." Imagine that you are staying at a dude ranch. Write a journal entry describing a day at the ranch. Use words from the *Words to Know* list in your journal entry.

AT A GUEST RANCH

Howdy, partner! That may sound corny, but it's appropriate because my family and I are at a ranch that lets people pay to stay here and see what ranch life is like. Guests are called dudes. That's what the cowhands called people from back East. Some dude ranches are just for entertaining visitors, excuse me, dudes. Some are real cattle or sheep ranches that take in a few dudes on the side.

Our ranch, the Double K near Bozeman, Montana, is a working cattle ranch. We went with the cowhands on a roundup. It was exciting to watch. With just a touch of his spurs, a cowhand moved his horse into the herd and cut out one cow. It was hot, dusty, and noisy too. The cattle were mooing, and the calves were bawling.

We also rode out on a trail and camped out under the stars. Dinner from a chuckwagon, a bedroll by the campfire, and a coyote howling in the distance — I felt as if I were in a Western movie!

Your Turn!

 Need a Review? For help with using a dictionary or glossary to determine the meanings of unknown words, see *Words!*

▶ **Ready to Try It?** Read *Coyote School News* on pp. 202–219.

 **Genre**

Historical fiction is a story that is made up around real events in history. Decide what those real events might have been as you read about children in a southern Arizona country school in 1938–1939.

COYOTE SCHOOL NEWS

by Joan Sandin

Question of the Week

How can we work together to achieve a goal?

Rancho San Isidro

UNITED STATES

•Rancho San Isidro

MEXICO

My name is Ramón Ernesto Ramírez, but everybody calls me Monchi. I live on a ranch that my great-grandfather built a long time ago when this land was part of Mexico. That was before the United States bought it and moved the line in 1854. My father has a joke about that. He says my great-grandfather was an *americano,* not because he crossed the line, but because the line crossed him.

In my family we are six kids: me, my big brother Junior, my big sister Natalia, my little tattletale brother Victor, my little sister Loli, and the baby Pili. My *tío* Chaco lives with us too. He is the youngest brother of my father.

The real name of our ranch is Rancho San Isidro, after the patron saint of my great-grandfather, but most of the time everybody calls it the Ramírez Ranch.

On our ranch we have chickens and pigs and cattle and horses. The boys in the Ramírez family know

204

how to ride and rope. We are a family of *vaqueros.* In the fall and spring we have roundup on our ranch. Many people come to help with the cattle and the horses. Those are the most exciting days of the year, even more exciting than Christmas.

The things I don't like about our ranch are always having to get the wood for the fire, and the long and bumpy ride to school.

My tío Chaco drives the school bus.

"It's not fair," I tell him. "We have to get up earlier than all the other kids at Coyote School, and we get home the latest too."

"Don't forget," says my tío, "you get first choice of seats."

Ha, ha. By the time the last kid gets in, we are all squeezed together like sardines in a can. And the bus is shaking and bumping like it has a flat tire.

"I wish President Roosevelt would do something about these roads," I tell my tío.

"Hey, you know how to write English," he says. "Write him a letter."

"Maybe I will," I say.

americano (*AH-mair-ee-CAHN-oh*)—
    American
tío (TEE-oh)—uncle
rancho (RAHN-choe)—ranch
san (sahn)—saint
vaqueros (bah-CARE-rose)—cowboys

205

Coyote School

"*Mira, mira,* Monchi," Natalia says, pinching my cheek. "There's your little *novia.*"

She means Rosie. I like Rosie, but I hate it when Natalia teases me. Rosie lives at Coyote Ranch, close enough to school that she can walk. Always she waits by the road so she can race the bus.

"*¡Ándale! ¡Ándale!* Hurry up!" we yell at my tío Chaco, but every time he lets her win.

Rosie wasn't first today anyway. Lalo and Frankie were. Their horses are standing in the shade of the big mesquite tree.

Yap! Yap! Yap! Always Chipito barks when he sees us, and Miss Byers says, "Hush, Chipito!" Then she smiles and waves at us.

Miss Byers is new this year. Her ranch is a hundred miles from here, in Rattlesnake Canyon, so five days of the week she and Chipito live in the little room behind the school. All of us like Miss Byers, even the big kids, because she is young and nice and fair. We like that she lives on a ranch, and we like her swell ideas:

1. Baseball at recess,
2. The Perfect Attendance Award,
3. *Coyote News.*

mira (MEER-ah)—look
novia (NOVE-ee-ah)—girlfriend
ándale (AHN-dah-lay)—come on; hurry up

Coyote News

All week we have been working on our first *Coyote News*. Natalia made up the name, and Joey drew the coyote. First we looked at some other newspapers: the *Arizona Daily Star*, *Western Livestock Journal*, and *Little Cowpuncher*. That one we liked best because all the stories and pictures were done by kids.

"Monchi," said Loli, "put me cute."

"What?" I said. Sometimes it's not easy to understand my little sister's English.

"Miss Byers says you have to help me put words to my story," she said.

"Okay," I told her. "But I have my own story to do, so hurry up and learn to write."

Loli's story was *muy tonta,* but one thing was good. She remembered how to write all the words I spelled for her.

Even if Victor is my brother, I have to say he is a big tattletale—*chismoso.* When Gilbert was writing his story for *Coyote News,* Victor told on him for writing in Spanish. But Miss Byers did not get mad at Gilbert. She smiled at him! And then she said Spanish is a beautiful language that people around here have been speaking for hundreds of years, and that we should be proud we can speak it too!

Ha ha, Victor, you big chismoso!

When we finished our stories and pictures, Miss Byers cut a stencil for the mimeograph. Then she printed copies of *Coyote News* for us to take home, and we hung them up on the ceiling to dry the ink. My tío Chaco said it looked like laundry day at Coyote School.

muy (MOO-ee)—very
tonta (TONE-tah)—silly
chismoso (cheese-MOE-soe)—tattletale
señor (sin-YORE)—Mr.
grandote (grahn-DOE-tay)—great, big, huge

Issue Number One   September 15, 1938

COYOTE NEWS

Stories and Pictures by the Students of Coyote School, Pima County, Arizona

Something New at Coyote School

Coyote News was the idea of our teacher, but we write the stories and draw the pictures. The big kids help the little kids...Rosie Garcia, Grade 3

About Coyote School

This year we have 12 kids and all the grades except Grade 5...Billy Mills, Grade 3

We Ride Our Horses to School

The road to Rancho del Cerro is a very big problem for the bus of Mr. Ramirez. For that reason Lalo and I ride our horses to school--16 miles all the days. The year past it was 2,352 miles. We had to put new shoes on the horses 5 times...Frankie Lopez, Grade 6

The Perfect Attendance

Miss Byers will give a prize to anybody who comes to school all the days, no matter what. The prize is called The Perfect Attendance Award and it is a silver dollar! For me perfect attendance is not easy, but oh boy, I would like to win that silver dollar...........Monchi Ramirez, Grade 4

Chipito

The dog of the teacher is called Chipito. He is very cute. He likes Loli best.....story by Loli Ramirez, Grade 1 with help by Monchi Ramirez, Grade 4

Señor Grandote

Our bus driver ran over a big rattlesnake. We took the skin and gave it to our teacher. She measured him with the yardstick. He was 5 feet and 7 inches! She hung him on the wall next to President Roosevelt. We kids call him Señor Grandote because in Spanish it means Mr. Huge...............Gilbert Perez, Grade 6

Chiles

Every day I am asking my father when we will have roundup. He says I am making him *loco* with my nagging and that first we have to pick *todos los chiles.*

All of us kids are tired of picking the chiles. It doesn't matter that we get home late from school, we still have to do it. And then, before the chiles dry out, we have to string them to make the *sartas.*

Last night we were taking about 600 pounds of the chiles to my tío Enrique's ranch. I was in the back of the truck when it hit a big rock.

All the heavy sacks fell on me. Oh boy, it hurt so much! But I did not tell my father. He had told me not to ride in the back of the truck, and I was afraid he would be mad.

My hand was still hurting this morning when Miss Byers did Fingernail Inspection.

"Monchi," she said, "what happened to your wrist? It's all black-and-blue and swollen."

"The chiles fell on him," Victor told her. "My father told him not to ride in the back."

"¡Chismoso!" I hissed at him.

Miss Byers called my tío Chaco over, and they had a long talk.

"Back in the bus, *mi'jo,*" my tío said. "I have to take you to Tucson."

"Tucson!" I said. "Why?"

"You got to see the doctor," he said. So we drove all the way to Tucson to my *tía* Lena's house. At first my aunt was surprised and happy to see us, but then my tío told her why we were there.

"Monchi!" my tía said. "*¡Pobrecito!*" Then she told my tío Chaco to go back with the bus and she would take care of me.

My tía took me to a doctor. He moved my hand around. It hurt when he did that.

"I'm afraid the wrist is broken," he told my tía. "I need to set it and put it in a cast."

So I got a cast of plaster on my arm, and I had to stay in Tucson. But for me that was no problem! My tía felt very sorry for me. She cooked my favorite foods, and I got to pick the stations on her radio. That night Miss Byers called on the telephone to ask about me. She said she would come early Monday morning to drive me to school.

On Sunday my tía took me to the Tarzan picture show at the Fox Theater. It was swell! After the show we got ice cream and walked around downtown to look in the windows of the stores. I saw many things I liked. The best was a silver buckle with a hole to put a silver dollar. *¡Ay caramba!* I wish I had a buckle like that.

loco (LOW-coe)—crazy
todos (TOE-dose)—all
los (lohs)—the
chiles (CHEE-less)—chile peppers
sartas (SAR-tahs)—strings of chile peppers
mi'jo (MEE-hoe)—my son, sonny
tía (TEE-ah)—aunt
pobrecito (pobe-ray-SEE-toe)—
    poor little thing
¡ay caramba! (EYE car-RAHM-bah)—
    oh boy!

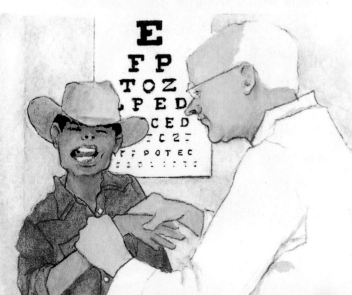

Nochebuena

For *Nochebuena* we are many people. Some are family I see only at Christmas and roundup and weddings and funerals. The day before Nochebuena my cousins from Sonora arrived. Now we could make the *piñata!*

First we cut the strips of red, white, and green paper. Then we paste them on a big *olla*. When the piñata is ready, we give it to my mother to fill with the *dulces* she hides in her secret places.

On Nochebuena, Junior and my tío Chaco hung the piñata between two big mesquite trees and we kids lined up to hit it, the littlest ones first. My mother tied a *mascada* over my little brother Pili's eyes and my tía Lena turned him around and around. She gave him the stick and pointed him toward the piñata. My tío Chaco and Junior made it easy for him. They did not jerk on the rope when he swung.

"*¡Dale! ¡Dale!*" we were yelling, but Pili never came close. None of the little kids could hit it. Then it was Loli's turn.

BAM.

Some peanuts fell out. Gilbert and I dived to get them. One by one, the other kids tried and missed. Then it was Natalia's turn. She took a good swing and—*BAM*.

The piñata broke open, and all the kids were in the dirt, screaming and laughing and picking up gum and nuts and oranges and candies.

Just before midnight we got into my tío Chaco's bus and my father's pickup to go to the Mass at Amado. When we got home my mother and my tías put out *tamales* and *menudo* and *tortillas* and cakes and coffee and other drinks. We had music and dancing. Nobody told us we had to go to bed.

Sometime in the night Santa Claus came and gave us our presents. Junior got a pair of spurs, Victor got a big red top, and Loli got a little toy dog that looks like Chipito. But I got the best present. It was a silver-dollar buckle, the one I had seen with my tía Lena in Tucson. It doesn't have a dollar yet, only a hole, but when I win the Perfect Attendance I will put my silver dollar in that hole.

Nochebuena (NO-chay-BUAY-nah)—
    Christmas Eve
piñata (peen-YAH-tah)—clay pot *(olla)*
    filled with treats
olla (OY-yah)—clay pot
dulces (DOOL-sehss)—sweets, candy
mascada (mas-KAH-dah)—scarf
¡dale! (DAH-lay)—hit it!
tamales (tah-MAH-less)—steamed,
    filled dough
menudo (men-OO-doe)—tripe soup
tortillas (tor-TEE-yahs)—flat Mexican bread

COYOTE NEWS

Happy New Year!

Stories and Pictures by the Students of Coyote School, Pima County, Arizona

Miss Byers' Radio

Miss Byers brought her new radio to school. It has a big battery, so it doesn't matter that Coyote School has no electricity. We got to hear President Roosevelt's speech to the Congress. He told them to be prepared for war. Then he said, "Happy New Year."........Monchi Ramirez, Grade 4

Our President

waw

by Joey Brown

Our President's Voice

None of us kids had heard the President's voice before. When he said "war" it sounded like "waw." We were all laughing because we never heard anybody who talked like that, but Billy said some of the dudes do............Rosie Garcia, Grade 3

Some Noisy Children

When the President was talking, Loli was noisy. Miss Byers gave her peanuts to make her quiet. I was quiet without the peanuts...Victor, Grade 2

Yap!

By Frankie López

Music on the Radio

We got to listen to the music on Miss Byers' radio. She has many stations, but I liked best to hear the one with the rancheras.........Gilbert Perez, Grade 6

No Earrings for Christmas

Santa Claus didn't bring me any earrings. Loli says it's because he knows that I don't have any holes in my ears like she does......Cynthia Brown, Grade 2

The Perfect Attendance Report

Miss Byers says Santa Claus must have given some of our kids the flu and chicken pox for Christmas. The only kids who still have perfect attendance are Natalia, Monchi, Victor, and me.........Billy Mills, Grade 3

La Fiesta de los Vaqueros Rodeo Parade

We are so excited because Miss Byers just told us something wonderful. Our school gets to be in the Tucson Rodeo Parade!...Natalia Ramirez, Grade 8

Roundup!

The vaqueros were hollering, "¡Ándale! ¡Ándale!" They were cutting through the cattle on their horses, swinging their lassoes in the air to rope out the steers. My tío Chaco threw his saddle up on his horse, Canelo, and joined them. We kids clapped and whistled. Sometimes we helped my father or my tíos. We brought them rope or a fresh horse or something to drink.

That night we boys got to eat with the vaqueros and sit by the fire and listen to them play their guitars and sing their *rancheras*. We got to hear their exciting stories and their bragging and their bad words. When my father came over to Junior and me, I thought he was going to tell us to go in to bed, but instead he said, "Tomorrow I want you boys to help with the branding." Junior had helped since he was eleven, but it was the first time my father had ever asked me.

"Tomorrow I have school," I said.

"School!" said Junior. "Monchi, don't you understand? You get to help with the branding!"

"He doesn't want to lose the Perfect Attendance," said Victor.

"The Perfect Attendance!" said Junior. "Monchi, you are crazier than a goat. You are a Ramírez. We are a family of vaqueros. Roundup is more important than the Perfect Attendance."

I knew Junior was right, but I touched the empty hole of my silver-dollar buckle and I sighed. *Adiós*, Perfect Attendance.

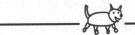

---

rancheras (rahn-CHAIR-ahs)—Mexican folk songs
fiesta (fee-ESS-tah)—party, celebration
de (day)—of
adiós (ah-DYOHSS)—good-bye

For two exciting days Junior and I helped with the roundup. First the vaqueros lassoed the calves and wrestled them down to the ground. Then Junior and I held them while my father and my *tío* Enrique branded them and cut the ears and gave them the shot.

¡Qué barullo! The red-hot irons were smoking, and the burned hair was stinking. The calves were fighting and bawling like giant babies. They were much heavier than Junior and me. It was hard work and dangerous to hold them down. I got dust in my eyes and in my nose, but I didn't care.

After the work of the roundup was over, we made the fiesta! First was a race for the kids. We had to ride as fast as we could to the chuck wagon, take an orange, and ride back again. Junior won on Pinto. He got a big jar of candies and gave some to all of us. Last came Victor and his little *burro*. All that day we had races and roping contests.

That night we had a big *barbacoa*. The kids got cold soda pops. When the music started, all the vaqueros wanted to dance with Natalia. The one they call Chapo asked her to be his *novia*, but Natalia told him she doesn't want to get married. She wants to go to high school.

Monday morning when we left for school, the vaqueros were packing their bedrolls. We waved and hollered from our bus, "*¡Adiós! ¡Adiós! ¡Hasta la vista!*"

qué (kaye)—what, how
barullo (bah-ROO-yoe)—noise, racket
burro (BOOR-row)—donkey
barbacoa (bar-bah-KOH-ah)—barbecue
hasta la vista (AH-stah lah VEE-stah)—
   see you

Stories and Pictures by the Students of Coyote School, Pima County, Arizona

Eduardo (Lalo) and Natalia Graduate!

Lalo and I have passed the Eighth Grade Standard Achievement Test! I am happy to graduate and I am excited about high school, but I will miss my teacher and all the kids at my dear Coyote School...Natalia Ramirez, Grade 8

I Lose the Perfect Attendance

I was absent from school to help with the roundup. It was very exciting, but now it is over and I am feeling sad. The vaqueros are gone and I will not get a silver dollar for my buckle....Monchi Ramirez, Grade 4

The Perfect Attendance Report

The only one who still has perfect attendance is Victor. Even Miss Byers has been absent, because when it was roundup on her ranch a big calf stepped on her foot. We had Miss Elias for 3 days. Miss Byers had to pay her 5 dollars a day to take her place.....Gilbert Perez, Grade 6

A Visit to the Boston Beans

Mr. and Mrs. Bean invited my family to visit them this summer in Boston. Boston is Back East. It is even bigger than Tucson. No other kid at Coyote School has ever gone that far away!.............Billy Mills, Grade 3

Earrings

My daddy is getting married. Joey and I will get a new mother and 4 new brothers. Laura is nice and she can cook, but the best part is she has pierced ears and now I will get to have them too!....Cynthia Brown, Grade 2

Last Issue for the School Year

This is the last issue before the summer vacation. I am saving all my Coyote News newspapers so that someday I can show my children all the swell and exciting things we did at Coyote School..........Rosie Garcia, Grade 3

The Last Day of School

On the last day of school Miss Byers gave us a fiesta with cupcakes and candies and Cracker Jacks and soda pops. We got to listen to Mexican music on her radio. I didn't have to dance with Natalia. I got to dance with Rosie.

Then Miss Byers turned off the radio and stood in the front of the room between President Roosevelt and Señor Grandote. She called Natalia and Lalo up to the front and told them how proud we were that they were graduates of Coyote School, and how much we would miss them. We all clapped and whistled.

Next, Miss Byers gave Edelia a paper and said, "Please read what it says, Edelia."

Edelia read: "Edelia Ortiz has been promoted to Grade Two." Miss Byers had to help her to read "promoted," but we all clapped and cheered anyway. Edelia looked very happy and proud.

Then Miss Byers asked Victor to come to the front of the room, and I knew what that meant. I didn't want to listen when she said how good it was that he had not missed a day of school, and I didn't want to look when she gave him the silver dollar. I knew I should be

happy that Victor won the Perfect Attendance, but I was not.

"And now, boys and girls," Miss Byers said, "it's time for the next award."

"What next award?" we asked.

"The *Coyote News* Writing Award for the student who has contributed most to *Coyote News* by writing his own stories and by helping others write theirs. The winner of the *Coyote News* Writing Award is Ramón Ernesto Ramírez."

"Me?" I said.

All the kids were clapping and whistling. I just sat there.

"Go up to the front," Natalia said and gave me a push.

Miss Byers smiled and shook my hand. "Congratulations, Monchi," she said, and then she gave me the award.

¡Ay caramba! The *Coyote News* Writing Award was a shiny silver dollar!

"Oh thank you, Miss Byers!" I said. "*¡Gracias!*" I was so surprised and happy. I pushed the silver dollar into the round hole on my buckle. It fit perfectly!

"*¡Muy hermosa!*" Miss Byers said.

She was right. It was very beautiful.

gracias (GRAHS-see-ahs)—thank you
hermosa (air-MOE-sah)—beautiful

219

Envision It! Retell

READING STREET ONLINE
STORY SORT
www.ReadingStreet.com

Think Critically

1. Imagine that your school is starting a school newspaper, and you've been asked to write an article for the first edition. What topic would you write about? Why? **Text to Self**

2. The author helps you get to know Monchi by narrating the story in his voice, in the first person. Find examples of how Monchi's words and actions help you get to know him. **Think Like an Author**

3. How do the members of Monchi's family feel about one another? How do they feel about being a family? Support your answer with details from the story. **Draw Conclusions**

4. What is the most important event that happens at the end of the story? Explain why this event is important. **Story Structure**

5. Look Back and Write Look back at *Coyote News*. What are some of the stories you enjoyed reading that made the news at Coyote School?

Key Ideas and Details • Text Evidence

Meet the Author

Joan Sandin

Joan Sandin grew up in Tucson, Arizona. "I walked a mile to grade school through the desert, with roadrunners and quail for company," she recalls. As a child, she loved to draw. Art was her favorite subject in school. As an adult, she has written several books and has illustrated many more.

Coyote School News is based on a real school newspaper called *Little Cowpuncher.* Schoolchildren in southern Arizona wrote articles for the paper from 1932 to 1943. Their teacher was Eulalia Bourne. Ms. Sandin explains, "Coyote School is a fictionalized school with fictionalized students, but it was inspired by the *Little Cowpuncher* papers and by conversations with my friend María." María Amado, Ms. Sandin's best friend in high school, lived on a ranch near Tucson when she was young. María attended Sópori School, "a school very much like Coyote School." María's brother, sister, and cousins all wrote articles for the *Little Cowpuncher.*

Here are other books about newspapers.

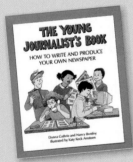

The Young Journalist's Book by Donna Guthrie and Nancy Bentley

Extra! Extra! The Who, What, Where, When, and Why of Newspapers by Linda Granfield

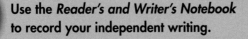

Use the *Reader's and Writer's Notebook* to record your independent writing.

221

Common Core State Standards

Writing 2. Write informative/explanatory texts to examine a topic and convey ideas and information clearly. **Also Writing 2.a., 2.b., Language 2.**

Let's Write It!

Key Features of a News Article

- reports real current events

- gives the most important information first

- has a headline, a byline, a lead, supporting details, and an ending

READING STREET ONLINE
GRAMMAR JAMMER
www.ReadingStreet.com

News Article

A **news article** gives readers information and facts about an important event. The student model on the next page is an example of a news article.

Writing Prompt Think about an event that happened recently in your school. Now write an article about it for a school newspaper.

Writer's Checklist

Remember, you should . . .

✓ write about a real event.

✓ make sure that the most important information comes first.

✓ include supporting sentences with simple facts, details, and explanations.

✓ have a headline and a byline.

✓ use plural, common, and proper nouns correctly.

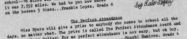

Brooks School Goes Green
by Cristi Santos

This week, Brooks School will launch "Go Green," a school-wide recycling project. "We want to do our part to save the environment," said science teacher Bill Burton. The project was planned by the **students** in Burton's science class. Recycling **bins** for paper and plastic are already in place in **classrooms**, **hallways**, and the cafeteria.

Student **volunteers** are helping to build and monitor compost **bins** outside the cafeteria. Sixth-grade science **students** will add shredded paper and leaves each week, and the cafeteria staff will add food waste every day. Members of the Brooks School Garden Club are looking forward to using the finished compost on their vegetable garden.

Students will formally launch "Go Green" at a school assembly on November 16 at 3:30 P.M. The presentation will be held in the auditorium and is open to the public.

Genre A **news article** features a headline and a byline.

Writing Trait Focus/Ideas The purpose of the article is to inform readers.

Regular plural nouns are used correctly.

Conventions

Regular Plural Nouns

Remember A **regular plural noun** is formed by adding -s or -es to the singular form. Some nouns that end in a consonant followed by a -y drop the -y and add -ies (family/families).

Common Core State Standards
Speaking/Listening 4. Report on a topic or text, tell a story, or recount an experience in an organized manner, using appropriate facts and relevant, descriptive details to support main ideas or themes; speak clearly at an understandable pace.
Also Foundational Skills 4.b., Language 4., 4.c.

READING STREET ONLINE
ONLINE STUDENT EDITION
www.ReadingStreet.com

Vocabulary

Unknown Words

Dictionary/Glossary When you look up a word in a glossary or a dictionary, you can find out how to pronounce it by using the pronunciation key. And, if you are using a dictionary, the syllabication of each word can also help you pronounce the word.

Practice It! Choose two or three words from the Glossary and carefully copy the pronunciations shown in the parentheses. Exchange pronunciations with a partner and use the pronunciation key to identify each other's words. Then tell how many syllables are in each word. Remember to check the meanings of any unknown words.

Fluency

Expression

Partner Reading Reading with expression makes a story more exciting. Stressing some words with more feeling and others with less feeling makes the story lively and more interesting.

Practice It! With a partner, practice reading aloud *Coyote School News*, page 219. Read the page once with no expression. Then read the page again with expression. Which way makes the story more exciting?

226

Media Literacy

When you give a presentation, make eye contact with the audience.

Newscast

In a newscast, a TV or radio reporter tells about important stories that are happening now. The purpose of a newscast is to inform the audience about current events.

Practice It! Work with students to create a newscast about events that are happening at your school. Focus on a problem, such as litter on school property. Explore the causes and effects of the problem and suggest solutions. Interview teachers and students. Rehearse your newscast and present it to the class.

Tips

- News directors use different camera angles to convey not only the words of the people speaking but the emotional messages of their stories as well.

- A close-up is when the camera shows only the face of who is being filmed. The viewer focuses his or her attention on the subject.

- A wide-angle view shows a landscape. It sets the scene of the report.

- Sound effects make the viewer feel as if he or she were at the actual scene.

- When reporting, make sure to use singular and plural nouns correctly.

227

Oral Vocabulary

Let's Talk About

Team Accomplishments

- Describe what teams can accomplish that one person cannot.

- Speak so everyone can hear you.

- Build on the ideas of others as you speak.

READING STREET ONLINE
CONCEPT TALK VIDEO
www.ReadingStreet.com

229

Common Core State Standards

Informational Text 1. Refer to details and examples in a text when explaining what the text says explicitly and when drawing inferences from the text.

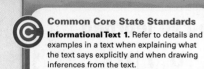

Skill

Strategy

Comprehension Skill

Draw Conclusions

- Facts and details are the small pieces of information in an article or story.

- Facts and details "add up" to a conclusion— a decision or opinion the reader forms that makes sense.

- Use this graphic organizer to draw conclusions about why Bodie would be interesting to visit as you read "Visiting a California Ghost Town."

| Facts and Details | + | Facts and Details | → | Conclusion |

Comprehension Strategy

Questioning

Active readers ask and answer questions before, during, and after reading. When you ask a literal question, the answer can be found in the text. An interpretive question is answered by using other information in the text to figure out an answer on your own. An evaluative question is answered by making a judgment. You will go beyond the text to answer the question.

Visiting a California Ghost Town

If you have ever wondered what a real ghost town looks like, you can visit Bodie, California. A ghost town is an abandoned town that has been deserted for many years. In 1859, when gold was discovered in Bodie, the whole town had only about twenty miners. By 1880—just over twenty years later—the town's population had grown to around ten thousand. A few years later, the boom was over, and by 1882 people started moving away.

In 1962, Bodie became a California State Historic Park. The park service keeps Bodie in a state of "arrested decay." This means that things are kept just as they were found many years ago. About 170 buildings are still standing and most of them are kept locked so that things inside can be kept the same as they were when the last residents left the town. If you look inside some of the buildings, it may appear that the people just left. You may even see books left open on desks or a store filled with goods.

Bodie is an incredible place to go if you like learning about the past. Walk around this town and see if you can imagine what it was like living in the Old West.

Strategy What is a "ghost town"?

Skill Why is Bodie called a ghost town?

Skill What conclusion can you draw about visiting a ghost town?

Your Turn!

❚❚ Need a Review? See the *Envision It! Handbook* for help with drawing conclusions and questioning.

▶ Ready to Try It? Use what you've learned about drawing conclusions as you read *Scene Two*.

SCENE TWO

231

Common Core State Standards

Language 4. Determine or clarify the meaning of unknown and multiple-meaning words and phrases based on grade 4 reading and content, choosing flexibly from a range of strategies. **Also Language 4.b.**

argument

descendants

script

Screenplay

advice

arrangements

dishonest

snag

Vocabulary Strategy for

Affixes: Prefixes

Word Structure Prefixes are word parts that are added to the beginning of words. A prefix changes a word's meaning. For example, the Middle English prefix *dis-* means "not." If you *disagree*, you do not agree with someone or something. Knowing what a prefix means can help you figure out the meaning of an unknown word as you read.

1. Find a sentence with a word that has a prefix. Cover the prefix with your finger.

2. Look at the base word. See if you know what it means.

3. Add the meaning of the prefix.

4. Check to see if this meaning makes sense in the sentence.

Read "Writing a Play About History." Use prefixes to help you determine the meanings of words you do not know.

Words to Write Reread "Writing a Play About History." Write a paragraph about a historical event you would like to see performed as a play. Use words from the *Words to Know* list in your paragraph.

Writing a Play About History

If you decide to write a play about history, make arrangements to spend a lot of time on research. Sometimes there is some argument about which facts are true. Although few writers mean to be dishonest, they may not always check their facts. Be a little distrustful of what you read.

It might be interesting to write about the descendants of the people who sailed on the *Mayflower*. Some of our Presidents, including Presidents John Adams, John Quincy Adams, and Franklin Roosevelt, had ancestors on the *Mayflower*. Astronaut Alan Shepard Jr. is also part of this special group. I'm sure you'll be able to discover more names to add to this list!

Your work can hit a snag if you don't make your information interesting. Take this advice and make sure your script tells a good story. You'll learn a lot while writing your play. You'll want to work hard to make sure your audience enjoys every minute of it!

Your Turn!

❚❚ Need a Review? For additional help using prefixes, see *Words!*

▶ Ready to Try It? Use what you've learned about prefixes as you read *Scene Two* on pp. 234–247.

Genre

Dramas, or plays, are stories performed in front of an audience. As you read, think about how one character can play two parts.

SCENE TWO

by Don Abramson and Robert Kausal

Question of the Week
What can teams accomplish?

CHARACTERS

JASMINE DELORES KERRY ANGIE

MITCH HAP MS. KEELER *a teacher* MR. BROWN *a teacher*

SETTING: *A room next to the stage in a school auditorium. It is bare, except for a table and chairs, perhaps clothes racks, a makeup table and mirror, some boxes, etc.*

AT RISE: *Mr. Brown enters, carrying a clipboard. He shows in Mitch, Jasmine, Hap, Angie, Kerry, and Delores, all carrying books, backpacks, etc. Ms. Keeler follows.*

MR. BROWN: All right, kids, you can work on your script in here while the others rehearse on the stage.

JASMINE: Thank you, Mr. Brown.

MS. KEELER: And how's that script coming along?

ANGIE: Oh, we're doing fine, Ms. Keeler.

MS. KEELER: Good, good. How many scenes are you planning?

KERRY: We were going to do a scene for each year of Riverside's history, but we thought 134 scenes would run long.

MR. BROWN: You think? Just keep in mind it's a skit in our Founders' Day talent show. You're sharing the stage with—(*He consults his clipboard.*) Betty and Beverly Tanner singing "If I Ain't Got You"—

MS. KEELER: "Don't Have." Sorry! Force of habit.

MR. BROWN (*still reading*): Milton the Miraculous Magician—oh, by the way, if you see an escaped rabbit come by here, try to corner him or something—Gloria Newman and her Hula Hoop™ Extravaganza—well, you get my point. It's a talent show. Nobody's going to win an acting award.

MS. KEELER: We'll let you work now.

KERRY: Right, thanks. (*MR. BROWN and MS. KEELER leave.*) Okay, so where are we?

ANGIE: We finished scene one.

DELORES: Who's got scene two?

MITCH AND JASMINE (*together*): I do. (*They look at each other.*)

MITCH: I was supposed to write it.

JASMINE: I told you I was going to write it.

MITCH: Two too?

JASMINE: Yes.

DELORES: Two twos?

JASMINE: I guess.

KERRY (*like a train*): Too-too-too-*tooo!* (*They all look at him; he grins and shrugs.*)

ANGIE: Cool it, Kerry.

HAP: I wrote a scene too. No, I mean it's *also* a scene, not two a scene—I mean—

DELORES: Don't get Kerry started again.

JASMINE: We'll see, Hap. Let's get this scene two business straightened out first.

KERRY: You guys could arm-wrestle for who goes first.

DELORES: Kerry!

JASMINE: I'll go first. Here, I made copies of the script. *(She distributes the scripts.)* Kerry, you play Joshua Wilkins; Angie, you read Becky Isaacs; and Hap, play Gunther Isaacs for now. *(They all take their scripts and move down center.)* This is scene two, now. After Gunther Isaacs and his wife and two daughters have moved to Riverside—except it isn't Riverside yet—and they've built their cabin and planted their crops. Lights up.

KERRY: Huh?

JASMINE: Begin.

KERRY *(JOSHUA):* Becky, I must tell you I truly appreciate your family's hospitality this week.

ANGIE *(BECKY):* Joshua, in truth, my mother bade you stay because she is so eager to hear news from the East.

MITCH *(interrupting):* Hold up. What does that mean, "bade you stay"?

JASMINE: It's a past tense of "bid."

MITCH: Like an auction?

JASMINE: No, no! Like in "invite." Go on.

MITCH *(to the others):* She reads too many books.

KERRY *(JOSHUA):* You know, Becky, I came west looking for land. If I could find the right spot, I might be of a mind—

MITCH *(interrupting):* Now, what does *that* mean—"of a mind"?

JASMINE: It means "to think; to have an opinion." Stop interrupting, Mitch.

MITCH: Well, why can't they talk regular English?

JASMINE: Because it's history, that's why. They're speaking—*(She searches for a word but can't find it.)*—historical. *(to the actors)* Please!

ANGIE (*BECKY*): My father owns all this land, Joshua. If you but talked to him—

HAP (*GUNTHER, enters*): If you talked to me about what?

ANGIE (*BECKY*): Hello, Papa!

KERRY (*JOSHUA*): About your land, Gunther. What if a young fellow desired to stay here?

HAP (*GUNTHER*): Why then, Joshua, I'm sure some sort of arrangements could be made. I can see more and more settlers moving into the area. Soon we'll have a town, and that town will become a city. And someday in the future—

MITCH (*interrupting*): You know what? I'm "of a mind" about this scene, Jasmine. It's bo-o-oring!

JASMINE: Well, that's too bad—it's *his-tor-y*.

KERRY: This skit should *be* history.

BO-O-ORING!

239

MITCH: Yeah, but you've got to read *my* scene about Gunther Isaacs. *(handing out scripts)* Here, Hap, you're still Gunther—Delores, you're Gunther's wife, Amity Isaacs, and Kerry, you're Peter Marlon. *(They all move to their places.)* Scene Two. And—action!

KERRY *(Peter)*: Gunther, it's been awesome doing business with you.

HAP *(Gunther)*: You made my day, Peter. High five. *(Following the script, he raises his hand, but unsurely. Kerry high-fives him.)*

JASMINE *(interrupting):* Now, wait a minute! The Founders did *not* high-five each other.

MITCH: How do you know? *(He holds up his hand; Kerry high-fives him. Then quickly, before Jasmine can think of an answer, he continues.)* Action, action!

HAP (GUNTHER): So, Pete, when are you going to start clearing your land?

KERRY (PETER): First, I think I'll get my wife and son in Philly.

DELORES (AMITY, *enters):* Take my advice, Peter, build first. Your family'll thank you for it.

HAP (GUNTHER): Yo, Amity, you never complained before.

DELORES (AMITY): About sleeping outdoors while you built a barn for the horses? What good would that do me?

HAP (GUNTHER): Good point. You know how much those horses are worth? *(to* PETER) Anyway, if you head east now, it'll be winter before you get back.

KERRY (PETER): Cool, I'll go give them a call now.

DELORES *(dropping character):* Give them a call? Mitch, even I know they didn't have telephones back then.

MITCH: Um—I guess you're right. We'll make it a telegraph. Action, action, action!

KERRY: How did we ever get scene one written? *(as* PETER): Well, I'll go start my cabin. And I'm sure looking forward to fishing in that river.

HAP (GUNTHER): Me too. Later, dude. (PETER, *exits)*

DELORES (AMITY): What's this about fish? You know there are no fish in that river!

HAP (GUNTHER): I made that mighty river by damming that sorry-looking creek.

DELORES (AMITY): True, but what about the fish?

HAP (*GUNTHER*): I thought—you know—if you dam it, they will come.

DELORES (*AMITY*): The fish? They'll have to crawl through the forest to get here.

HAP (*GUNTHER*): But you've got to admit, the dam helped.

DELORES (*AMITY*): Oh, that pathetic creek looks like a real river now. But Gunther, what if the settlers find out?

HAP (*GUNTHER, shrugs*): Good point.

JASMINE: Mitch, you can't put that on stage!

MITCH: Why not?

JASMINE: Because it's not true, that's why not! (*holding up a book she has dug out of her backpack*) I've read all the way through *The History of Riverside,* and I know it's not in here. Besides, Gunther Isaacs was a Founding Father. He would never—

MITCH: I got it off the Internet. Look, I got a printout— (*He digs in his backpack and finds several pages of printout. He hands them to Jasmine.*)

JASMINE (*scanning the article quickly*): ". . . another tale told of Gunther Isaacs, but probably an apocryphal one. . . ." Don't you know what that means?

MITCH: I thought it meant—like, "secret."

JASMINE: No—it means—it means—oh, wait a minute. (*She digs in her backpack to find her electronic dictionary. She punches in the word and reads the screen.*) It means "of doubtful authorship or authenticity." See, it's made up!

MITCH: Well, so?

DELORES: I think what Jasmine is getting at, Mitch, is that it's a lie.

KERRY: It *is* a good story, though.

HAP: But this is a play about history!

KERRY: Do you think anybody'll know the difference?

DELORES: I think a lot of the audience will know about the town's history.

JASMINE *(waving her book):* Some of them might even have read *The History of Riverside.*

MITCH: But face it, Gunther Isaacs was a shady character.

DELORES: You're saying he was dishonest?

MITCH: If he was, at least he wasn't dull!

JASMINE: The scene's out, and that's final!

MITCH: If the scene's out, I'm out. And you can't use scene one either.

243

HAP: Come on, Mitch. We all worked on that scene together.

MITCH: Well then, I'll just take back the lines I wrote.

DELORES: That's silly. You can't just take back some lines!

MITCH: Sure I can. They're my lines. So—who's with me?

HAP: Mitch, don't do this.

MITCH: Whose side are you on, Hap? Come on.

DELORES: This isn't about sides.

MITCH: Sure it is.

ANGIE (*in a surprisingly sharp voice*): Will you all stop this! (*They all fall silent and look at her.*) I'm sorry. But my mom's a family counselor, and if there's one thing I learned, it's how to settle arguments.

MITCH: That's a lot of hooey!

ANGIE: No, it isn't!

DELORES: Be quiet, Mitch.

KERRY: Me, I enjoy a good argument.

DELORES: We can tell.

ANGIE: You can talk about what you really want. But then you really have to listen. Jasmine, Mitch, why do you want to put on this skit?

JASMINE: Well, I guess I want to bring history alive.

MITCH: I want people to be entertained.

ANGIE: Does the skit have to have this scene to be entertaining?

MITCH: I was just trying to add a little humor.

ANGIE: Well then, can't we all work together—?

MITCH: Look, we don't need another lecture on teamwork.

KERRY: Yeah, when I hear the word *teamwork*, I just want to punch somebody.

DELORES: Look, I've got an idea. If this story about damming up the creek is apoc—uh—made up, why does the Web site even run it?

ANGIE: Well, they do *say* the story probably isn't true.

DELORES: So why can't we do the same thing? Then we could keep Mitch's scene.

MITCH: Yeah—we could have the narrator say—um— "There's another story about Gunther Isaacs—"

JASMINE: "Some say it's true, and some say it's untrue—"

MITCH: "But we say—it's a good story."

HAP: Yes!

KERRY: Write that down. *(Mitch does so.)*

ANGIE: Can we move on now?

DELORES: Yes!

HAP: Would you like to hear *my* scene?

MITCH: I suppose we've got to.

JASMINE: If we're really cooperating now—

MS. KEELER *(enters):* Teamwork, yes.

(KERRY quickly and secretly punches MITCH's arm.)

MITCH: Hey!

(KERRY grins and shrugs as if to say: "I couldn't help myself.")

MS. KEELER *(not noticing):* That's so important when you're doing this sort of thing. How're things going?

ANGIE: We—uh—hit a snag, but we solved it.

MS. KEELER: Good. We're going to have a great show. Dixie's tap dancing to the "Star-Spangled Banner" is going to bring down the house. Now tell me, I hope you're all contributing to this script.

DELORES: Yes, we've all been working together.

HAP: Now we're going to read my scene.

MS. KEELER: Hap, did you write about your ancestor, Cornelius Hapgood?

HAP: Yes, I did.

MS. KEELER: I'm so glad. Kids, I don't know if you know this, but Hap's family are descendants of Riverside's earliest settlers.

KERRY: The buffalo?

HAP: No, my great, great, great, great—I don't know how many *greats*—grandfather was Cornelius Hapgood.

ANGIE: Wow, that's *great*, Hap.

DELORES: Who's Cornelius Hapgood?

HAP: He opened Riverside's first shoe store—for people *and* horses.

DELORES: Okay. So what's your scene about, Hap?

HAP: Picture this: the curtain rises. Sunset. Cornelius Hapgood is talking to his faithful horse Bucketmouth—

ANGIE: Bucketmouth?

JASMINE: Wait a minute! Where are we going to get a horse?

HAP: Good point. Okay—picture this: the curtain rises. Sunset. Cornelius Hapgood walks on stage, talking to himself—
(reads, as CORNELIUS): Oh, my dogs are tired—

KERRY: Dogs? I thought he had a horse.

HAP: They're his *feet*. Okay—picture this: the curtain rises—

KERRY: I know! Sunset, dogs, feet. Get on with it!

HAP *(CORNELIUS):* I plum wore out these boots down to my socks. Where can a person buy full-grain leather shoes that are rugged, yet stylish?

MITCH: Ms. Keeler, I think we're going to need another hour. Or two.

HAP *(CORNELIUS):* I'm talkin' comfortable, yet affordable. Maybe a waterproof moccasin with fringes. . . .
(As he talks, the lights fade out.)

Common Core State Standards

Literature 1. Refer to details and examples in a text when explaining what the text says explicitly and when drawing inferences from the text. **Also Literature 2., Writing 9.**

Envision It! Retell

READING STREET ONLINE
STORY SORT
www.ReadingStreet.com

Think Critically

1. Many people are interested in the history of the town they live in. Why do you think people are interested in events of the past that took place in their town? **Text to World**

2. Why do you think the authors have Jasmine always checking everyone's facts?
   Think Like an Author

3. What conclusions can you come to about the way history can be told?
   Draw Conclusions

4. What do you think the students learned about teamwork? Use evidence from the story to support your answer. **Questioning**

5. **Look Back and Write** Look back at page 236. As with all plays, there is a list of characters and information about the setting and time. Why is it important to know these things before you begin reading? What might happen if you didn't know them?
   Key Ideas and Details • Text Evidence

Meet the Authors

DON ABRAMSON & ROBERT KAUSAL

Don Abramson became involved in theater as a high school freshman. He directed and acted in plays and designed and built theatrical sets. His plays written for children and adults have been performed in cities in the United States and England. He also enjoyed writing books and lyrics for musical theater. His children's musical *The Well of the Guelphs* was produced in Iowa and Nebraska. Recently, he combined versions of Cinderella from different cultures into a musical entitled *Who Is Cinderella?*

Robert Kausal also started working in theater while in high school. Since then, he has acted in local theaters before eventually becoming a high school English teacher. Mr. Kausal says, "My students enjoyed reading and performing plays, so when I had the chance to work with Don Abramson on *Scene Two*, I jumped at it." *Scene Two* is Mr. Kausal's first play.

Here are some other books you might enjoy.

Use your *Reader's and Writer's Notebook* to record your independent reading.

Descriptive

Key Features of Poetry

- sometimes written in meter

- often uses figurative language

- may use a pattern of verse

**READING STREET ONLINE
GRAMMAR JAMMER
www.ReadingStreet.com**

Poem

A **poem** is a piece of writing that expresses the writer's imagination. In a poem, the patterns made by the sounds of the words have special importance. There are many forms of poetry, such as free verse and cinquain. A cinquain is a five-line stanza in which each line has a specific number of syllables. The student model on the next page is an example of a cinquain.

Writing Prompt Write a poem about a person who has helped you.

Writer's Checklist

Remember, you should . . .

☑ express your imagination.

☑ include sensory details.

☑ use the correct pattern of verse for the form of poetry you are writing.

☑ write about a personal experience.

☑ use plural nouns correctly.

Student Model

Ms. James
understanding,
helpful, encouraging
teacher who helps the **children** in
her class.

Writing Trait Word Choice Descriptive language shows subject's personality.

Irregular plural nouns are used correctly.

Genre A cinquain is a form of **poetry** that begins and ends with a two-syllable line.

Conventions

Irregular Plural Nouns

Remember Irregular plural nouns have special plural forms. They are not made plural by adding *-s* or *-es*. Irregular plural forms must be learned.

Common Core State Standards

Language 4.b. Use common, grade-appropriate Greek and Latin affixes and roots as clues to the meaning of a word (e.g., *telegraph, photograph, autograph*). **Also Foundational Skills 4.b., Speaking/Listening 1.c., Language 4.**

Let's Learn It!

READING STREET ONLINE
ONLINE STUDENT EDITION
www.ReadingStreet.com

Vocabulary

Affixes: Prefixes

Word Structure A prefix at the beginning of a word can help you figure out the word's meaning. Knowing that the Greek prefix *tele-* means "far off" helps you figure out the meaning of *telescope*. A *telescope* is a device to see objects that are far away.

Practice It! Read page 241 in *Scene Two* to find words with the prefix *tele-*. Write the words and their meanings. Then think of other words you know with the prefix *tele-*. Use what you know about the meaning of *tele-* to write a definition for each word. Check your definitions in a dictionary.

Fluency

Expression

Partner Reading When you change the pitch of your voice as you read, you are using intonation. Speaking in higher and lower tones adds interest to what you are reading.

Practice It! With a partner, practice reading aloud *Scene Two*, page 242. Take turns reading the lines. First, read the dialogue with no intonation. Then read with intonation. Which way helps you understand the story?

254

Listening and Speaking

When you perform for an audience, speak clearly and loudly.

Readers' Theater

The purpose of Readers' Theater is to show the characters, setting, and action in a way that brings a story to life for the audience.

Practice It! With a small group, describe how plays and other dramas are structured differently from fiction. Assign roles from *Scene Two*. How will you portray your character's personality? Practice your lines with the group. Follow the stage directions in *Scene Two*. Perform for the class.

Tips

Listening ...

- Listen attentively to the speakers.
- Make comments related to the performance.

Speaking ...

- Look directly at the other characters as you speak.
- Use singular and plural nouns correctly.

Teamwork ...

- As you rehearse, answer questions with detail.
- Make suggestions that build upon the ideas of other students.

255

Common Core State Standards

Speaking/Listening 1. Engage effectively in a range of collaborative discussions (one-on-one, in groups, and teacher-led) with diverse partners on grade 4 topics and texts, building on others' ideas and expressing their own clearly. **Also Language 6.**

Oral Vocabulary

Let's Talk About

Animals and Teamwork

- Share ideas about people and animals that work as a team.

- Contribute pertinent comments to ideas.

- Support opinions with accurate information.

READING STREET ONLINE
CONCEPT TALK VIDEO
www.ReadingStreet.com

Common Core State Standards

Informational Text 1. Refer to details and examples in a text when explaining what the text says explicitly and when drawing inferences from the text. **Also Informational Text 8.**

Envision It! | Skill Strategy

Skill

Strategy

READING STREET ONLINE
ENVISION IT! ANIMATIONS
www.ReadingStreet.com

Comprehension Skill

🎯 Fact and Opinion

- A statement of fact can be proved true or false.

- A statement of opinion cannot be proved true or false. It is a belief or judgment.

- Use the graphic organizer to distinguish facts and opinions as you read "Bug Boys."

Statement	Fact? How Can It Be Checked?	Opinion? What Are Clue Words?

Comprehension Strategy

🎯 Monitor and Clarify

While you read, it's important to know when you understand something and when you don't. If you are confused, stop and reread the section aloud. Looking back and rereading is one way to clarify, or "adjust," your understanding of what you are reading.

Bug * Boys

In the sport of horse racing, a jockey is the one who rides the horses. Jockeys start out when they are young. An apprentice jockey is called a "bug boy" because a mark called an asterisk appears after his name in the race program. Some people think that the mark looks like a bug!

Willie Shoemaker was one of the most well-known jockeys in racing. He won his first horse race at the age of seventeen. He was small in size, weighing under one hundred pounds. Many people believe he was the greatest jockey of all time. He won the Kentucky Derby four times. Another jockey, Pat Day, started out as a rodeo cowboy. Because he was 4 feet 11 inches tall, people thought he would do well as a jockey. In 1989, he set a record when he won eight of nine races in a single day!

Chris McCarron was called the best jockey of the year in 1974. After a career as a jockey, Chris McCarron worked on the 2003 film *Seabiscuit*. The movie was about a real race.

Skill What three facts did you learn about jockeys? How can they be checked?

Skill What opinion did people have about Willie Shoemaker?

Strategy Why would his height make him a good jockey? Reread the selection for details to help understand this.

Your Turn!

⏸ **Need a Review?** See the *Envision It! Handbook* for additional help with fact and opinion and monitoring and clarifying.

▶ **Ready to Try It?** Establish your own purpose for reading *Horse Heroes* based upon your desired outcome to enhance comprehension.

Common Core State Standards

Language 4.c. Consult reference materials (e.g., dictionaries, glossaries, thesauruses), both print and digital, to find the pronunciation and determine or clarify the precise meaning of key words and phrases. **Also Language 4.**

Envision It! | Words to Know

infested

landslide

roamed

ambition

quicksand

resistance

rickety

vast

Vocabulary Strategy for

🎯 Unknown Words

Dictionary/Glossary When you are reading, you may come across a word you don't know. If you can't use the context, or words and sentences around the unknown word, to figure out its meaning, you can use a dictionary or glossary for help.

Choose one of the *Words to Know* and follow these steps.

1. Look in the back of your book for the glossary.

2. Find the entry for the word. The entries are in alphabetical order.

3. Use the pronunciation key to pronounce the word. Do you see how the word is broken into syllables?

4. Read all the meanings given for the word.

5. Choose the meaning that makes the best sense in the sentence.

Read "Racing Dreams." Use the glossary to help you figure out the meanings, syllabications, and pronunciations of this week's *Words to Know*.

Words to Write Reread "Racing Dreams." Imagine that you're a reporter at a horse race. Write a news article on the race. Use words from the *Words to Know* list in your article.

RACING Dreams

One summer my parents sent me to camp in Wisconsin. I spent a lot of time taking horseback-riding lessons. It was my ambition to become a great rider. As we roamed down the trails, I dreamed about being a famous rider.

First, my imaginary horse and I would gallop over the vast plains. We would leap over rickety gates and pass untouched through fields infested with locusts. My horse would amaze everyone with his bravery. He would leap over quicksand without the slightest resistance. My horse would be so fast that he could outrun a landslide. Nothing would scare him!

Everyone would want us to run in a great race. My horse and I would train for long hours. We would work hard. The day would come, and all the fastest horses and their riders would be there to see who was the best. My horse and I would fly around the track. We would pass all the other horses.

Your Turn!

❚❚ Need a Review? For help with using a dictionary/glossary to determine the meanings of unknown words, see *Words!*

▷ Ready to Try It? Read *Horse Heroes* on pp. 262–273.

261

HORSE HEROES

True Stories of Amazing Horses

Written by Kate Petty

Genre

Expository Text recounts a true event or series of events. Think about your own desired outcome for reading this selection to establish your own purpose for reading.

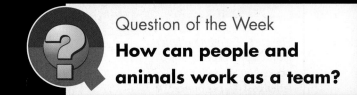

Question of the Week

How can people and animals work as a team?

Horses and humans have worked together for thousands of years. From the vast wilderness to the Hollywood movie set, horses have served us faithfully while playing an important role in history. Horses can be found in our art, religion, and mythology. Let's look at some of history's most famous horse heroes.

UNITED STATES
California   Missouri

Long Journey
Pony Express riders took the mail 2,000 miles from Missouri to California.

Pony Express

When the little mustang came into view, the crowd began to cheer.

Her rider, Johnny Fry, led her into the packed town square of St. Joseph, Missouri, that warm April evening in 1860. Johnny checked the mail pouch on the mustang's back for the last time as she snorted excitedly.

A cannon boomed. They were away! The mustang raced off into the evening twilight,

This poster for the Pony Express service dates from 1861.

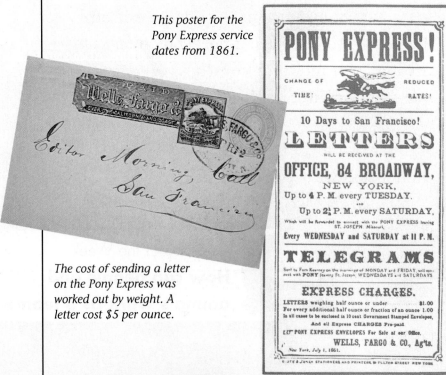

First Delivery
Johnny Fry's mail sack held 49 letters and three newspapers.

The cost of sending a letter on the Pony Express was worked out by weight. A letter cost $5 per ounce.

leaving the cheering crowds far behind.

Horse and rider had entered history as the first ever Pony Express team.

In 1860, there were no such things as telephones and fax machines. If you lived on the West Coast of the United States, keeping up to date with the latest news on the East Coast was almost impossible. It could take more than a month for mail to travel across the continent by wagon.

The Pony Express was a horse relay designed to keep the mail moving day and night. It cut down the time taken for mail to reach California to just eight days.

Each horse and rider galloped at top speed to the next station. The rider leaped off the exhausted horse shouting, "Pony rider coming!" The mail was transferred to a fresh horse, and the rider galloped off again on his new mount.

There were 157 relay stations, and riders changed horses about six to eight times.

The teams risked death together on a daily basis.

Much of the route lay through the homelands of American Indians, some of whom declared war on the invaders of their territory.

Mustang

This hardy breed is descended from the horses brought to America by Spanish explorers.

Express Riders

Pony Express riders had to be under 18 years old and weigh less than 126 pounds, so as not to slow down their horses.

Transfer

It took a rider two minutes to transfer between horses.

Saddle Up

Mail pouches were sometimes sewn into the rider's saddle.

One of the bravest riders was "Pony Bob" Haslam. In May 1860, he arrived at a station in Nevada to find the keeper dead and all the horses gone. He set out for the next station, which was 40 miles away.

"I knew I had to carry on. As I rode through the night, I kept watching my pony's ears. I knew he'd hear any ambush before I did."

At the next station he persuaded the keeper to leave with them. Bob and his tireless horse saved the man's life—the next night that station was attacked.

Express riders carried rifles in case of trouble.

The Pony Express teams rode across rocky mountain passes and wide, empty plains in scorching sun, pouring rain, and freezing blizzards. If their rider fell off, some brave horses carried on alone to the next station.

The final stop was Sacramento, California. Crowds of eager people would gather to watch the arrival of the last rider on the route bringing them their mail and newspapers.

The success of the Pony Express teams proved that it was possible for the East and West coasts to keep in touch. It was a milestone on the way to modern America. The horses and riders that ran the Pony Express were real pioneers.

The Pony Express is remembered today by horse lovers who ride the Express's desert tracks for pleasure. Their journeys pay tribute to the riders of 1860, who insisted that "the mail must get through."

The Pony Express closed down when the transcontinental telegraph system opened in 1861. Stagecoach operators Wells, Fargo & Company took over the route.

Lincoln
In 1860, Abraham Lincoln's first speech as U.S. President was carried by the Pony Express.

267

Aimé Tschiffely

Aimé Tschiffely
was a Swiss teacher
living in Argentina.

Americas

Tschiffely wanted to ride
from South to North
America across the
Panama Canal.

Tale of Two Horses

When Aimé Tschiffely (Ay-may Shiff-ell-ee) told people about his idea early in 1925, they thought he had gone mad.

"Impossible! It can't be done!"

Tschiffely wanted to be the first man ever to ride from Buenos Aires in Argentina all the way to Washington, D.C.

He realized that the 10,000-mile journey would be full of difficulties, but it had been his secret ambition for years.

Tschiffely knew that he needed two tough and resourceful horses if he was to succeed. He chose Gato and Mancha, Criollo horses ages 15 and 16. They had belonged to an Argentinian Indian chief and roamed free on the plains.

They were not handsome and they were headstrong, but they knew how to survive in the wild.

Tschiffely and the horses set off in April 1925. After four months, the travelers crossed over into Bolivia.

In that time the trio had learned to trust each other and to work together as a team.

One day, as they rode along the shore of a lake in Peru, they reached a shallow strip of water. Gato reared up and refused to go on.

A man rushed toward them, shouting that the water hid dangerous quicksand. He led them to a safe trail. Tschiffely was amazed. The horse had saved their lives!

As they rode on through Peru, they began to climb the Andes—a huge range of snow-capped mountains.

One morning, they came to a sight that made Tschiffely's blood run cold. The way forward was along a rickety old rope bridge that stretched over a deep gorge. One slip would prove fatal.

When they reached the middle, the bridge swayed violently. If Mancha panicked and turned back, they would both fall to their deaths. But Mancha waited calmly for the bridge to stop moving, and then went on. When Gato saw his companions safe on the other side, he crossed the bridge as steadily as if he were walking on solid ground.

Criollo

These horses are very tough and can carry heavy weights over long distances.

Horse Sense

People believe that horses have a sixth sense that warns them about danger.

Herd Instincts

Wild horses stay in groups, or herds. Mancha and Gato would instinctively follow each other, whatever the dangers.

From Peru, Tschiffely headed into Ecuador and followed a series of tracks through lush forests over high mountains and down into valleys. At night, Tschiffely never tied up the horses. He knew they would not run. The three travelers were sharing a great adventure, each showing the others the way.

Zigzagging up a narrow trail one day, Tschiffely saw that the path ahead had been swept away by a landslide, leaving a sheer drop. There was no choice but to turn back and find another route. Tschiffely tightened Gato's packs to get ready for a long detour.

But Mancha had other ideas. Tschiffely saw with horror that Mancha was preparing to jump the gap. His heart rose in his mouth as Mancha sailed through the air and landed on the other side.

The horse turned and neighed to his companions not to be afraid. Tschiffely and Gato soon followed. As their adventure stretched on, the three travelers reached the Panama Canal and crossed into Costa Rica and then Mexico.

Moving through dense jungle, the trio had to cope with mosquito bites and attacks by vampire bats and poisonous snakes.

Once Mancha slipped into a crocodile-infested river. He only just managed to find a foothold and pull himself up the bank as Tschiffely clung on for dear life.

Two and a half years after setting out from Buenos Aires, Tschiffely reached Washington, D.C. He had achieved his lifelong ambition.

"I could never have done it," he said, "without Mancha and Gato. My two pals have shown powers of resistance to every hardship."

Tschiffely was given a hero's welcome, even meeting President Coolidge in the White House. Admirers suggested that the horses should live in a city park. But Tschiffely took Mancha and Gato back to Argentina and set them free.

Dense Jungle
The jungles of Central and South America are home to some of the world's most dangerous snakes, such as the 30-foot (10 meter) anaconda.

Born Free
Horses who grow up in the country can become sad and listless if confined in a city.

Horses seem to remember that their ancestors were hunted by crocodiles and know to be afraid of them.

Hollywood Hero

In 1932, a star was born. He was a beautiful golden color with a white, flowing mane and tail. Son of a palomino mare and a racehorse, Golden Cloud was to become the most famous horse of his day.

Golden Cloud made his big-screen debut in 1938. His owners, Hudkin Stables, lent him out to play a part in the Hollywood film *The Adventures of Robin Hood.*

Later that year, Republic Studios decided to make a series of Westerns featuring the singing cowboy actor, Roy Rogers. They brought several horses round for Roy to audition. He fell for Golden Cloud the moment he climbed on the horse's back.

While they were making their first film, *Under Western Stars,* Golden Cloud was renamed "Trigger" because he was so quick.

Roy loved Trigger so much that after their third film, he bought Trigger for $2,500. From then on, they became full-time partners.

Trigger loved the camera. He often stole the show from Roy Rogers with a well-timed yawn or a graceful dance step.

He knew more than 60 tricks. He could walk 150 steps on his hind legs, stamp his hoof to count, and draw a gun from a holster.

Trigger became one of the most popular characters in show business. He starred in 887 films and 101 TV shows, and once even had a party in the Grand Ballroom of the Astor Hotel in New York City.

Like a true star, Trigger made special personal appearances. He always traveled in style, carried his own horse-sized passport, and signed his name with an X in hotel registers.

Trigger finally retired in 1957, and died in 1965, age 33. Roy Rogers was heartbroken. He said he had lost "the greatest horse who ever came along."

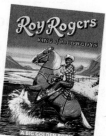

Trigger's fan club produced hundreds of books and toys for its members.

Today, we may be less dependent on the horse for transportation and work, but we continue to be amazed by stories of its strength, speed, and intelligence. Humans and horses will always make a great team.

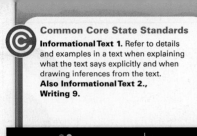

Common Core State Standards

Informational Text 1. Refer to details and examples in a text when explaining what the text says explicitly and when drawing inferences from the text. **Also Informational Text 2., Writing 9.**

Envision It! Retell

READING STREET ONLINE
STORY SORT
www.ReadingStreet.com

Think Critically

1. The illustration on page 267 shows excited people welcoming a Pony Express rider. How is mail delivery today different from mail delivery in 1860? **Text to World**

2. On page 271, the author quotes what Tschiffely said about Mancha and Gato: "My two pals have shown powers of resistance to every hardship." Why do you think the author included this quote? **Think Like an Author**

3. The statement "He was a beautiful golden color with a white, flowing mane and tail" contains statements both of fact and of opinion. Which part of the sentence is a statement of fact? Which part is a statement of opinion? Explain how to verify what is a fact and what is an opinion.
   Fact and Opinion

4. "Pony Bob" Haslam kept watching his pony's ears. What did he think his horse might hear? **Monitor and Clarify**

5. **Look Back and Write** Look back at pages 268–271. What made Gato and Mancha so amazing? Provide evidence to support your answer.
   Key Ideas and Details • Text Evidence

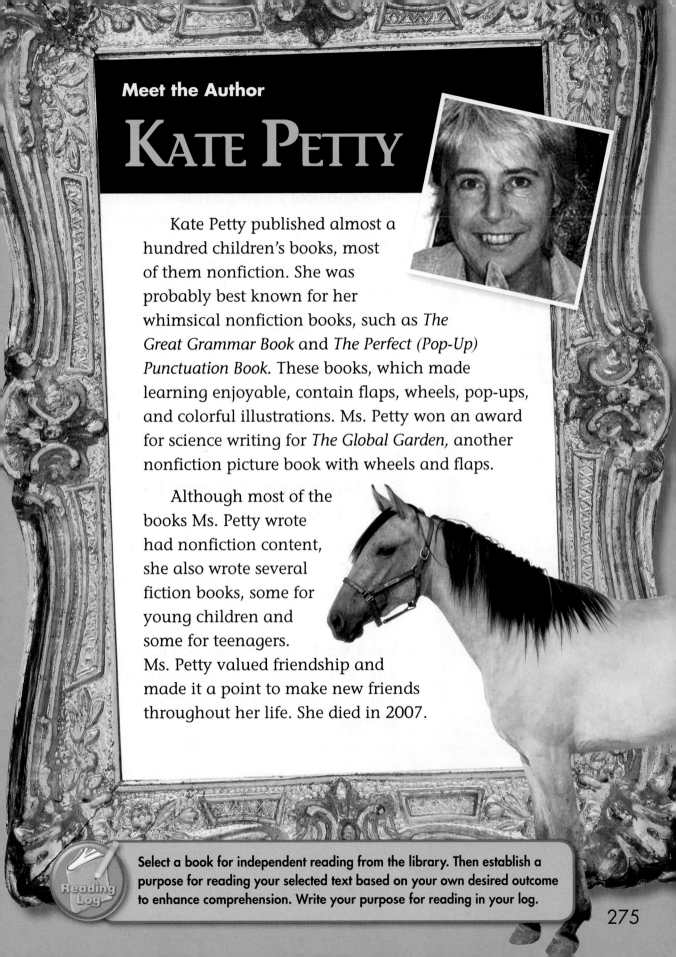

Meet the Author

KATE PETTY

Kate Petty published almost a hundred children's books, most of them nonfiction. She was probably best known for her whimsical nonfiction books, such as *The Great Grammar Book* and *The Perfect (Pop-Up) Punctuation Book.* These books, which made learning enjoyable, contain flaps, wheels, pop-ups, and colorful illustrations. Ms. Petty won an award for science writing for *The Global Garden,* another nonfiction picture book with wheels and flaps.

Although most of the books Ms. Petty wrote had nonfiction content, she also wrote several fiction books, some for young children and some for teenagers. Ms. Petty valued friendship and made it a point to make new friends throughout her life. She died in 2007.

Select a book for independent reading from the library. Then establish a purpose for reading your selected text based on your own desired outcome to enhance comprehension. Write your purpose for reading in your log.

Reading Log

Common Core State Standards
Writing 2. Write informative/explanatory texts to examine a topic and convey ideas and information clearly.
Also Writing 2.a., Language 1.

Expository

Let's Write It!

Key Features of an Expository Composition

- made up of factual information

- often includes text features such as photos, labels, sidebars, or charts

- usually written in third person

READING STREET ONLINE
GRAMMAR JAMMER
www.ReadingStreet.com

Expository Composition

An **expository composition** recounts a true event or series of events or tells information about the real world. The student model on the next page is an example of an expository composition.

Writing Prompt Write an expository composition about an animal that has done something remarkable.

Writer's Checklist

Remember, you should . . .

☑ have a central idea in your topic sentence.

☑ use facts, details, and explanations to support your central idea.

☑ know your audience and purpose for writing.

☑ include an introduction, body, and concluding statement.

☑ use singular nouns correctly.

Hero of Brookfield Zoo

On August 16, 1996, a gorilla at the Brookfield Zoo near Chicago, Illinois, became a hero. Binti Jua rescued a 3-year-old boy who had slipped and fallen more than 18 feet into the gorilla exhibit below!

After the boy fell, Binti Jua walked over to the unconscious boy, and the people who were watching screamed. They thought the gorilla would hurt the boy. But she lifted the **boy's** arms as if she were looking for signs of life. Though other gorillas came close, Binti Jua grunted until they went away.

Taking the boy in her strong arms, Binti Jua carried him to the **zookeeper's** entrance. She waited with him until paramedics came to take him to the hospital. **Binti Jua's** 17-month-old baby, Koola, clutched her back the entire time.

The boy spent four days in the hospital with a concussion, but he recovered fully. **Binti Jua's** gentleness and concern for the little boy make her a special animal.

Writing Trait Organization
The introductory paragraph sets up the composition.

Genre An **expository composition** tells about real people and events.

Singular possessive nouns are used correctly.

Conventions

Singular Possessive Nouns

Remember A possessive noun shows ownership. A **singular possessive noun** shows that one person, place, or thing has or owns something. Add an apostrophe (') and the letter s to a singular noun to make it possessive.

Common Core State Standards

Language 3.c. Differentiate between contexts that call for formal English (e.g., presenting ideas) and situations where informal discourse is appropriate (e.g., small-group discussions).
Also Writing 6.

21st Century Skills
INTERNET GUY

E-mail Texting is fun, but e-mail can be even better. Share documents and work on a project in school. E-mail skills get you ready for the world of work.

- E-mail, or "electronic mail," is a message sent through the Internet. You can e-mail Web sites for information or just to answer your questions.

- The "To:" box shows to whom the message is going. The "Subject:" box tells what the topic is.

- The message itself looks like a letter.

- Read "Riding the Pony Express." Compare the language in these e-mails with the language you read in a Web-based news article.

RIDING THE PONY EXPRESS

by Sophia DeRosa

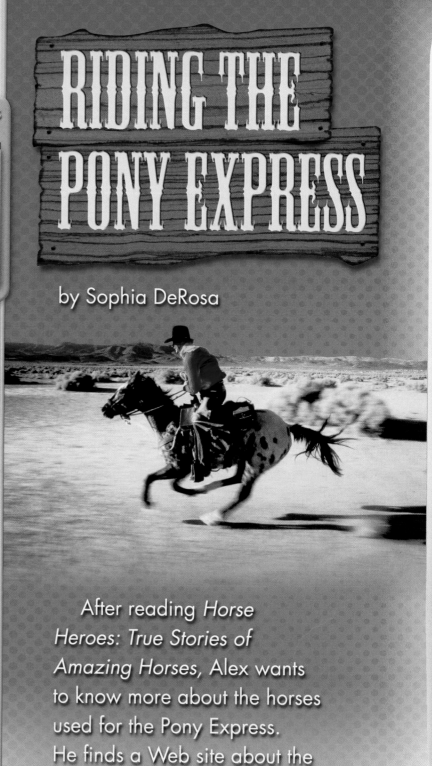

After reading *Horse Heroes: True Stories of Amazing Horses*, Alex wants to know more about the horses used for the Pony Express. He finds a Web site about the history of the Pony Express.

In order to find information about a topic, first you might send an e-mail to an expert. Alex decides to search the Web site to find an e-mail address.

File   Edit   View   Favorites   Tools   Help

http://www.url.here

THE PONY EXPRESS

Type the e-mail address of the person to whom you are writing here.

Send   Attach   Address

To: Receiver's e-mail address goes here

Cc:

Subject: Pony Express Horses

Begin with a greeting. If you do not know to whom to address your e-mail, use "Dear Sir or Madam."

Dear Sir or Madam:

I just read about how the Pony Express got started. Now I want to know more about the different types of horses used by the Pony Express. I have to give an oral report for class. Can you tell me where I might find more information about the horses? Thank you.

Alex Gonzales

In your e-mail to an expert, ask questions that will help you get details and information about your topic. When you are finished, click the "Send" button to send your e-mail.

Common Core State Standards

Language 4.c. Consult reference materials (e.g., dictionaries, glossaries, thesauruses), both print and digital, to find the pronunciation and determine or clarify the precise meaning of key words and phrases. **Also Foundational Skills 4.b., Speaking/Listening 1.b., Language 4.**

Let's Learn It!

READING STREET ONLINE
ONLINE STUDENT EDITION
www.ReadingStreet.com

Vocabulary

Unknown Words

Dictionary/Glossary Turn to the Glossary on page 464. Remember that when you look up a word in a glossary or a dictionary, you can also find out how to pronounce it by using the pronunciation key.

Practice It! Choose two or three glossary words and carefully copy the pronunciations shown in parentheses. Exchange pronunciations with a partner and use the pronunciation key to identify each other's words. Remember to check the meanings of any unknown words.

Fluency

Expression

Partner Reading Reading with expression makes a story more exciting. Stressing words differently, saying some words with more feeling than others, makes the story lively.

Practice It! With your partner, practice reading aloud pages 264–265 of *Horse Heroes*. Read them once with no expression. Then read them with expression. Which way is more exciting?

Listening and Speaking

> When you participate in a discussion, always ask and answer questions with detail.

Interview

In an interview, one person asks another questions. The purpose of an interview is to find out what the person being interviewed knows about or did.

Practice It! With a partner, conduct an interview in front of the class. One person can be Aimé Tschiffely as he arrives in Washington, D.C. The other can be a radio reporter. Write Tschiffely's answers to your questions in a notebook. Then change roles.

Tips

Listening ...

- Be ready to ask relevant questions that include details about the topic. For example, "How did you decide what interview questions to ask?"

Speaking ...

- Express an opinion supported by accurate information.
- Make eye contact when you speak.

Teamwork ....

- Answer questions with details.
- If necessary, ask your partner to restate what he or she has said.

Common Core State Standards

Speaking/Listening 1.c. Pose and respond to specific questions to clarify or follow up on information, and make comments that contribute to the discussion and link to the remarks of others. **Also Language 6.**

Oral Vocabulary

Let's Talk About

U.S. Government

- Express opinions about the rewards of being the U.S. President.

- Ask relevant questions.

- Look others in the eye when sharing opinions.

READING STREET ONLINE
CONCEPT TALK VIDEO
www.ReadingStreet.com

Common Core State Standards

Informational Text 2. Determine the main idea of a text and explain how it is supported by key details; summarize the text. **Also Informational Text 1.**

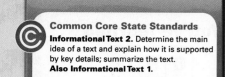

Skill

Strategy

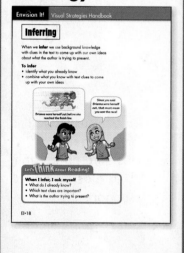

READING STREET ONLINE
ENVISION IT! ANIMATIONS
www.ReadingStreet.com

Comprehension Skill

Main Idea and Details

- The focus of a paragraph or an article is the topic, or what the paragraph or article is about.

- The most important thing an author has to say about the topic is the main idea.

- Small pieces of information that tell more about the main idea are supporting details.

- Use the graphic organizer to summarize the main ideas and details in "A White House History."

Comprehension Strategy

Inferring

When you infer, you combine your background knowledge with clues in the text to come up with your own idea about what the author is writing about. Good readers often infer the ideas, morals, lessons, and themes of a story or an article.

A WHITE HOUSE HISTORY

The White House, in Washington, D.C., is where the President of the United States lives and works. Although our first President, George Washington, chose the spot where the White House would be built, he never even lived there! The building began in 1792, but it wasn't finished until Washington was out of office.

Skill Summarize the main idea of the first paragraph. Find a detail that supports it.

Our second President, John Adams, moved into the White House in 1800. The building still wasn't really finished. As a result, it was somewhat uncomfortable for daily life. The President's wife, Abigail, had nowhere to hang the family's laundry, so she used the East Room. Today that room is the biggest, grandest room in the White House.

Strategy What clues in the text can you use to help you infer what the East Room might be used for today?

In 1814, while our fourth President, James Madison, was in office, the United States was again at war with England. The British burned the White House, and it had to be rebuilt.

Skill Summarize the main idea of the third paragraph. Find a detail that supports it.

By 1902, so many people worked in the White House that Theodore Roosevelt built the West Wing. The new wing freed up space for his six lively children and their pets.

Even though Presidents live in the White House, it really belongs to the American people.

Your Turn!

❚❚ Need a Review? See the *Envision It! Handbook* for help with main idea and inferring.

▶ Ready to Try It? Use what you've learned about main idea as you read *So You Want to Be President?*

287

Common Core State Standards

Language 4.c. Consult reference materials (e.g., dictionaries, glossaries, thesauruses), both print and digital, to find the pronunciation and determine or clarify the precise meaning of key words and phrases. **Also Language 4.**

Envision It! | Words to Know

Constitution

howling

politics

humble

responsibility

solemnly

vain

Vocabulary Strategy for

🎯 Unknown Words

Dictionary/Glossary When you are reading, you may come across a word you don't know. If you can't use the context, or words and sentences around the word, to figure out the word's meaning, you can use a dictionary or glossary to help you.

1. Check the back of your book for a glossary. If there is no glossary, look up the word in a dictionary.

2. Find the entry for the word. The entries are in alphabetical order.

3. To yourself, say the word broken into syllables or use the pronunciation key to help you pronounce the word. Saying the word may help you recognize it.

4. Read all the meanings given for the word.

5. Choose the meaning that makes sense in the sentence.

Read "Class Election." Use context clues, a dictionary, or the glossary to help you determine the meanings, syllabications, and pronunciations of this week's *Words to Know*.

Words to Write Reread "Class Election." Imagine that you have just been elected class president. Now you need to write your acceptance speech. Use words from the *Words to Know* list in your speech.

Class Election

The students in Grade 4 are electing class officers. Four students are running for president.

Steven is vain about his looks. He puts just his name and his face on his signs. He says politics is dull, but winning is fun. Suzanne acts humble about how well she plays sports. Yet all her signs show her making the winning goal in last year's soccer championship. Omar solemnly promises that he will run a clean campaign. Then he makes fun of the other candidates. Still, his speeches are a howling success. Maya says that unlike the President of the United States, the president of Grade 4 does not have to "protect and defend the Constitution of the United States." However, she says the Grade 4 president does have a responsibility to all the students in Grade 4, not just the ones who voted for him or her. Maya was Grade 3 president and is captain of the softball team. If you were a student in Grade 4, whom would you vote for?

Suzanne
She is a winner!

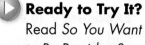

Your Turn!

⏸ **Need a Review?** For additional help with using a dictionary or glossary to determine the meanings of unknown words, see *Words!*

▶ **Ready to Try It?** Read *So You Want to Be President?* on pp. 290–301.

So You Want to Be President?

289

Expository Text gives information about real people and events. As you read, note new or surprising information about our country's Presidents.

So You Want to Be President?

by Judith St. George
illustrated by David Small

Question of the Week

**What is the job of the
President of the United States?**

There are good things about being President, and there are bad things about being President. One of the good things is that the President lives in a big white house called the White House.

Another good thing about being President is that the President has a swimming pool, bowling alley, and movie theater.

The President never has to take out the garbage.

The President doesn't have to eat yucky vegetables. As a boy, George H. W. Bush had to eat broccoli. When George H. W. Bush grew up, he became President. That was the end of the broccoli!

One of the bad things about being President is that the President always has to be dressed up. William McKinley wore a frock coat, vest, pin-striped trousers, stiff white shirt, black satin tie, gloves, a top hat, and a red carnation in his buttonhole every day!

The President has to be polite to everyone. The President can't go anywhere alone. The President has lots of homework.

People get mad at the President. Someone once threw a cabbage at William Howard Taft. That didn't bother Taft. He quipped, "I see that one of my adversaries has lost his head."

Lots of people want to be President. If you want to be President, it might help if your name is James. Six Presidents were named James. (President Carter liked to be called Jimmy.) Four Johns, four Williams (President Clinton liked to be called Bill), three Georges, two Andrews, and two Franklins—all became President.

If you want to be President, your size doesn't matter. Presidents have come in all shapes and sizes. Abraham Lincoln was the tallest—six feet four inches. (His stovepipe hat made him look even taller.)

James Madison was the smallest—five feet four inches and only one hundred pounds. William Howard Taft was the biggest—more than three hundred pounds. He was so big that he had a special tub built for his White House bathroom. (Four men could fit in the tub!)

Though the Constitution says you'll have to wait until you're thirty-five, young, old, and in between have become President. Theodore (Teddy) Roosevelt at forty-two was the youngest. He had pillow fights with his children and played football on the White House lawn. "You must always remember that the President is about six," a friend said. Ronald Reagan was the oldest. When he first ran for President, he was sixty-nine. He joked that it was the thirtieth anniversary of his thirty-ninth birthday.

Do you have pesky brothers and sisters? Every one of our Presidents did. Benjamin Harrison takes the prize—he had eleven! (It's lucky he grew up on a six-hundred-acre farm.) James Polk and James Buchanan both had nine. George Washington, Thomas Jefferson, James Madison, and John Kennedy each had eight. (Two Presidents were orphans, Andrew Jackson and Herbert Hoover.)

A President in your family tree is a plus. John Quincy Adams was John Adams's son. George W. Bush was the son of George H. W. Bush. Theodore Roosevelt and Franklin Roosevelt were fifth cousins. Benjamin Harrison was William Harrison's grandson. James Madison and Zachary Taylor were second cousins.

Do you have a pet? All kinds of pets have lived in the White House, mostly dogs. Herbert Hoover had three dogs: Piney, Snowflake, and Tut. (Tut must have been a Democrat. He and his Republican master never got along.) Franklin Roosevelt's dog, Fala, was almost as famous as his owner.

George H. W. Bush's dog wrote MILLIE'S BOOK: ADVENTURES OF A WHITE HOUSE DOG (as reported to Mrs. Bush!). Ulysses Grant had horses, Benjamin Harrison's goat pulled his grandchildren around in a cart, the Coolidges had a pet raccoon, Jimmy Carter and Bill Clinton preferred cats.

Theodore Roosevelt's children didn't just have pets, they ran a zoo. They had dogs, cats, guinea pigs, mice, rats, badgers, raccoons, parrots, and a Shetland pony called Algonquin. To cheer up his sick brother, young Quentin once took Algonquin upstairs in the White House elevator!

Though most Presidents went to college, nine didn't: George Washington, Andrew Jackson, Martin Van Buren, Zachary Taylor, Millard Fillmore, Abraham Lincoln, Andrew Johnson, Grover Cleveland, and Harry Truman. (Andrew Johnson couldn't read until he was fourteen! He didn't learn to write until after he was married!)

Thomas Jefferson was top-notch in the brains department—he was an expert on agriculture, law, politics, music, geography, surveying, philosophy, and botany. In his spare time he designed his own house (a mansion), founded the University of Virginia, and whipped up the Declaration of Independence.

Almost any job can lead to the White House. Presidents have been lawyers, teachers, farmers, sailors, engineers, surveyors, mayors, governors, congressmen, senators, and ambassadors. (Harry Truman owned a men's shop. Andrew Johnson was a tailor. Ronald Reagan was a movie actor!)

There they are, a mixed bag of Presidents! What did they think of being head man? George Washington, who became our very first President in 1789, worried about his new line of work. "I greatly fear that my countrymen will expect too much from me," he wrote to a friend. (He was a howling success.) Some loved the job. "No President has ever enjoyed himself as much as I," Theodore Roosevelt said. Others hated it. "The four most miserable years of my life," John Quincy Adams complained.

Every President was different from every other and yet no woman has been President. No person of color has been President.* No person who wasn't a Protestant or a Roman Catholic has been President. But if you care enough, anything is possible. Thirty-four Presidents came and went before a Roman Catholic—John Kennedy—was elected. Almost two hundred years passed before a woman—Geraldine Ferraro—ran for Vice President.

*On November 4, 2008, Barack Obama, an African American, was elected President.

—Pearson Editor

299

It's said that people who run for President have swelled heads. It's said that people who run for President are greedy. They want power. They want fame.

But being President can be wanting to serve your country—like George Washington, who left the Virginia plantation he loved three times to lead the country he loved even more.

It can be looking toward the future like Thomas Jefferson, who bought the Louisiana Territory and then sent Lewis and Clark west to find a route to the Pacific. (They did!)

It can be wanting to turn lives around like Franklin Roosevelt, who provided soup and bread for the hungry, jobs for the jobless, and funds for the elderly to live on.

It can be wanting to make the world a better place like John Kennedy, who sent Peace Corps volunteers around the globe to teach and help others.

Every single President has taken this oath: "I do solemnly swear (or affirm) that I will faithfully execute the office of President of the United States, and will to the best of my ability, preserve, protect and defend the Constitution of the United States."

Only thirty-five words! But it's a big order when you're President of this country. Abraham Lincoln was tops at filling that order. "I know very well that many others might in this matter as in others, do better than I can," he said. "But . . . I am here. I must do the best I can, and bear the responsibility of taking the course which I feel I ought to take."

That's the bottom line. Tall, short, fat, thin, talkative, quiet, vain, humble, lawyer, teacher, or soldier—this is what most of our Presidents have tried to do, each in his own way. Some succeeded. Some failed. If you want to be President—a good President—pattern yourself after the best. Our best have asked more of themselves than they thought they could give. They have had the courage, spirit, and will to do what they knew was right. Most of all, their first priority has always been the people and the country they served.

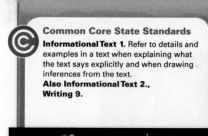

Common Core State Standards

Informational Text 1. Refer to details and examples in a text when explaining what the text says explicitly and when drawing inferences from the text. **Also Informational Text 2., Writing 9.**

Envision It! Retell

Think Critically

1. The life and accomplishments of George Washington, our first President, have been featured in many books, movies, and legends. Do you think that he deserves all the interest people have in him? Why?
Text to Text

2. Why do you think the author used silly illustrations and a fun, friendly style of writing to tell about the Presidents? Explain your answer. **Think Like an Author**

3. Reread page 297. What sentence states the main idea of this page? What supporting details can you find? **Main Idea and Details**

4. Reread page 294. What can you infer about Theodore Roosevelt's personality from his actions with his children? Provide information from the text to support your answer.
Inferring

5. **Look Back and Write** Look back at page 293. What do you think are the most important qualities a President should have? Why?

Key Ideas and Details • Text Evidence

Meet the Author and the Illustrator

Judith St. George & David Small

Judith St. George first discovered writing when she wrote a play in sixth grade. Since then she has gone on to write more than forty books. After publishing several books about American history, she decided to write about the presidency. She thought, "How about making my book on Presidents amusing and fun as well as informative?"

David Small, the illustrator, draws political cartoons for newspapers and illustrates children's books. *So You Want to Be President?* was a perfect opportunity for him to combine these two pursuits. "I hope readers will laugh first, and then begin to think a little more deeply," Mr. Small says. "Caricatures are not only funny pictures of people. The best ones make us see familiar faces in a new way. They exaggerate prominent aspects of a face to make us re-examine our heroes and other public figures in a different, more human light. The book concerns Presidents as the human beings they all are."

Here are other books you may enjoy.

So You Want to Be an Inventor?

Imogene's Antlers

Use the *Reader's and Writer's Notebook* to record your independent reading.

303

Common Core State Standards

Writing 1. Write opinion pieces on topics or texts, supporting a point of view with reasons and information.
Also Writing 1.a., 1.d., 3.c., Language 1.

Let's Write It!

Key Features of a Persuasive Essay

- tries to influence the reader's opinion

- uses facts and examples as supporting details

- may urge readers to take action

READING STREET ONLINE
GRAMMAR JAMMER
www.ReadingStreet.com

Persuasive

Persuasive Essay

A **persuasive essay** presents an opinion on a topic and tries to convince readers to agree. The student model on the next page is an example of a persuasive essay.

Writing Prompt Choose the president you think was most important to our country. Now write a persuasive essay to convince others to agree with your choice.

Writer's Checklist

Remember, you should ...

✓ state your position in a topic sentence.

✓ include supporting details to try to persuade your audience.

✓ use words that appeal to the reader's emotions.

✓ end by using a transition and restating your opinion or position.

Our Most Important President

Thomas Jefferson is clearly the president who was most important to our country. He was there at the very beginning, writing the Declaration of Independence and helping make our country what it is today.

Then, when he was president, Jefferson helped to shape the country—literally! If he hadn't purchased the Louisiana Territory, we might still be sharing the continent with France and Spain!

In addition, Jefferson sent Lewis and Clark out to explore the Louisiana Territory because he knew that was the best hope for the United States to become a great nation. Jefferson was right; the westward expansion that followed led to Americans' many successes.

If you have any doubt that Jefferson was the most important president to our country, you should think again! Just ask yourself: Where would we be today without the Declaration of Independence or the Louisiana Purchase?

Writing Trait Organization
Transition words connect ideas.

Possessive plural nouns are used correctly.

Genre The ending of this **persuasive essay** restates the writer's opinion.

Conventions

Plural Possessive Nouns

Remember A **plural possessive noun** is formed in two ways. Add an apostrophe to a plural noun ending in -s. Add an apostrophe and an -s to a plural noun that does not end in -s.

Common Core State Standards

Informational Text 5. Describe the overall structure (e.g., chronology, comparison, cause/effect, problem/solution) of events, ideas, concepts, or information in a text or part of a text. **Also Informational Text 1., 8.**

Social Studies in Reading

Genre
Expository Text

- Expository text contains facts and information about a subject.

- Some authors will state their purpose for writing. Others do not. When a purpose is not stated, and the author has implied the purpose, a reader needs to figure it out.

- Some authors may compare information to explain ideas. The comparisons may be explicit or implicit.

- Read "Our National Parks." Look for elements that make this article an expository text. Is the author's purpose stated or implied? Are there comparisons? Provide evidence for your answers.

OUR NATIONAL PARKS

by Susan Gavin

Did you know that the President of the United States has the power to set aside land for national parks? Ulysses S. Grant helped create the world's first national park, Yellowstone National Park, in 1872. In 1864, Abraham Lincoln set aside land that became Yosemite National Park in 1890.

Visit one of the 55 parks in the U.S. national park system. (A sampling is on page 307.) Walk through caves, climb mountains, and see wildlife, rain forests, and glaciers. As you enjoy these natural areas, remember that U.S. Presidents helped protect them.

Sequoia
CALIFORNIA

Established: 1890
Size: 456,552 acres
Highlights: giant sequoia trees; Mt. Whitney (14,491 feet)

Mammoth Cave
KENTUCKY

Established: 1941
Size: 52,830 acres
Highlight: world's longest known network of caves

Everglades
FLORIDA

Established: 1947
Size: 1,399,078 acres
Highlight: largest subtropical wilderness in the United States

Death Valley
CALIFORNIA, NEVADA

Established: 1994
Size: 3,367,628 acres
Highlights: largest national park outside of Alaska; desert, dunes, gorges

Big Bend
TEXAS

Established: 1944
Size: 801,163 acres
Highlights: desert land; on the Rio Grande; dinosaur fossils

Let's **Think** About...

Identify the author's purpose. Explain how you knew whether it was implied or stated.
Expository Text

Let's **Think** About...

Describe three implicit relationships among the ideas about the parks that you could use to compare them.
Expository Text

Let's **Think** About...

Reading Across Texts "Our National Parks" and *So You Want to Be President?* tell about things Presidents have done. List some other things Presidents have done.

Writing Across Texts Make a list of three or four Presidents and tell something each did that was good for the country.

307

Common Core State Standards

Language 5.a. Explain the meaning of simple similes and metaphors (e.g. *as pretty as a picture*) in context. **Also Literature 2., 5., 10.**

Poetry

- Poets use **metaphors** to create images. A metaphor is a comparison stating that a thing "is" or things "are" something else. *You are a rock* is a metaphor.

- Poets arrange words and sounds in a way that creates a **meter**. The meter is the poem's beat.

- Read "His Hands" and "Homework." Look for metaphors. Listen for the poems' meter or beat. Explain how the structure of a poem helps convey how the poet thinks and feels.

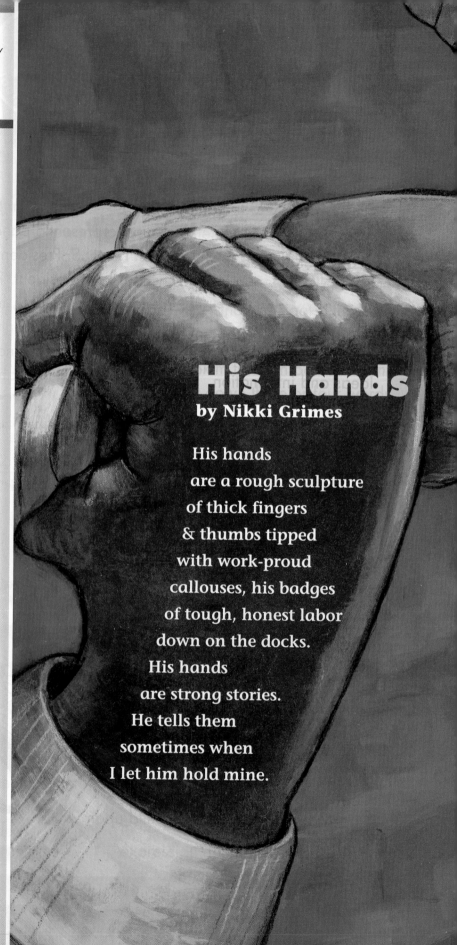

His Hands
by Nikki Grimes

His hands
are a rough sculpture
of thick fingers
& thumbs tipped
with work-proud
callouses, his badges
of tough, honest labor
down on the docks.
His hands
are strong stories.
He tells them
sometimes when
I let him hold mine.

Homework

by Russell Hoban

Homework sits on top of Sunday, squashing Sunday flat.
Homework has the smell of Monday, homework's very fat.
Heavy books and piles of paper, answers I don't know.
Sunday evening's almost finished, now I'm going to go
Do my homework in the kitchen. Maybe just a snack,
Then I'll sit right down and start as soon as I run back
For some chocolate sandwich cookies. Then I'll really do
All that homework in a minute. First I'll see what new
Show they've got on television in the living room.
Everybody's laughing there, but misery and gloom
And a full refrigerator are where I am at.
I'll just have another sandwich. Homework's very fat.

Let's **Think** About...

Nikki Grimes uses metaphors to create images in "His Hands." Give an example of a metaphor she uses. Explain how you know it is a metaphor.

Let's **Think** About...

"Homework" has a strong meter or beat. Read a line of the poem. Can you hear the meter? How does the meter make you feel? Explain how the poet uses meter to create that feeling.

311

Lem Lonnigan's Leaf Machine

by Andrea Perry

Lem Lonnigan's Leaf Machine cleans lawns with ease
by vacuuming all that falls down from the trees.
And as you might guess, he's quite busy in autumn.
Just look in a yard full of trees and you'll spot 'im!

He uses a special attachment to get
those few stubborn leaves that have not fallen yet,
extending its claws to reach sky-scraping heights
for snatching up stragglers and sometimes stray kites.

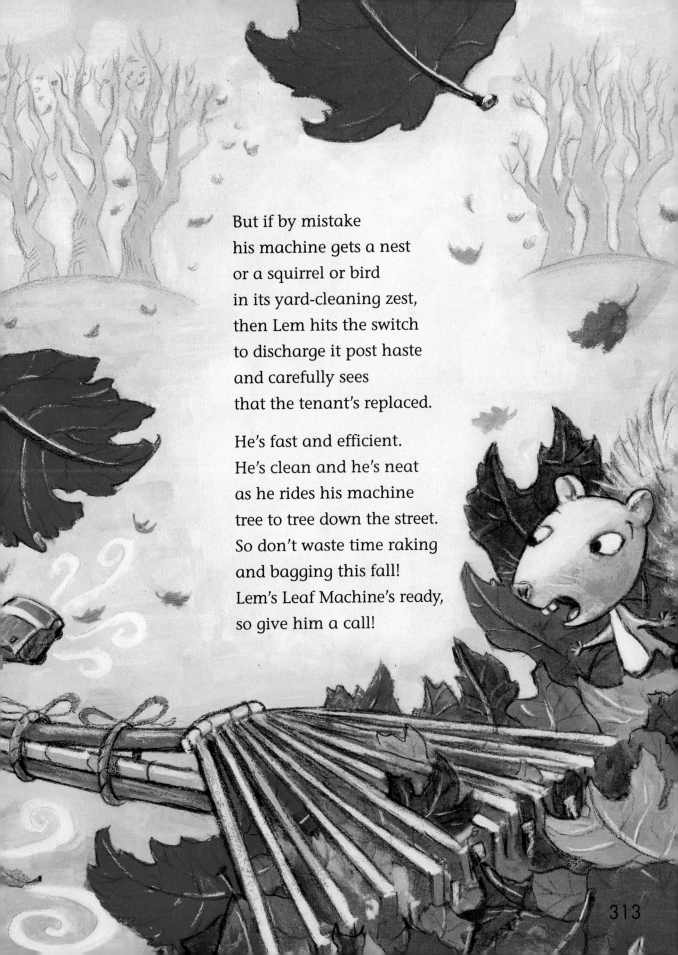

But if by mistake
his machine gets a nest
or a squirrel or bird
in its yard-cleaning zest,
then Lem hits the switch
to discharge it post haste
and carefully sees
that the tenant's replaced.

He's fast and efficient.
He's clean and he's neat
as he rides his machine
tree to tree down the street.
So don't waste time raking
and bagging this fall!
Lem's Leaf Machine's ready,
so give him a call!

313

Patterns

in Nature

Reading Street Online

www.ReadingStreet.com
- Big Question Video
- eSelections
- Envision It! Animations
- Story Sort

THE BIG

What are some patterns in nature?

Let's Talk About

Clouds

- Share what you know about cloud formations.

- Ask questions about different kinds of clouds.

- Listen attentively to others.

READING STREET ONLINE
CONCEPT TALK VIDEO
www.ReadingStreet.com

Common Core State Standards

Informational Text 7. Interpret information presented visually, orally, or quantitatively (e.g., in charts, graphs, diagrams, time lines, animations, or interactive elements on Web pages) and explain how the information contributes to an understanding of the text in which it appears. **Also Informational Text 2.**

Envision It! | Skill Strategy

Skill

Strategy

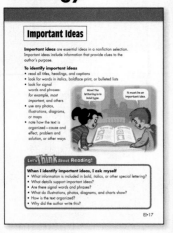

Comprehension Skill

Graphic Sources

- A graphic source shows or explains information in the text. Illustrations, photographs, maps, diagrams, charts, and time lines are all examples of graphic sources.

- As you read, use graphic sources to help you understand information. Compare information in the text with information in the graphic sources.

- Use the photographs below to help you understand the information in "Measuring the Invisible."

Level 2   Level 6

Comprehension Strategy

Important Ideas

Important ideas are essential ideas and supporting details in a nonfiction selection. Important ideas include information and facts that provide clues to the author's purpose. To identify important ideas, identify all the headings, look for words in special type, and use the graphics in the text.

Measuring the Invisible

How can you measure what you cannot see? For years, people depended on their powers of observation to guess the speed of wind. Today, we have instruments we use to measure wind speed accurately.

One is called an anemometer (an-uh-MOM-i-ter). As the wind blows past the cups of the anemometer, the cups rotate. The faster the winds blow, the faster the cups rotate. A device then figures out the number of times the cups rotate and turns the information into scientific units of measurement for wind, called knots. One knot is a little more than one mile per hour.

Another instrument is the Beaufort scale. In 1805, a British admiral named Sir Francis Beaufort invented a way to measure wind speed while he was at sea. By watching the effect of wind on the ocean, Beaufort created a scale that classified wind speed from 1 to 12. People changed the scale slightly, but it is still used today to measure wind speed on water, as well as on land.

Skill Look at the photograph of the anemometer at work. Explain how the cups show how fast the wind blows.

Skill Look at the images of Level 2 and Level 6 of the Beaufort scale on p. 318. Which number represents the stronger wind speed?

Strategy Summarize the most important idea of this paragraph.

Your Turn!

Need a Review? See the *Envision It! Handbook* for help with graphic sources and important ideas.

Let's Think About..

Ready to Try It? Use what you've learned about graphic sources as you read *The Man Who Named the Clouds*.

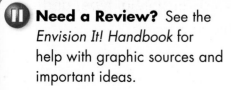

Common Core State Standards

Language 4.a. Use context (e.g., definitions, examples, or restatements in text) as a clue to the meaning of a word or phrase. **Also Language 4.**

Envision It! | Words to Know

atmosphere

chemical

scales

apprentice

club

essay

manufacturing

pressure

Vocabulary Strategy for

🎯 Multiple-Meaning Words

Context Clues When you read you might see a word whose meaning you know, but the word doesn't make sense in the sentence. The word may have more than one meaning. You can look for clues, such as an example or definition, in the text to help you decide which meaning the author is using.

1. First, try the meaning you know. Does it make sense in the sentence?

2. If that meaning doesn't make sense, reread the words and sentences around the word. Use context clues to try to figure out a meaning for the word.

3. Try that meaning in the sentence to see if it makes sense.

Read "And the Winner Is. . . ." Use context clues to help you figure out the meanings of this week's *Words to Know* and multiple-meaning words.

Words to Write Reread "And the Winner Is . . . ." Imagine that you are a TV meteorologist. Write your script for tonight's weathercast. Use words from the *Words to Know* list.

And the Winner Is . . .

Rob's twin, Jill, ran into the family room where Rob and his friend Ryan were working on homework. Waving an envelope, she yelled, "Rob! It's from the Forecaster Club, the club you wanted to join! Do you think it's about the essay you wrote? You know, the one about using pine-cone scales to predict weather?"

Rob ripped the letter out of the envelope. "Yes! My essay won! I'm going to be a meteorologist's apprentice for a day! Remember I told you that some scientists have been manufacturing a new weather detector? Well, I'll be one of the first people to watch them use it!"

Ryan was the one who told Rob about the contest. He knew how crazy his friend was about forecasting the weather, so he really put the pressure on Rob to enter. Ryan was thrilled when Rob won, even though he knew he'd have to put up with Rob's constant weather updates! Just then, Rob announced, "A severe cold front will be moving across our region later today, so get out your winter jackets! The chemical composition of the gases in the air will change significantly as the day goes on...."

Suddenly the room's atmosphere changed, as Ryan groaned jokingly and muttered to Jill, "At least we'll know what clothes to wear—every single minute of the day!"

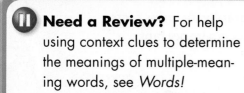

Your Turn!

Need a Review? For help using context clues to determine the meanings of multiple-meaning words, see *Words!*

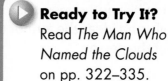 **Ready to Try It?** Read *The Man Who Named the Clouds* on pp. 322–335.

Cirrus

Stratus

Genre

A biography is an account of a person's life written by another person. A biography includes facts, details, and ideas the author thinks are important about the person.

The Man Who Named the Clouds

by Julie Hannah and Joan Holub

illustrations by Paige Billin-Frye

umulus

Let's
Think
About
Reading!

A person who daydreams is sometimes said to have his or her "head in the clouds." But daydreams can lead to great accomplishments. As a boy, Luke Howard wondered about the weather and daydreamed about clouds. He began to study them as a hobby. When he grew up, he created the first practical scientific system for naming clouds.

Luke Howard was born on November 28, 1772, in the city of London, England. When he was young, he noticed there were different kinds of clouds. Some were high and feathery. Some were puffy on top and flat on the bottom. Others looked like gray blankets.

Luke didn't get serious about studying clouds until he was ten years old. That's when he began keeping a weather journal to describe what he saw in the sky.

Luke had three younger brothers, one younger sister, and three older half-brothers. Many of them helped in the family's ironworks business. Their father didn't want his children to be lazy. He taught them the importance of working hard and learning.

When Luke was a boy, it was popular to study science and nature. People wanted to know more about metals and chemicals that might help in manufacturing and making medicines.

And Luke wasn't the only one who was curious about the weather. Many people kept weather journals, hoping to learn more about what caused clouds, rain, and fog. One theory was that clouds were bubbles of air and that the sun's rays gave them the power to float.

In the 1700s, the causes of weather were a mystery. Sailors and farmers could only watch for signs in nature to help them predict storms.

Let's Think About...

What questions about predicting weather do you have so far?
Questioning

In dry, sunny weather, they noticed a pine cone's scales opened outward. If its scales folded inward, rain might be on the way.

Rhymes like this one also helped in predicting the weather:

Red sky at night, sailor's delight.
Red sky at morning, sailors take warning.

Sailors like red sunsets because it means the air in the west (where the sun sets) is dry. Wind usually moves weather from west to east, so dry air is coming, and the sky will be clear.

If the sunrise sky is red-colored, it means dry air has already moved from the west to the east (where the sun rises). There is a good chance clouds, rain, or even storms will soon come from the west.

People made up sayings comparing clouds to shapes in nature, such as horses' tails or fish scales.

Mares' tails bring storms and gales.

Clouds are blown into wispy, horse-tail shapes by strong, stormy winds.

Mackerel sky, mackerel sky,
Never long wet, never long dry.

Clouds shaped like the pattern of scales on a mackerel fish often bring quick showers that come and go.

Let's **Think** About...

Have you ever looked for shapes of animals in clouds? Why would people try to connect a cloud's shape with the weather?
Background Knowledge

Luke and his family were members of a religion called the Religious Society of Friends, or Quakers. Because Quakers didn't belong to the Church of England, England's main church, they weren't allowed to go to the same schools as people who did. Instead, eight-year-old Luke and his younger brother William attended a Quaker boarding school in Burford, England. They lived at the school year-round, except for a short vacation each summer.

As part of his lessons, Luke had to recite Latin words over and over. This wasn't interesting or fun at the time, but it came in handy years later.

Luke finished school at age fifteen and moved back home to live with his parents. He happily began his weather studies outside in the family garden.

Twice a day in his journal, he recorded the weather conditions. He used a thermometer to learn the temperature of the air, a weather vane to check the wind direction, a rain gauge to measure the rainfall, and a barometer to measure the pressure of the atmosphere on the Earth's surface.

Let's **Think** About...

What do you want to know about weather instruments?
Questioning

327

Luke was still very interested in clouds. Since there were no scientific names for different types of clouds, it was hard to write about them. He painted pictures of clouds instead. These are some of his paintings.

Cloud study by Luke Howard, painted sometime between 1808 and 1811

Landscape and cloud study by Luke Howard, painted sometime between 1808 and 1811

Luke's father thought cloud-watching was a waste of time. He wanted his son to learn a trade so he could get a good job. After a few weeks at home, Luke was sent away to work as an apprentice in a Quaker chemist shop, where medicines were made and sold.

Luke worked long hours at the shop for seven years. He didn't have time to study the weather, so he was unhappy.

When he finally returned home, he went to work for another chemist for a few months. One day, he cut his hand badly when a glass bottle of poisonous chemicals he was holding broke. After he was well again, his father loaned him the money to open his own small chemist shop.

Let's **Think** About...

Will Luke's interest in clouds continue even though his father doesn't approve?
Predict

At age twenty-four, Luke married a woman named Mariabella Eliot. Their first daughter, Mary, was born the following year.

About that time, Luke became the manager of a large chemical factory and shop in the English village of Plaistow. He and his new family moved into a house there. Plaistow wasn't crowded with tall buildings as London had been. There were wide spaces where Luke could see lots of sky. Upstairs in his new house, he had a weather-watching room with big windows. He filled the shelves with his science books and instruments for recording conditions in the atmosphere.

This was a happy time in Luke's life. He had a good job and he had made friends who liked to study science. Now he could get back to his hobby of weather study.

Let's **Think** About...

Why was Luke's new house better for weather watching?
◉ **Important Ideas**

Let's **Think** About...

Describe implicit relationships among ideas in this text organized by sequence. What did Luke do before he joined the Askesian Society?

Inferring

Luke was determined to find new ways to study the weather. In 1796, he joined a club called the Askesian Society. The word *askesian* comes from a Greek word that means "philosophical exercise" or "training."

Most of the club's members were Quakers who wanted to learn about science. They did experiments and brainstormed to try to answer questions about weather, astronomy, electricity, and other branches of science. They wrote their ideas in reports and read them aloud at club meetings held twice a month. At every meeting, each member had to read a paper he had written or pay a fine!

It wasn't easy to discuss clouds because everyone described their shapes differently. Luke knew clouds needed to be classified and named. But scientists had tried this before and failed because their systems weren't exact enough.

Luke studied the work of a Swedish botanist named Carl von Linné, also known as Linnaeus. In 1735, Linnaeus had created a system for scientifically classifying plants and animals using Latin names. This gave Luke an idea for a way to classify clouds.

At a society meeting in 1802, Luke read an essay he'd written called "The Modification of Clouds." (At the time, *modification* meant "classification" or "naming by categories.") In his paper, Luke described three main cloud shapes and gave them Latin names.

Cirrus (a Latin word that means "curl of hair")— "Parallel, flexuous, or diverging fibres, extensible by increase in any or in all directions."

Cumulus (a Latin word that means "heap")— "Convex or conical heaps, increasing upward from a horizontal base."

Stratus (a Latin word that means "layer")— "A widely extended, continuous, horizontal sheet, increasing from below upward."

He also described four other types of clouds, which were combinations of the three main ones: *cirro-cumulus, cirro-stratus, cumulo-stratus,* and *cumulo-cirro-stratus* or *nimbus. (Nimbus* means "rain.") Everyone in the Askesian Society was excited about his essay. Finally, someone had a good idea for a system to name clouds!

Let's **Think** About...

What details help you understand the importance of Carl von Linné?
🔊 **Important Ideas**

331

Unknown to Luke, a Frenchman named Jean Baptiste Lamarck had made up another cloud classification system earlier that same year. Lamarck believed there were many cloud types. He planned to name each of them in French.

At first, there were arguments about which system was better. Was Latin, French, or maybe English the best language for the system?

Latin was the official language of the Roman Empire for over five hundred years, beginning about 31 B.C.E. Because of Rome's widespread influence, many other European languages were based on Latin. So scientists pointed out that people would probably understand Latin cloud names more easily than French ones.

Let's **Think** About...

Why was using Latin cloud names more popular? You can reread to find out. **Monitor and Clarify**

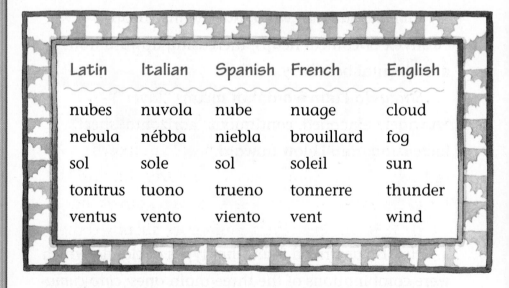

Latin	Italian	Spanish	French	English
nubes	nuvola	nube	nuage	cloud
nebula	nébba	niebla	brouillard	fog
sol	sole	sol	soleil	sun
tonitrus	tuono	trueno	tonnerre	thunder
ventus	vento	viento	vent	wind

In 1803, Luke's essay was printed in a magazine many scientists read and trusted called *Philosophical Magazine.* Soon his cloud-naming system became more popular than Lamarck's.

Luke's essay was printed and sold in bookstores. His cloud-naming system appeared in the *Encyclopedia Americana* in the early 1800s.

Still, scientists argued about his system. Was it really possible there were only seven cloud types as Luke claimed? Although some people proposed different classification ideas, Luke never changed his list of seven cloud types. But, over time, others did.

In 1896, an important conference about weather was held in Paris, France. Scientists who attended agreed on a list of ten types of clouds. Each cloud type was given a name based on its shape and the height of its base. Five of Luke's original names were used on the new list. The other five were combinations or revisions of his cloud names.

Let's **Think** About...

What details help you understand that Luke's system was accepted by other scientists?

⊙ **Important Ideas**

333

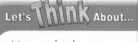
Let's Think About...

Use multiple text features to locate information. How do the diagram and caption help you understand the different clouds?
Text Structure

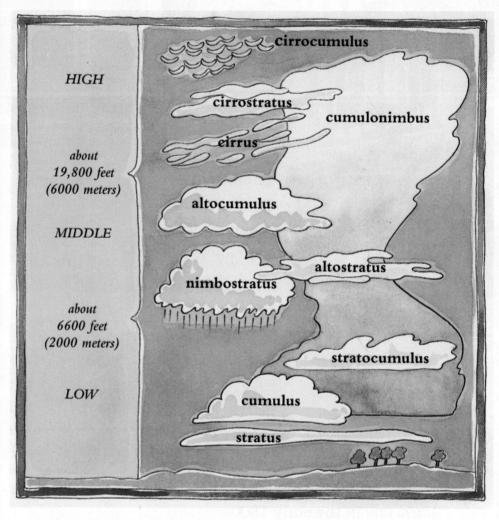

HIGH

about
19,800 feet
(6000 meters)

MIDDLE

about
6600 feet
(2000 meters)

LOW

cirrocumulus

cirrostratus

cumulonimbus

cirrus

altocumulus

altostratus

nimbostratus

stratocumulus

cumulus

stratus

You can tell different kinds of clouds apart by their shape and by how high they are in the sky. The sky often contains a mix of the ten types of clouds.

Today, the World Meteorological Organization (WMO), an agency of the United Nations located in Switzerland, is the authority on clouds and weather. The WMO still uses these ten basic names.

As news of his cloud-naming system spread, scientists asked him to give speeches about weather. Luke's weather observations were published in 1818 in two book volumes called *The Climate of London. Seven Lectures on Meteorology,* his textbook about the science of meteorology, was published in 1837.

Many people admired and praised Luke, but he always tried to be a good Quaker and stay humble.

Luke and Mariabella had a long marriage, and he enjoyed spending time with their eight children. Two of his sons worked in his chemist shop when they grew up. Luke's sister, Elizabeth, said that in his later years, he was "always having some of his children and grandchildren with him."

Even as a very old man, Luke loved to watch the sky. By the time he died on March 21, 1864, at the age of ninety-one, he and his cloud-naming system were famous around the world.

Let's Think About...

What information did the author provide about Luke's life and character? How would you describe Luke Howard?
Summarize

Common Core State Standards

Informational Text 1. Refer to details and examples in a text when explaining what the text says explicitly and when drawing inferences from the text. **Also Informational Text 2., 7., Writing 9.**

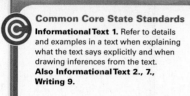

Envision It! Retell

Think Critically

1. When Luke Howard was a boy, he daydreamed about clouds. Have you ever daydreamed about something? Do you think you might want to study more about it when you get older? Why? **Text to Self**

2. Look back at the rhymes on page 326. Why do you think the author included rhymes in a nonfiction article?

Think Like an Author

3. Look at the chart on page 334. How does this chart help you understand the text?

Graphic Sources

4. Reread page 334. Why did the World Meteorological Association use Luke's original cloud names? What does this tell you about Howard's cloud-naming system?

Important Ideas

5. Look Back and Write Look back at pages 324–325. Do you think Luke's interest in clouds was just a hobby or something more? Provide evidence from the article to support your answer.

Key Ideas and Details • Text Evidence

Meet the Author and the Illustrator

Joan Holub

For years, Joan Holub dreamed of working as a children's book author. She moved to New York City to work in publishing while writing and sending out books to publishers. So many of her manuscripts were returned that she began calling them "boomerangs." Eventually, she sold three books—in one year! Today, Ms. Holub has written and illustrated more than 120 children's books.

Joan worked with her mother, Julie Hannah, to write *The Man Who Named the Clouds*. Both authors hope that *The Man Who Named the Clouds* will spark children's interest in science.

Paige Billin-Frye

Paige studied design at Washington University in St. Louis, and now she lives in Washington, D.C., with her family. The thrill of illustration for her is in taking real places and activities and turning them into artwork. She researches her books thoroughly so that she can show what clothes people really wear and what things really look like.

Here are other books by Joan Holub.

Use your Reading Log in the *Reader's and Writer's Notebook* to record your independent writing.

337

Common Core State Standards

Writing 3. Write narratives to develop real or imagined experiences or events using effective technique, descriptive details, and clear event sequences. **Also Writing 3.a.**

Narrative

Narrative Poem

A **narrative poem** is a poem that tells a story. The student model on the next page is an example of a narrative poem.

Writing Prompt Write a narrative poem about Luke Howard and his achievements.

Let's Write It!

Key Features of a Narrative Poem

- tells a story
- often focuses on a specific person or event
- usually has regular rhyme scheme and meter

READING STREET ONLINE
GRAMMAR JAMMER
www.ReadingStreet.com

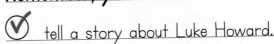

Writer's Checklist

Remember, you should . . .

- ✓ tell a story about Luke Howard.
- ✓ use figurative language to show sensory details.
- ✓ make use of rhyme and meter in your poem.
- ✓ write legibly in either cursive or manuscript printing.
- ✓ use verbs correctly.

Luke **was** a dreamer—he loved looking at clouds,
his face always turned to the sky.
In his journal each night, he **recorded** the shapes
of fluffy clouds that **floated** on high.

A chemist by trade, a dreamer at heart,
to his window he would **go**
to **watch** the wonderful shapes **roll** by,
whose names he did not **know**.

"I'll **name** them in an essay," **said** Luke,
"and I'll **gain** both fame and status
for giving to clouds these fine Latin names:
Cirrus, Cumulus, and Stratus."

Writing Trait
The poem's **organization** includes four-line stanzas and a regular rhyme scheme.

Genre A **narrative poem** tells a story.

Action and linking verbs are used correctly.

Conventions

Action and Linking Verbs

Remember Words that show action are called **action verbs.**
Linking verbs do not show action. They tell what the subject is or what the subject is like.

Science in Reading

Genre
Procedural Text

- Most procedural texts explain how to do or make something.

- Procedural texts contain a sequence of steps needed to carry out the activity.

- Some procedural texts explain information using examples.

- Read "My Weather Journal." As you read, look for elements of procedural text. What steps does Grace follow to create her monthly weather journal?

My Weather Journal

by Julie Hannah and Joan Holub

My name is Grace. I'm keeping a weather journal like Luke did. It's my science fair project. Once a month during the school year, I'll write these things: the date, the time, the temperature, what kinds of weather I see outside, and interesting facts.

One thing I've learned is that temperature is measured with a Fahrenheit thermometer in the United States. Most other countries use a Celsius thermometer.

My Weather Journal

September 25 Time: 9:15 A.M.

Temperature: 75° Fahrenheit or 23.9° Celsius

The weather today is: Cloudy

Here's how clouds are made:

1. Sun heats the earth.

2. Water evaporates from the surface of oceans, ponds, lakes, and rivers. Evaporation means a liquid changes to a gas. When water gets warm enough, it evaporates and becomes water vapor, the gas form of water.

3. The water vapor rises.

4. As the vapor meets higher, cooler air, it condenses into tiny drops of liquid water. Condensation means a gas changes to a liquid.

5. A cloud is made of a bunch of those drops hanging in the sky.

My Weather Journal

October 23 Time: 9:35 A.M.

Temperature: 68° Fahrenheit or 20° Celsius

The weather today is: Foggy

Today I walked through a cloud on the way to school! Fog is a cloud near the ground. It forms in the same way other clouds do, except for one thing—warm air doesn't rise and get cooled by the higher, cool air. Instead, the warm air stays low and passes over cool land, making water droplets form. That's why fog clouds are at ground level, instead of high in the sky.

Let's Think About...

Does Grace follow her own instructions in this first weather journal entry?
Procedural Text

Let's Think About...

Reading Across Texts Connect what you have learned about Luke Howard and Grace. Do you think they are both scientists? Explain your reasons.

Writing Across Texts Write a brief report with interesting facts about clouds. Use facts from both selections.

Common Core State Standards

Speaking/Listening 4. Report on a topic or text, tell a story, or recount an experience in an organized manner, using appropriate facts and relevant, descriptive details to support main ideas or themes; speak clearly at an understandable pace. **Also Foundational Skills 4.b., Writing 1., Language 4., 4.a.**

Let's Learn It!

Vocabulary

Multiple-Meaning Words

Context Clues Multiple-meaning words have more than one meaning. Sometimes the definition of a multiple-meaning word is given in the same sentence.

Practice It! Reread *The Man Who Named the Clouds*, page 331. The definition of the word *modification* as it was used in Luke Howard's time is given in the same sentence in which the word appears. What does the word *modification* mean today? Make a list of other words you know whose meanings have changed over time.

Fluency

Expression

Partner Reading Changing the volume of your voice as you read brings drama to a story. Reading in a soft or a loud voice helps you understand the emotions the author is trying to convey.

Practice It! With a partner, practice reading aloud page 326. Use punctuation to adjust the loudness or softness of your voice. Read the weather poems in a different tone of voice from the one you use to read the text.

Listening and Speaking

When you give a presentation to a group, speak clearly and loudly.

Persuasive Speech

The purpose of a persuasive speech is to try to persuade an audience to agree with the speaker's opinion or point of view.

Practice It! Use information from the selection to write a speech in which you convince people that Luke Howard's cloud-naming system should become the official way of naming clouds. Include details about Howard's system to support your point of view. Present your speech to the class.

Tips

Listening ...

- Listen attentively to the speaker.
- Be ready to ask relevant questions.

Speaking ...

- Use accurate information to express your opinion.
- Raise or lower your voice to emphasize your points.
- Speak clearly and purposefully to communicate your ideas.
- Use verbs correctly.

Teamwork ...

- Ask and answer questions with detail.

Let's Talk About

Animal Migration

- Ask questions about why birds migrate.

- Offer information about where they may go.

- Contribute to others' ideas about migration.

READING STREET ONLINE
CONCEPT TALK VIDEO
www.ReadingStreet.com

Common Core State Standards

Informational Text 5. Describe the overall structure (e.g., chronology, comparison, cause/effect, problem/solution) of events, ideas, concepts, or information in a text or part of a text. **Also Informational Text 1., 8.**

Envision It! | Skill Strategy

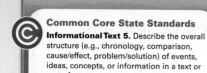

Skill

Strategy

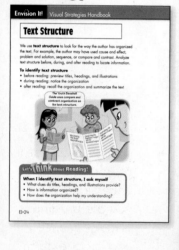

READING STREET ONLINE
ENVISION IT! ANIMATIONS
www.ReadingStreet.com

Comprehension Skill

Fact and Opinion

- A statement of fact can be correct or incorrect. You can check a fact by doing research.

- A statement of opinion should be supported. A valid opinion is supported by facts or good logic. A faulty opinion is not supported.

- Some sentences contain both statements of fact and statements of opinion.

- Use this graphic organizer to identify facts and opinions, and whether the opinions are valid, in "Something Must Be Done."

Statement	Support	True or False/ Valid or Faulty
Statement of fact	Other facts	True
Statement of opinion	Logic or known facts	Valid
Statement of opinion	Weak opinion or incorrect facts	Faulty

Comprehension Strategy

Text Structure

Use the text structure to help understand what you read. A nonfiction article may put events in sequence. An explicitly stated sequence uses clue words such as *first* or *next*. Or the sequence may be implicit, and the reader has to figure out the order of what happens. When you preview a text, look for features such as titles, headings, bold print, and photos to know what to expect.

346

SOMETHING MUST BE DONE

What is the largest animal that ever lived? Is it an elephant? Not even close. This animal can be as big as four elephants. Is it a dinosaur? No!

The largest animal in the world is the blue whale. This beautiful animal can grow to be one hundred feet long! You might think that an animal so enormous could survive anything. Not so.

Skill Some sentences contain both a statement of fact and a statement of opinion. Find the fact and opinion in this paragraph.

In the 1800s and early 1900s, whaling was big business. People killed whales to make things such as oil and candles. Whales were hunted almost to extinction. In time, other ways of lighting houses and workplaces were developed. People realized how the whaling business hurt the whales. Now, most countries ban whaling, but even so, many species are still endangered.

Skill How can the author support this statement?

Whales face other challenges too. They can get tangled in fishing nets and drown. (Remember, whales are mammals; they need to breathe air.) Also, they can get sick from pollution. Sometimes, they collide with ships.

We need to find ways to protect whales. People can write letters to newspapers and to politicians to inform others that saving whales is important. We all can do something to help the whales and save their habitats. We can make a difference!

Strategy How does the order, or sequence, of events in this paragraph help you understand what you are reading? Is the sequence implicit or explicit? What about the last paragraph?

Your Turn!

⏸ **Need a Review?** See the *Envision It! Handbook* for help with fact and opinion and text structure.

▶ **Ready to Try It?** Use what you've learned about fact and opinion as you read *Adelina's Whales*.

Adelina's Whales

347

Common Core State Standards

Language 4.a. Use context (e.g., definitions, examples, or restatements in text) as a clue to the meaning of a word or phrase. **Also Foundational Skills 4.c.**

bluff

lagoon

tropical

biologist

massive

rumbling

Vocabulary Strategy for

Multiple-Meaning Words

Context Clues When you read, you may find that the meaning of a word you know does not make sense in a sentence. The word may have multiple meanings. You can look for clues to decide which meaning the author is using.

1. Try the meaning you know to see if it makes sense in the sentence.

2. If it doesn't make sense, think of another meaning for the word. Does that meaning make sense?

3. If that meaning doesn't make sense either, reread the words and sentences around the word. Use the context to help you figure out a meaning for the unknown word.

4. Try that meaning in the sentence. Check that it makes sense in the sentence.

As you read "Paradise Island," look for words that can have more than one meaning. Use context clues to help you figure out which meaning is being used.

Words to Write Reread "Paradise Island." Imagine you are visiting Paradise Island. Write a letter to a friend describing what the place is like. Use words from the *Words to Know* list in your writing.

PARADISE ISLAND

Welcome to Paradise Island! To find out more about what you can do on our island, check out these exciting activities.

• Walk or run on the gorgeous white sand beaches that ring the whole island. They were voted the Best Beaches in the World last year by *Touring* magazine!

• Swim in the beautiful blue-green waters of our lagoon. Protected from the ocean by a reef, the lagoon is also perfect for canoeing and kayaking.

• Take a walk with our staff biologist. You can learn about the many strange and colorful birds and other animals that live on the island.

• Climb the bluff for wonderful views of the island and the ocean. We offer climbs for beginners and experts.

• Take a day trip to the volcano. You can ride or hike to the top and look down into the massive crater. It has always been quiet (except for a rumbling noise every once in a while).

Paradise Island is a tropical paradise. Come see it for yourself and have the best vacation of your life!

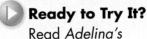

Your Turn!

❚❚ Need a Review? For additional help with using context clues to determine the meanings of multiple-meaning words, see *Words!*

▷ Ready to Try It? Read *Adelina's Whales* on pp. 350–361.

349

Adelina's Whales

text and photographs by Richard Sobol

350

La Laguna is the name of a quiet, dusty fishing village on the sandy shore of Laguna San Ignacio, in Baja California, Mexico. A few dozen homesites are scattered along the water's edge. These little houses are simple one- or two-room boxes patched together with plywood and sheet metal. Drinking water is stored outside in fifty-gallon plastic barrels, and electricity is turned on for only a few hours each day.

Adelina Mayoral has lived her whole life in La Laguna. She is a bright ten-year-old girl. She loves the ocean and the feeling of the ever-present wind that blows her long, dark hair into wild tangles. She knows what time of day it is by looking at the way the light reflects off the water. Adelina can tell what month it is by watching the kind of birds that nest in the mangroves behind her home. She can even recognize when it is low tide. Simply by taking a deep breath through her nose, she can smell the clams and seaweed that bake in the hot sun on the shoreline as the water level goes down.

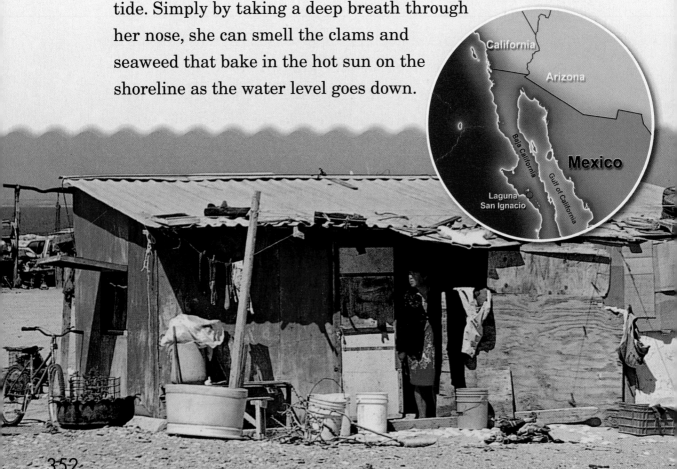

In late January, every afternoon after school, Adelina walks to the beach to see if her friends—the gray whales—have returned. At this same time every year the whales come, traveling from as far away as Alaska and Russia. They slowly and steadily swim south, covering more than five thousand miles along the Pacific Coast during November, December, and January.

One night Adelina is awakened by a loud, low, rumbling noise. It is the sound of a forty-ton gray whale exhaling a room-size blast of hot wet air. As she has always known they would, the gray whales have come again to visit. Adelina smiles and returns to her sleep, comforted by the sounds of whales breathing and snoring outside her window. At daybreak she runs to the lagoon and sees two clouds of mist out over the water, the milky trails of breath left by a mother gray whale and her newborn calf.

The waters of the protected lagoon are warm and shallow. The scientists who have come to visit and study the whales have explained that Laguna San Ignacio is the perfect place for the mother whales to have their babies and then teach them how to swim. But Adelina knows why they really come—to visit her!

Adelina's family lives far away from big cities with highways and shopping malls. Her little village does not have any movie theaters or traffic lights, but she knows that her hometown is a special place. This is the only place on Earth where these giant gray whales—totally wild animals—choose to seek out the touch of a human hand. Only here in Laguna San Ignacio do whales ever stop swimming and say hello to their human neighbors. Raising their massive heads up out of the water, they come face-to-face with people. Some mother whales even lift their newborns up on their backs to help them get a better view of those who have come to see them. Or maybe they are just showing off, sharing their new baby the way any proud parent would.

The whales have been coming to this lagoon for hundreds of years, and Adelina is proud that her grandfather, Pachico, was the first person to tell of a "friendly" visit with one. She loves to hear him tell the story of that whale and that day. She listens closely as he talks about being frightened, since he didn't know then that the whale was only being friendly. He thought he was in big trouble.

Adelina looks first at the tight, leathery skin of her grandfather, browned from his many years of fishing in the bright tropical sun. From his face she glances down to the small plastic model of a gray whale that he keeps close by. As he begins to tell the story of his first friendly whale encounter, there is a twinkle in his eye and a large smile on his face. Adelina and her father, Runolfo, smile too, listening again to the story that they have heard so many times before.

In a whisper, her grandfather begins to draw them in. Adelina closes her eyes to imagine the calm and quiet on that first afternoon when his small boat was gently nudged by a huge gray whale. As the boat rocked, her grandfather's and his fishing partner's hearts pounded. They held tight and waited, preparing themselves to be thrown into the water by the giant animal. The whale dove below them and surfaced again on the opposite side of their boat, scraping her head along the smooth sides. Instead of being tossed from the boat, they were surprised to find themselves still upright and floating. For the next hour the whale glided alongside them, bumping and bobbing gently— as gently as possible for an animal that is as long as a school bus and as wide as a soccer goal. As the sun started to set behind them, the whale gave out a great blast of wet, snotty saltwater that soaked their clothes and stuck to their skin. The whale then rose up inches away from their boat and dove into the sea. Her first visit was over.

As her grandfather finishes the story, he looks to Adelina, who joins him in speaking the last line of the story: "Well, my friend, no fish today!" they say before breaking into laughter.

After this first friendly visit with the whales, word quickly spread of the unique encounter between a wild fifty-foot whale and a tiny fishing boat. Scientists and whale watchers started to come to Laguna San Ignacio to see the whales themselves. Perhaps word spread among the whales, too, because now dozens of whales began to approach the small boats. With brains as large as a car's engine, gray whales might even have their own language. They "talk" in low rumbles and loud clicks, making noises that sound like the tappings of a steel drum or the ticking that a playing card makes as it slaps against the spokes of a turning bicycle wheel. Maybe they told each other that it was safe to visit here.

Adelina's favorite time of the day is the late afternoon, when her father and grandfather return from their trips on the water, guiding visitors to see the whales. They sit together as the sun goes down behind them, and she listens to stories of the whales. She asks them lots and lots of questions.

Adelina has learned a lot about the gray whales. She knows that when a whale leaps out of the water and makes a giant splash falling back in, it's called breaching. When a whale pops its head straight up out of the water, as if it is looking around to see what is going on, it is called spyhopping. Adelina also learned how the whale's wide, flat tail is called a fluke, and when it raises its tail up in the air as it goes into a deep dive, that is called fluking.

Although her home is a simple shack on a sandy bluff hugging the edge of the Pacific Ocean, Adelina has many new friends who come to share her world. She has met people who come from beyond the end of the winding, bumpy road that rings the lagoon. Some are famous actors. Some are politicians. Some speak Spanish. Some speak English. Those that weigh forty tons speak to her in their own magical style. The whales have taught her that the world is a big place.

Adelina knows that she has many choices in her future. Sometimes she giggles with delight at the idea of being the first girl to captain a panga (a small open fishing boat) and teach people about the whales in the lagoon. Or sometimes she thinks she may become a biologist who studies the ocean and can one day help to unlock some of the mysteries of the whales in her own backyard. Or maybe she will take pictures like the photographer whom she watches juggling his three cameras as he stumbles aboard the whale-watching boat. But no matter what she chooses, the whales will always be a part of her life.

For these three months Adelina knows how lucky she is to live in Laguna San Ignacio, the little corner of Mexico that the gray whales choose for their winter home. This is the place where two worlds join together. She wouldn't trade it for anything.

In the early spring the lagoon grows quiet. One by one the whales swim off, heading north for a summer of feeding.

On their heads and backs they carry the fingerprints of those they met, the memories of their encounters in Mexico. Maybe, as the whales sleep, they dream of the colorful sunsets of Laguna San Ignacio.

Every afternoon Adelina continues to gaze across the water. Sometimes now, when she closes her eyes, she can still see the whales swimming by. And if she listens *really* closely, she can even hear their breathing.

Common Core State Standards

Writing 9. Draw evidence from literary or informational texts to support analysis, reflection, and research. **Also Informational Text 1., 2.**

Envision It! | Retell

Think Critically

1. The gray whales of Adelina's village are wild animals that seem to have formed a special relationship with humans. What other stories about bonding between humans and wild animals have you read about? **Text to Text**

2. Why do you think the author tells you about gray whales from Adelina's point of view? **Think Like an Author**

3. Reread page 353. Is it a fact or an opinion that the gray whales come to Laguna San Ignacio every year? How do you know? **Fact and Opinion**

4. On page 350, you read that this article is an example of expository text. Skim through the article, taking note of the photos. Why do you think the author chose to structure and support the text with photos? How do the photos help you understand the sequence of Adelina's story? **Text Structure**

5. **Look Back and Write** Look back at pages 360–361. Do you believe that the whales will always be part of Adelina's life? Why or why not? Provide evidence from the text to support your answer.

Key Ideas and Details • Text Evidence

Richard Sobol

Richard Sobol says he "started photography in high school and never stopped." This passion led to a fast-paced career taking pictures of politicians and wildlife. Then he decided to write photo essays. He explains, "I was always insecure about my writing, but I was reluctant to leave the storytelling to someone else."

Mr. Sobol got the idea for *Adelina's Whales* while in Baja California, where Adelina's father was his whale guide. To take photographs for the book, he says, "I spent each morning and afternoon on a small boat waiting for the whales to approach. Most often, I was within twenty feet of the whales. Sometimes, though, they were right on the side of the boat!"

When asked what it was like to be so close to whales, Mr. Sobol answers, "I am still amazed that these totally wild animals chose to come so close to humans. I will never forget the slick rubbery sensation of rubbing the forehead of a huge gray whale that swam from one side of my boat to the other." He hopes his books inspire kids to value and protect the gray whale and other rare and endangered animals.

Here are other books by Richard Sobol.

An Elephant in the Backyard

Seal Journey (with Jonah Sobol)

Reading Log

Use the *Reader's and Writer's Notebook* to record your independent reading.

Common Core State Standards
Writing 2.a. Introduce a topic clearly and group related information in paragraphs and sections; include formatting (e.g., headings), illustrations, and multimedia when useful to aiding comprehension. **Also Language 3.**

Let's Write It!

Key Features of an Invitation

- gives important information about an event
- tells details about the time, place, and purpose of the event
- asks for a response

READING STREET ONLINE
GRAMMAR JAMMER
www.ReadingStreet.com

Invitation

An **invitation** is a written offer asking someone to come to a party, gathering, or special event. The student model on the next page is an example of one kind of invitation.

Writing Prompt Imagine you are Adelina. Write an invitation to a friend inviting him or her to come to Laguna San Ignacio.

Writer's Checklist

Remember, you should . . .

☑ use language that is tailored to your audience and purpose.

☑ include a date, salutation, and closing.

☑ give the details about the time, place, and purpose of the event.

☑ include the date by which you would like a response.

January 23, 20__

Dear Ana,

Come help me celebrate the return of the gray whales!

When: February 12 until February 18
Where: My family's house in Laguna San Ignacio

Ask your parents if you can visit over school break. We can sit on the beach and watch the whales leaping and diving. I **have asked** my father to take us out on the lagoon in his boat to visit with the whales, and he **has agreed!** Don't forget to bring your camera!

Please call me at 555-1234 by February 5 to let me know if you can come, OK? I can't wait to hear! I've got my fingers, toes, and eyes crossed hoping that your folks will say yes—well, maybe not my eyes!

Sincerely,
Adelina

Genre An **invitation** gives details about time, place, and purpose of an event.

Main and helping verbs are used correctly.

Writing Trait Voice The writer's personality comes through in the language.

Conventions

Main and Helping Verbs

Remember A verb phrase is made up of a **main verb** and one or more **helping verbs.** The main verb shows action. A helping verb or verbs tells more about the action.

Science in Reading

Genre
Expository Text

- Expository texts give facts and details about real people, places, animals, and things.

- Most expository texts contain a main idea (the most important idea about the topic) with details that support it.

- Expository texts may use features to organize information. For example, guide words such as headings give you clues about what you will be reading.

- Read "Sea Animals on the Move." Look for elements that make this article a good example of expository text.

Sea Animals on the Move

by Joanne Wachter

Some families take a trip to see relatives every Thanksgiving. Other families go to a cabin in the mountains every summer. Certain sea animals take trips to the same place year after year too. The trips these animals take are called *migration.*

Line Up!

One sea animal that migrates is the spiny lobster. Usually, the lobster stays close to its home, a crack in a rock deep in the ocean. When the first winter storm hits, however, something strange happens. Groups of up to 60 lobsters line up, head to tail. Then they travel day and night, going 30 or more miles in a few days.

Other sea animals that migrate are sharks, eels, turtles, and whales. Sea turtles may travel more than 7,000 miles, one-third of the way around the Earth. Some fish have special ways to rest on their long trips. Lampreys use their sucking mouths to hold on to rocks for short breaks.

Trips with a Purpose

Why would an animal make such a trip? Spiny lobsters and sharks move to warmer or cooler waters when the seasons change. Flashlight fish migrate in search of food. This fish moves from deep to shallow water in order to feed. It uses a light that shines out of its body to find its way.

Many migrate to find safe places to lay eggs. Salmon live in the salty sea but travel to fresh water to have their young. The fish digs a hole in the river floor with its tail. Then it lays as many as 14,000 eggs. Sea turtles swim thousands of miles to have their babies on the same beaches where they hatched.

Let's Think About...

Summarize the main idea of this article. Summarize the details that support the main idea. **Expository Text**

Let's Think About...

Describe a reason one type of sea animal migrates in comparison to the reason another one does. Is this comparison explicit, or stated, or is it implied, or unstated? **Expository Text**

Common Core State Standards

Speaking/Listening 1.c. Pose and respond to specific questions to clarify or follow up on information, and make comments that contribute to the discussion and link to the remarks of others. **Also Foundational Skills 4.b., Language 4., 4.a.**

Vocabulary

Multiple-Meaning Words

Context Clues Use the words and phrases around a multiple-meaning word to help you figure out which meaning the author is using. Remember, some meanings are uncommon.

Practice It! With a partner, find the word *covering* in *Adelina's Whales*, page 353. Decide which meaning of *covering* is used. Explain to your partner how you decided. Then, on page 357, figure out which meaning of the word *word* is being used. Discuss how you figured out the correct meaning.

Fluency

Expression

Partner Reading Reading with expression helps show the emotions of the people in a story or an article. Showing emotions makes the story more real. It also makes it easier to understand the story.

Practice It! With a partner, practice reading aloud *Adelina's Whales*, pages 356 and 357 (first paragraph). As you read, express the emotions that Adelina's grandfather and his fishing partner feel when they meet the gray whale.

Listening and Speaking

Get Ready For Middle School

When you participate in a discussion, ask and answer questions with detail.

Interview

In an interview, one person asks another person questions about a specific topic. The purpose of an interview is to find out what the person knows or did.

Practice It! With a partner, conduct an interview. One person can be Adelina and the other, a TV reporter. Ask questions about the visits of the gray whales. Think of questions that prompt thoughtful answers. Write Adelina's answers to your questions in a notebook. Then switch roles.

Tips

Listening ...

- Listen attentively to the speaker.
- Ask detailed questions about the topic.

Speaking ...

- Express an opinion supported by accurate information.
- Make eye contact with your partner as you speak.

Teamwork ...

- Ask detailed questions.
- Answer questions with specific details and examples.

Common Core State Standards

Speaking/Listening 1.c. Pose and respond to specific questions to clarify or follow up on information, and make comments that contribute to the discussion and link to the remarks of others. **Also Language 6.**

Oral Vocabulary

Let's Talk About

Day and Night

- Ask questions about why night occurs.

- Discuss what you like about both day and night.

- Speak clearly so others can understand.

READING STREET ONLINE
CONCEPT TALK VIDEO
www.ReadingStreet.com

You've learned

1 2 0

Amazing Words

so far this year!

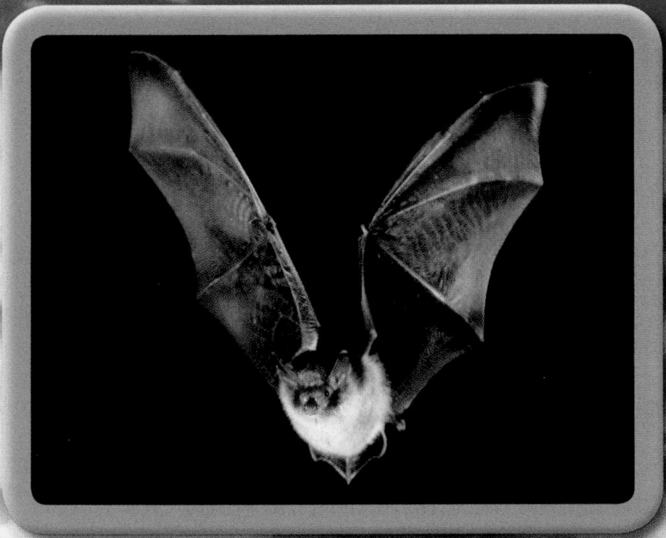

Common Core State Standards

Informational Text 1. Refer to details and examples in a text when explaining what the text says explicitly and when drawing inferences from the text.

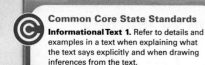

Skill

Strategy

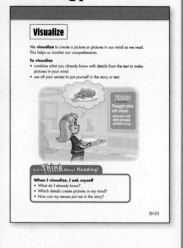

Comprehension Skill

Generalize

- A generalization is a broad statement that applies to many examples.

- Clue words, such as *all, most, always, usually,* or *generally,* signal that an author is making a generalization.

- Some generalizations are valid, which means that they are supported by facts or details. Some are faulty, which means that they are not supported.

- Use the graphic organizer to help you identify generalizations as you read "Call It a Day."

Generalization	Clue Word?

Comprehension Strategy

Visualize

Good readers visualize, or make pictures in their mind, as they read. These mental pictures can help you understand the ideas and information in the text. As you read, use the author's words to help you picture in your mind information that is unfamiliar to you.

Call It a Day

When we say *day*, we often mean daytime, when it is light out—as opposed to nighttime, when it is dark. Daytime can vary. It depends on where you are and what time of year it is. Along the equator the length of day is always the same—about 12 hours.

North or south of the equator, hours of daylight change throughout the year. In general, the farther north or south you are, the greater the change. The longest "day" of the year in the Northern Hemisphere is usually June 21. On that day, New York has about 13 hours of daylight. The North Pole has 24!

Of course, 24 hours is another meaning of day. Daytime and nighttime together make up one day. We have day and night because of the Earth's spin, or rotation.

The Earth orbits around the sun. It also spins on its axis at a tilted angle. It takes about 24 hours for the Earth to spin around once. As it spins, the side of the Earth that is facing the sun has daylight. The side that is facing away from the sun has nighttime. And for the half of the year that the Northern Hemisphere tilts toward the sun, daylight there is longer than darkness.

Skill Look for a generalization in this paragraph. The word *often* is a clue word.

Skill Find two generalizations in this paragraph. Clue words signal them.

Strategy What could you visualize at this point to help you understand what you read?

Your Turn!

⏸ **Need a Review?** See *Envision It! Handbook* for help with generalizing and visualizing.

▶ **Ready to Try It?** Use what you've learned about generalizing as you read *How Night Came from the Sea: A Story from Brazil.*

Common Core State Standards

Language 4.a. Use context (e.g., definitions, examples, or restatements in text) as a clue to the meaning of a word or phrase. **Also Language 4.**

brilliant

chorus

shimmering

coward

gleamed

Vocabulary Strategy for

🎯 Unfamiliar Words

Context Clues Sometimes when you read, you come to a word you do not know. The context, or the words and sentences around the unfamiliar word, may give you clues to the word's meaning.

1. Read the words and sentences around the unfamiliar word. The author may have included a definition, a synonym, or another clue to the word's meaning.

2. If not, say what the sentence means in your own words.

3. Predict a meaning for the unfamiliar word.

4. Try that meaning in the sentence to see if it makes sense.

Read "At the Edge of the Sea." Use context clues to help you determine the meanings of unfamiliar words.

Words to Write Reread "At the Edge of the Sea." Imagine you are on the coast of a tropical sea. Write a letter home describing what you see and how you feel. Use words from the *Words to Know* list in your writing.

At the Edge of the Sea

The two boys hesitated at the edge of the forest. They looked out at the sea. Waves caught the morning sun and sparkled in a thousand points like brilliant jewels. The white sand gleamed as though some servant of the wind had been polishing it all night. The boys knew it would soon be too hot to tread.

Still, they stood gazing out. The scene was like a painting. Its colors were bright and already shimmering with heat. Other than the waves and a few seabirds, nothing moved. It was all too radiant. Perhaps it also did not seem real because a great journey lay ahead of them. They hoped for some omen of good luck.

At their backs, a chorus of birds began their songs. "May your travels be safe," they seemed to chant. "May your hearts be true and brave. May you never know the shame of a coward. Firm in purpose, may you find what you seek."

The boys smiled then. They shifted the canoe on their shoulders and stepped forward onto the white sand.

Your Turn!

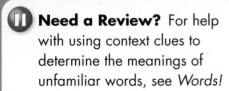 **Need a Review?** For help with using context clues to determine the meanings of unfamiliar words, see *Words!*

 **Ready to Try It?** Read *How Night Came from the Sea* on pp. 378–391.

377

Genre

Myths are traditional stories that try to explain how things in nature came to be. Think about how you would explain the cycle of day and night as you read this story.

How Night Came from the Sea

A Story from Brazil

retold by Mary-Joan Gerson
illustrated by Carla Golembe

 Question of the Week
**How have people explained
the pattern of day and night?**

379

Long, long ago, at the very beginning of time, when the world had just been made, there was no night. It was always daytime.

No one had ever heard of sunrise or sunset, starlight or moonbeams. There were no night creatures such as owls and tigers, and no night flowers that secretly open their petals at dusk. There was no soft night air, heavy with perfume. Sunlight always filled the sky. The light jumped from the coconuts at the top of the palm trees, and it gleamed from the backs of the alligators wading at the edge of the sea. Everywhere there was only sunlight and brightness and heat.

In that time, the great African goddess Iemanjá dwelt in the depths of the sea. And Iemanjá had a daughter who decided to marry one of the sons of the earth people. With sorrow and with longing, the daughter left her home in the deep ocean and came to live with her husband in the land of daylight.

Iemanjá's daughter loved her husband, and she loved the magic of daylight that he showed her: the shimmering sand of the beach, the rows and rows of cocoa and sugarcane baking in sunlight, and the sparkling jewels and feathered costumes worn in harvest festivals.

381

But with time, the light became too bright and hard for Iemanjá's daughter. The sight of the workers bent over in the fields day after day hurt her eyes and her heart.

And finally even the brilliant colors worn by the dancers at the festivals burned through her drooping lids.

"Oh, how I wish night would come," she cried. "Here there is always daylight, but in my mother's kingdom there are cool shadows and dark, quiet corners."

Her husband listened to her with great sorrow, for he loved her. "What is this night?" he asked her. "Tell me about it, and perhaps I can find a little of it for you."

"Night," she said, "is like the quiet after crying or the end of the storm. It is a dark, cool blanket that covers everything. If only we could have a little of the darkness of my mother's kingdom to rest our eyes some of the time."

Her husband called at once his three most faithful servants. "I am sending you on a very important journey," he told them. "You are to go to the kingdom of Iemanjá, who dwells in the depths of the seas. You must beg her to give you some of the darkness of night so that my wife will stop longing to return to her mother's kingdom and will be able to find happiness on land with me."

The three servants set forth. After a long, dangerous journey through the surging waves of the ocean, over the cliffs of underwater sand, and past the razor-sharp reefs of coral, they arrived at the palace of Iemanjá. Throwing themselves at the feet of the goddess, they begged her for some night to carry back with them. "Stand up, you foolish men," she commanded. "How can you beg a mother whose child is suffering?" And without a second lost, she packed a big bag of night for them to carry through the circling currents of water. "But," she said, "you must not open this until you reach my daughter, because only she can calm the night spirits I have packed inside."

The three servants pulled the big bag alongside them as they swam back through the cool, swirling sea. Finally they emerged into the bright sunlight of the shore and followed the path home, bearing the big bag upon their heads. Soon they heard strange sounds. They were the voices of all the night creatures squeezed inside. The servants had never heard this strange chorus of night screeching before, and they shook with fear.

The first servant stared at the screaming bag of voices and began to tremble.

"Let us drop this bag of night and run away as fast as we can," said the second servant.

"Coward!" said the third, trying to sound brave. "I am going to open the bag and see what makes all those terrible sounds."

385

He laid the bag on the ground and opened its sealing wax with his teeth. **Out rushed** the **night beasts,** the **night birds,** and all the **night insects. Out jumped** the **stars** and the **moon.** The servants ran terrified into the jungle.

387

But the servants were in luck, because Iemanjá's daughter was standing at the shore, waiting and waiting for their return. Ever since they had set out on their journey, she had stood in one spot under a palm tree at the edge of the sea, shading her eyes with her hand and praying for the darkness. And she was still standing in that spot when the servants let night escape.

"Night has come. Night has come at last," she cried as she saw the blue-black shadows gather on the horizon. "I greet you, my kinship spirits." And when she spoke, the night spirits were suddenly calmed, and there was hushed darkness everywhere.

Then the gentle hum of the night creatures began, and moonbeams flickered across the sky. The creatures of the night appeared before her: the owl hunting by moonlight and the tiger finding its way through the forest by smelling the dark, damp earth. The soft air grew heavy with the smell of night perfume. To Iemanjá's daughter, this coming of night was indeed like the quiet after crying or the end of the storm. It was like a dark, cool blanket covering everything, and just as if a soft hand had soothed her tired eyes, Iemanjá's daughter fell fast asleep.

She awoke feeling as if she were about to sing. How rested she was after the coolness of her night dreams! Her eyes opened wide to the brightness of the glistening day, and in her heart she knew she would find peace in her husband's land. And so to celebrate the beauty of her new home, Iemanjá's daughter made three gifts.

To the last bright star still shining above the palm tree she said, "Glittering star, from now on you will be our sign that night is passing. You shall be called the morning star, and you will announce the birth of each day."

To the rooster standing by her, she said, "You shall be the watchman of the night. From this day on, your voice will warn us that the light is coming."

And to the birds all about her she called, "You singing birds, you shall sing your sweetest songs at this hour to announce the dawn of each day."

To this day, the gifts of Iemanjá's daughter help celebrate each new sunrise. In Brazil the early morning is called the *madrugada*. As the *madrugada* slides onto the horizon, the morning star reigns in the sky as queen of the dawn. The rooster announces the day's approach to the sleeping birds, and then they sing their most beautiful songs.

And it is also true that in Brazil night leaps out quickly like a bullfrog just as it leapt quickly out of the bag in the beginning of time. The night flowers suddenly open their petals at dusk. And as they do, the owl and tiger begin their hunt for food.

The beasts and birds and insects of the night begin to sing their gentle chorus. And when the dark, cool blanket of night covers everything, the people of the earth take their rest.

Common Core State Standards

Literature 1. Refer to details and examples in a text when explaining what the text says explicitly and when drawing inferences from the text. **Also Writing 9., Language 5.a.**

Envision It! | Retell

Think Critically

1. Folk tales from different cultures seek to explain certain things that occur in nature. Why do you think natural occurrences are often the subject of folk tales? **Text to World**

2. On page 383, what simile does the author use to describe night? What similes would you use? **Think Like an Author**

3. What generalization could you make about the story or one of the characters in it? What examples support that generalization? **Generalize**

4. After the servants let the night escape, they run "terrified into the jungle." What might the jungle at night be like? Describe what the servants might see, hear, smell, and feel. **Visualize**

5. **Look Back and Write** Look back at page 390. The text explains how three things came to be. Write what they are and why they are there at the end of the night. Provide evidence to support your answer.

Key Ideas and Details • Text Evidence

Meet the Author and the Illustrator

Mary-Joan Gerson and Carla Golembe

Mary-Joan Gerson became interested in writing books for children when she and her husband were in Nigeria serving with the Peace Corps. After she returned to the United States, she wanted to write books so that American children could learn about Africa.

Ms. Gerson travels to learn about cultures. *How Night Came from the Sea* grew out of a trip she made to Brazil, where she went to experience the Yoruba culture. The tale shows the importance of women in Yoruba religion. In addition to her work as a writer, Ms. Gerson is a psychologist and on the faculty at New York University.

Carla Golembe is an artist, writer, and teacher. Her paintings have been displayed in art galleries. Of her art she says, "My paintings are the product of my dreams and experiences." Ms. Golembe loves to travel to warm places. When she paints jungles or oceans, she thinks of her experiences in Mexico, Belize, and Hawaii. She likes to use tropical colors in her illustrations.

Here are other books by Mary-Joan Gerson.

Why the Sky Is Far Away: A Nigerian Folktale

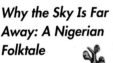

People of Corn: A Mayan Story

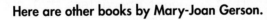

Use the *Reader's and Writer's Notebook* to record your independent reading.

Common Core State Standards
Writing 3.a. Orient the reader by establishing a situation and introducing a narrator and/or characters; organize an event sequence that unfolds naturally. **Also Language 1.**

Let's Write It!

Key Features of a Myth

- a story that usually explains how something in nature came to be

- characters often represent some part of nature

- often passed down by word of mouth

READING STREET ONLINE
GRAMMAR JAMMER
www.ReadingStreet.com

Myth

A **myth** is a story that often tries to explain something about nature. Some myths have been passed down through generations by word of mouth. The student model on the next page is an example of a myth.

Writing Prompt *How Night Came from the Sea* tells how people long ago explained the concept of night and day. Think about how you might explain the pattern of night and day. Now write a myth that includes your explanation.

Writer's Checklist

Remember, you should . . .

- ☑ create an imaginative story.

- ☑ build the plot to a climax.

- ☑ invent characters that are connected to natural forces.

- ☑ use details to describe the setting.

- ☑ have subject-verb agreement in both simple and compound sentences.

Night and Day

Long, long ago, when **Earth was** young, night and day did not exist. It was dark all the time, and people's hearts and **deeds were** also dark. One day, Sun climbed high in the sky and let his warm, bright light shine. But when Sun looked down and saw how badly **people were** behaving, he became sad and hid himself away in a cave. Again, Earth was plunged into darkness.

One young girl, Allegra, wanted Sun to return, so she went to find Sun in his cave. Allegra begged Sun to give people another chance. Sun finally agreed to climb into the sky again. He said he would travel across the sky and then he would rest in his cave for a while. Allegra told the people that if they misbehaved, Sun would go away for good. Most people gave up their bad ways, and that is how we came to have night and day.

Subjects and verbs agree in number.

Writing Trait Sentences
A variety of compound and simple sentences are used.

Genre
Myths explain something in the natural world.

Conventions

Subject-Verb Agreement

Remember Subject-verb agreement means that the subject and verb of a sentence agree in number: both are plural or both are singular.

Common Core State Standards
Literature 2. Determine a theme of a
story, drama, or poem from details
in the text; summarize the text.
Also Literature 1., 3., 9.

ᎯᏇ ᎯᏇ ᎯᏇ ᎯᏇ ᎯᏇ ᎯᏇ ᎯᏇ ᎯᏇ ᎯᏇ ᎯᏇ ᎯᏇ ᎯᏇ ᎯᏇ

Science in Reading

Genre
Myth

- Myths are stories that explain how things in nature came to be.

- Most myths are passed from generation to generation until they are finally written down.

- Many cultures from around the world have their own myths. Myths are an important part of a culture's traditions.

- Read "The Ant and the Bear." Look for elements that make this story a myth.

THE ANT AND THE BEAR

from SPIRIT OF THE CEDAR PEOPLE

MORE STORIES AND PAINTINGS OF CHIEF LELOOSKA

Into the newly created world came Whone, the Changer. It was he who set the world right. Whone piled up earth and made the mountains. He planted trees on the hills and in the valleys. He planted all the edible roots that we now use for food. Then Whone took a stick and dug the rivers, and he called the salmon forth from the sea to feed the children of men.

ᎯᏇ ᎯᏇ ᎯᏇ ᎯᏇ ᎯᏇ ᎯᏇ ᎯᏇ ᎯᏇ ᎯᏇ ᎯᏇ ᎯᏇ ᎯᏇ ᎯᏇ

After Whone had grown weary of all his good work, he called upon the animal people to help him make rules for the new world. One of the most important decisions was the proper length for the daylight and the dark. For in that time the daylight came and went as it pleased. A day might last a whole season or be as quick as a blink of the eye. Clearly something needed to be done, so Whone chose Ant and Bear for the task.

Bear was big and fat and lazy. He yawned, scratched himself, and looked down at the tiny Ant, the little Sky Yack, and said in a deep, gruff voice, "I am Chetwin! I am the Bear! I think half the year should be dark and half of it light. Then we bears could sleep for half the year and eat for the other half."

Let's **Think** About…

What do you think this myth will try to explain? **Myth**

Let's **Think** About…

Compare and contrast the exploits and adventures of the characters in the classical tale *The Horned Toad Prince* with the characters in the traditional tale *The Ant and the Bear*. How are they alike and different? **Myth**

Let's **Think** About...

How are the characters of Bear and Ant alike? **Myth**

Ant was a scrawny little fellow, and he had a habit of tugging nervously at his belt when he talked. But Ant was also proud and stubborn. He was not about to let Bear decide anything for him. Ant pulled himself up as tall as he could and shouted up to the great Bear, "No, no! Never do! Never do! Never do! We must have *kai tacheelah, kai tacheelah, chowow, chaloose!* We must have daylight and dark, daylight and dark, every day!"

Bear, who was used to having his own way, leaned down and stared in Ant's face. "*Yo yoks! Sky ta che!*" he growled. "Half of the year dark and half of it light!"

And so the argument went on. Ant began to jump up and down in excitement, all the while yanking nervously at his belt and squeaking at the top of his voice, "Daylight and dark! Daylight and dark! Every day!"

Bear became very angry. He roared louder and louder, "Half the year dark and half of it light!"

On and on they shouted. How long they argued no one knows because there was no proper length for the daylight and the dark.

At last Bear grew weary. "All right, Ant, have it your way," he said. "Daylight and dark every day. But we bears will have it our way too! We will go into the mountains and sleep for half the year. Then we will wake up and eat."

Bear began to lumber away. Then he turned back to Ant. "And do you know what we will eat, Ant?" asked Bear with a big grin. "We will eat you! And all your relatives! We will tear open the old rotten logs and find you and eat you!"

"No, no, you will not," cried Ant. "We will grow wings and fly away!"

And so little Ant won the argument. There would be daylight and dark every day. Ant was pleased with himself, but then he looked down at his waist. In his excitement and all that yanking on his belt, Ant had cinched himself up so tight that he was almost cut in two. Ant had paid an awful price for his victory. He was left with the little skinny waist that all ants have to this very day.

We know this story must be true because ants do have tiny waists; they do grow wings and fly out of old rotten logs in the late summer; and bears do rumble off into the mountains and sleep for half the year. Most of all, we know it is true because we have daylight and dark every single day!

Let's **Think** About...

How are Bear and Ant different? **Myth**

Let's **Think** About...

Reading Across Texts Both *How Night Came from the Sea* and "The Ant and the Bear" are myths that explain the cycle of day and night. Summarize each explanation.

Writing Across Texts Which explanation of day and night do you like better? Write a paragraph that tells why you chose the one you did.

Common Core State Standards

Language 4.a. Use context (e.g., definitions, examples, or restatements in text) as a clue to the meaning of a word or phrase. **Also Foundational Skills 4., 4.b., Speaking/Listening 1.c., 4., Language 4.**

Let's

Learn

It!

READING STREET ONLINE
ONLINE STUDENT EDITION
www.ReadingStreet.com

Vocabulary

Unfamiliar Words

Context Clues Words, phrases, and sentences around an unfamiliar word may give you clues to the word's meaning. Using these context clues helps you figure out what the unfamiliar word means.

Practice It! Find the words *surging* and *currents* in the first paragraph, page 385. What do you think these words mean? How do the other words in each sentence and nearby sentences help you figure out what they mean? List other unfamiliar words in the story you figured out by using context clues.

Fluency

Appropriate Phrasing

Partner Reading Following the rhythm of the sentences as you read makes the story flow smoothly.

Practice It! With a partner, practice reading aloud *How Night Came from the Sea*, page 380. Notice the similar structure of the sentences in the description of the world without night. Read with rhythm to give meaning to the descriptions.

400

Listening and Speaking

When you participate in a performance, make eye contact with others.

Readers' Theater

In Readers' Theater, people read aloud from a script that portrays a scene from a story or play.

Practice It! With a small group, choose a scene from *How Night Came from the Sea*. Assign roles for the characters. Use details from the story to find clues about your character and how to speak his or her dialogue. Practice your lines with the group. Perform your scene for the class.

Tips

Listening ...

- Listen attentively as others speak.
- Make relevant comments.

Speaking ...

- Make eye contact with other characters as you speak.
- Raise or lower your voice to express excitement or disappointment.
- Use complete sentences with correct subject-verb agreement.

Teamwork ...

- Make suggestions to improve the performance of group members.

Oral Vocabulary

Let's Talk About

Storms

- Express opinions about liking or disliking storms.

- Describe how people protect themselves during a storm.

- Speak clearly and make eye contact.

READING STREET ONLINE
CONCEPT TALK VIDEO
www.ReadingStreet.com

Common Core State Standards
Language 4.b. Use common, grade-appropriate Greek and Latin affixes and roots as clues to the meaning of a word (e.g., telegraph, photograph, autograph).

Envision It! | Words to Know

destruction

shatter

surge

expected

forecasts

inland

**READING STREET ONLINE
VOCABULARY ACTIVITIES**
www.ReadingStreet.com

Vocabulary Strategy for

🎯 Word Origins: Roots

Word Structure When you read an academic word you do not know, try to identify the root. The word *transport* has the Middle English root *port*, which means "to carry," and the prefix *trans-*, which means "across." Now you know the meaning of *transport* is "to carry across." Use what you know about roots as you follow these directions.

1. When you read an unknown word, first try to identify its root. The word *construction* contains the root *struct*.

2. The root *struct* means "to build."

3. Look for a prefix, suffix, or ending in the word. The prefix *con-* means "with" or "together." The suffix *-ion* means "the act of" or "the result of." So *construction* means "the act of building together."

4. Try the meaning in the sentence to see if it makes sense.

As you read "Hurricanes," use what you know about roots to figure out the meanings of academic words such as *destruction* and *tropical*.

Words to Write Reread "Hurricanes." Have you ever been in a severe storm or seen one on TV? Write about the experience. Use words from the *Words to Know* list in your writing.

HURRICANES

A hurricane is a large storm with high winds and heavy rain. It needs heat and moisture to form, so the best hurricane-producing place is a tropical ocean. As warm, moist air rises, cooler air moves in. Then the air begins to spin. The winds spin around a calm center called the eye. The strongest winds are around the eye. They may have speeds of 200 miles per hour. A hurricane's winds may extend 250 miles from the eye.

If a hurricane stays over water, it keeps pulling heat and moisture from the ocean. But it begins to lose power as it reaches land, where the air is cooler and drier. Once it moves over land, it becomes weak very quickly.

The destruction from a hurricane comes from both wind and water. High winds shatter windows and uproot trees. Besides bringing heavy rain, a hurricane can cause a storm surge as winds push ocean water to areas far inland.

Meteorologists watch for and track hurricanes. They issue forecasts telling when a hurricane is expected to arrive so that people can prepare for the storm.

Your Turn!

⏸ **Need a Review?** For additional help with using root words and word structure to determine the meanings of unknown words, see *Words!*

▶ **Ready to Try It?** Read *Eye of the Storm* on pp. 408–419.

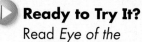

Eye of the

by Stephen Kramer
photographs by Warren Faidley

Genre

Expository Text gives information about real people and events. Be prepared for a few surprises as you read about a real person, Warren Faidley, who experiences a real storm, Hurricane Andrew.

Storm

Chasing Storms with Warren Faidley

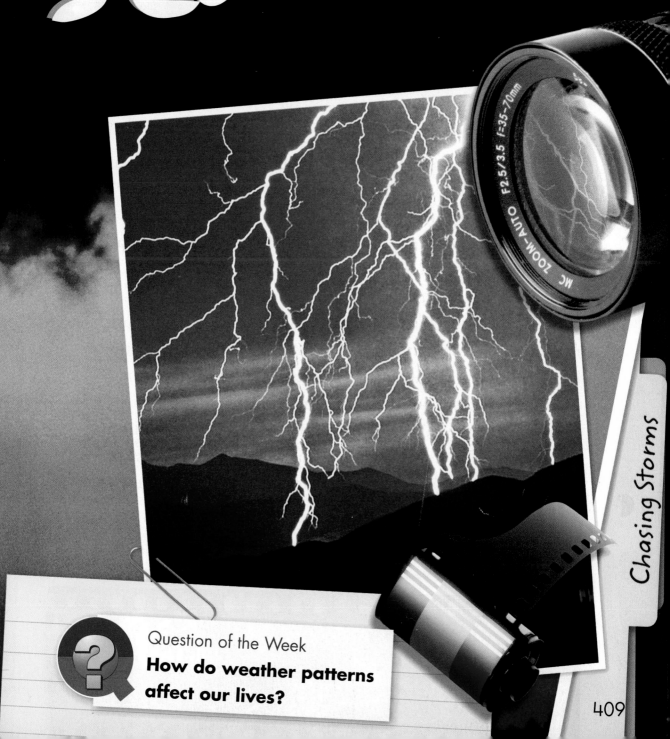

Chasing Storms

Question of the Week
How do weather patterns affect our lives?

Warren Faidley is a storm chaser. Beginning in April and continuing through November, he can be found on the trail of tornadoes, thunderstorms, and hurricanes, photographing their spectacular beauty and power. When he is not out chasing storms, Warren is at home in Tucson, Arizona, where he sells his photographs through his business, a stock photo agency.

SEVERE STORM SPOTTER

Storm Seasons and Chasing

Storms are caused by certain kinds of weather patterns. The same patterns are found in the same areas year after year. For example, every spring, large areas of cool, dry air and warm, moist air collide over the central United States. If the winds are right, tornado-producing thunderstorms appear. That's why tornadoes in the south central United States are most likely to happen in spring. During July and August, shifting winds push moisture from the south up into the Arizona desert. When the cool, moist air is heated by the hot desert, storm clouds form. That's why Tucson has summer thunderstorms. In the late summer and early fall, when oceans in the northern Atlantic are warmest, tropical storms form off the west coast of Africa. A few of these turn into the hurricanes that sometimes batter the east and gulf coasts of North America.

April	May	June	July	August	September	October	November

Tornadoes   Thunderstorms   Hurricanes

Because Warren is a storm chaser, his life also follows these weather patterns. Each spring, Warren goes on the road, traveling through parts of the United States likely to be hit by tornadoes. During the summer, he stays near Tucson so he can photograph the thunderstorms that develop over the desert. In the late summer and fall, he keeps an eye on weather activity in the Atlantic Ocean, ready to fly to the east coast if a hurricane appears.

Chasing Hurricanes

By the first or second week in September, Tucson's summer thunderstorms are ending. There won't be much lightning until the next summer. But that works out well for Warren, because August through November are months when hurricanes sometimes strike the east and gulf coasts of the United States.

Although Tucson is far from the areas where hurricanes hit, Warren begins his hurricane chases from home. He uses his computer to get information on tropical storms or hurricanes moving toward North America.

"I can't go out and look for a hurricane, or watch one develop, like I can with tornadoes and lightning," says Warren. "When a hurricane is forming, I look at satellite pictures, I listen to weather forecasters talk about it, and I pay attention to what scientists and meteorologists think the hurricane is going to do. Hurricane paths are very hard to predict. Often a hurricane will roar right up to the coast and then stop and go away. So I want to be sure that I'm going to have a storm to photograph before I travel all the way to the east coast!"

When weather forecasters predict that a hurricane will strike the eastern United States, Warren flies to a city near the place the storm is expected to arrive. Flying is faster than driving Shadow Chaser* all the way from Tucson. Besides, a vehicle would not be safe during a hurricane. Branches, boards, and other loose materials carried by hurricane winds quickly shatter windows and damage any cars left outside.

*Shadow Chaser is Warren's specially equipped four-wheel-drive vehicle.

"Hurricanes are the only type of storm where I'm shooting destruction in progress. With tornadoes, you're not usually close enough to shoot the destruction—if you are, you're in a very dangerous place! With hurricanes I'm shooting palm trees bending until they're ready to break and floodwaters splashing over the bank. Those kinds of shots really separate hurricane photos from the others. Most of my hurricane photos are wind shots with heavy rains.

"Finding a place to stay safe while I take hurricane photos is also a challenge. I like to find a solid garage. A good concrete garage is going to be able to withstand the high winds. Another danger with hurricanes is that the powerful winds can lift the seawater and carry it a long ways inland. This is called a storm surge, and it's like a flood from the ocean. When you're picking a spot to stay during the hurricane, you need to have some idea of how high the storm surge might be and how far inland it will go."

Hurricane Andrew

On Saturday, August 22, 1992, after a seven-hour flight from Tucson, Warren arrived in Miami, Florida. He had arranged to meet Mike Laca and Steve Wachholder, two other experienced hurricane chasers. Hurricane Andrew was expected to hit the Florida coast in two days, so Mike, Steve, and Warren had agreed to work together to predict where the storm was going to hit, scout out a safe place to stay, and photograph the storm.

When Warren arrived, the three compared notes. They knew, from weather reports and bulletins from the National Hurricane Center, that Andrew had the potential to become a very dangerous storm. The hurricane was about 520 miles from Miami. It was heading in their direction at about 14 miles per hour. The storm had sustained wind speeds of 110 miles per hour, and they were expected to increase. Warren, Mike, and Steve agreed to get a good night's sleep and meet at noon the next day to go over the latest forecasts. When they had a better idea of where the storm would hit, they could start looking for a safe place to stay.

Mike and Warren found a sturdy, seven-story parking garage in an area called Coconut Grove. It was built with thick concrete walls and looked like a fortress, but the outside walls also had large square openings that could be used for taking pictures. Fort Andrew, as Warren began calling the building, was located on a slight hill, which would help protect it from the storm surge.

Warren, Mike, and Steve find shelter in a seven-story parking garage.

Steve, Mike, and Warren set up a "command center" on the fifth floor of the garage. They stockpiled food, water, rope, and waterproof bags as well as their photography equipment. The three took turns monitoring the latest updates on TV and radios.

As the sun set, Warren and his friends waited anxiously. By 11:00 P.M., there was still no sign of the storm. They began to wonder whether the hurricane had changed direction. But reports on the TV and radio kept saying that Andrew was still headed straight for land—and its strongest winds were expected to hit the area where Warren, Steve, and Mike were staying.

About 2:30 A.M., Hurricane Andrew finally arrived. Warren was watching when bright flashes began appearing in the northeast. The lights looked like fireworks. Actually, they were sparks and explosions as the approaching winds knocked down power lines and transformers. Warren will never forget the sounds of that night:

"At first, there was just the noise of sparking electrical lines and trash cans rolling down the street. But as time passed, the wind just kept getting louder and louder and scarier and scarier."

415

During the next hour, Steve and Warren tried several times to measure the wind speeds with an instrument called an anemometer. Steve held the instrument out an opening in the wall and Warren used his flashlight to read the dial. When the wind reached 65 miles per hour they gave up.

"I can't hold on anymore," Steve called above the howling winds. "It's too dangerous! I can't hold on!" The winds were carrying raindrops sideways through the air.

"Around 3:45 A.M., we began to hear bursts of breaking glass, as the winds became strong enough to blow in windows. Sometimes the crack of breaking glass was followed by a tinkling sound, like wind chimes, as the wind blew the broken glass along the streets. Inside the garage, car alarm sirens wailed as cars were hit by blasts of wind. Later, even the sound of alarms and the crack of breaking glass disappeared in the roar of the hurricane winds."

As the wind wailed in the darkness, Warren wondered how he was ever going to get any pictures. He worried that by the time it became light, the hurricane winds would die down. He worried about missing the chance to see what was going on outside.

About 5:15 A.M., the hurricane winds reached their peak. The parking garage began to shake. Wind slammed into the concrete walls with the force of bombs. Large sprinkler pipes fastened to the ceilings in the garage began to work their way loose. Several pipes collapsed and fell to the floor.

Now the winds were blowing so hard inside the garage that it was impossible to walk even a few feet in areas that weren't blocked by walls. The roar of the wind turned into a sound like the constant blast of jet engines.

Finally, around 6:00 A.M., with the winds still howling, Warren saw the first faint light of the new day. As the sky gradually turned a strange blue color, Steve, Mike, and Warren looked out on a scene of terrible destruction. Broken boats, and parts of boats, had been carried by the storm surge from the marina almost to the garage. A tree that had been torn from the ground during the night had smashed into the side of a parked truck. Although most of the buildings around the garage were still standing, many had been heavily damaged.

When there was finally enough light for his camera, Warren headed outside. Leaning into the strong winds, he carefully made his way toward the marina. At times, gusts of wind knocked him to the ground. Wreckage from boats and buildings was still flying through the air. Warren took pictures of the wind bending the trees near the marina and the broken boats on the shore.

Warren continued walking along the beach, shooting more pictures as the sky turned light. After about an hour, the wind began to quiet and the rain became more gentle. Now Warren began to wade carefully toward the marina, taking more pictures of the wreckage ahead of him. Other people were arriving to look at the damage and to see if their boats had survived.

After a tour of the marina, Warren went back to the beach. It was littered with boat parts, clothing, and dead fish. There was even a photo album opened to a wet page. More and more people arrived to see what remained of their homes or boats.

Warren finally returned to his motel, where he slept for ten hours. The next day, when he drove back to the Miami airport, his camera bags were filled with rolls of exposed film. His arm ached where the wind had slammed him into a railing after he left the parking garage. Still, as the airplane took off from Miami, it was hard for Warren to imagine that two nights earlier he had been watching, listening to, and photographing the destructive winds of Hurricane Andrew.

Common Core State Standards

Informational Text 1. Refer to details and examples in a text when explaining what the text says explicitly and when drawing inferences from the text. **Also Informational Text 7., Writing 9.**

Think Critically

1. Storm chasing can be a dangerous job. What other jobs do you know of that are dangerous? Why do you think someone might choose to do one of these jobs?

Text to World

2. Reread pages 416–417. How does the author use details to help you understand the force of the winds? **Think Like an Author**

3. Reread pages 410–411. How do various weather patterns have an effect on the way a storm chaser lives his life?

Cause and Effect

4. Why do you think the author chose to use so many photos in his article? Do they help you predict what the life of a storm chaser is like? Why or why not?

Predict and Set Purpose

5. Look Back and Write Look back at page 413. Why does Warren Faidley need a safe place to stay when he photographs a hurricane? What does he look for in a shelter? Provide evidence to support your answer.

Key Ideas and Details • Text Evidence

Stephen Kramer

When Stephen Kramer interviewed Warren Faidley for this book, he was impressed by Warren's enthusiasm. "Warren loves the excitement of trying to be in the right place at the right time to capture the perfect photo of a storm. I also learned about Warren's respect for the danger of lightning, tornadoes, and hurricanes. Warren knows how to stay safe in dangerous weather."

About himself, Mr. Kramer says, "I've been picking up leaves, looking at flowers, and learning about animals for as long as I can remember." Mr. Kramer studied biology in college. While attending graduate school in Arizona, he did research on the songs of a bird called the Townsend's Solitaire. Now he teaches fourth grade near Vancouver, Washington. "I write science books because I love science and want to share my excitement with young readers," he says. "Science helps us uncover the beauty and wonder of nature. I also hope that my books might inspire some of my readers to become scientists!"

Here are other books by Stephen Kramer.

Use the *Reader's and Writer's Notebook* to record your independent reading.

421

Common Core State Standards

Writing 2.a. Introduce a topic clearly and group related information in paragraphs and sections; include formatting (e.g., headings), illustrations, and multimedia when useful to aiding comprehension. **Also Writing 4., Language 1., 3.c.**

Let's Write It!

Key Features of a Formal Letter

- includes a heading, address, salutation, body, closing, and signature

- focuses on one subject

- uses business-like tone

READING STREET ONLINE
GRAMMAR JAMMER
www.ReadingStreet.com

Expository

Formal Letter

A **formal letter** focuses on one subject and has a business-like tone. The student model on the next page is an example of a formal letter.

Writing Prompt Imagine you are creating a book about storms. Write a formal letter to Warren Faidley asking him for permission to use his photos.

Writer's Checklist

Remember, you should . . .

☑ include all six parts of a formal letter.

☑ use the appropriate language for your audience and purpose.

☑ give a short, simple explanation of why you are writing.

☑ write legibly in either cursive or manuscript printing.

785 Winthrop Street
Easton, PA 18040
January 11, 20__

Mr. Warren Faidley
14 Main Street
Tucson, Arizona 85705

Dear Mr. Faidley:

The book <u>Eye of the Storm</u> **inspired** me to make my own book about storms for a class project. I would like to add photographs to my book.

I am asking for your permission to use some of your wonderful storm photographs from <u>Eye of the Storm</u> in my project. My project is due at the end of March. I **will send** you a copy when it is finished.

I **look** forward to hearing from you about permission to use your photographs.

Sincerely,
Pat Stephanos

**Writing Trait
Organization**
A formal letter includes a heading and an address.

Genre A **formal letter** uses a business-like tone.

Past, present, and **future** tenses of verbs are used correctly.

Conventions

Past, Present, and Future Tenses

Remember The **past tense** expresses an action that took place in the past. The **present tense** expresses an action that is taking place now. **The future tense** expresses an action that will happen in the future.

423

Common Core State Standards

Informational Text 5. Describe the overall structure (e.g., chronology, comparison, cause/effect, problem/solution) of events, ideas, concepts, or information in a text or part of a text. **Also Language 3.c.**

21st Century Skills
INTERNET GUY

Web Site Want to quickly find information at a Web site? Type Control + F. Then type the information you are looking for. Hit return. A great trick!

- Every Web site has a home page, which introduces the site. You can move around a Web site by clicking on the links there.

- Links are buttons or underlined words or phrases set in a different color. When you click on a link, your computer will open a new Web page that contains the information indicated by the link.

- Read "Severe Weather Safety." Compare the writing on the Web pages with formal writing you practice in school.

Severe Weather Safety

After reading *Eye of the Storm*, Natalia wants to know more about storm safety. Where she lives, in northern Illinois, thunderstorms are frequent during the spring and summer. What should she do if she is caught outside during a thunderstorm, she wonders. And if she is inside during a storm, are there any things she shouldn't do?

Natalia decides to search for information on the Internet. Her search takes her to the Web site of a regional weather service office.

File   Edit   View   Favorites   Tools   Help

 http://www.url.here

Regional Weather Service Office

Staying Safe in Severe Weather

Contents

Tornado Safety

Flash Flood Safety

Lightning Safety

Winter Storm/Blizzard Preparedness and Safety

Hurricane Safety

Other Severe Weather Safety Links

In the United States, lightning causes about 100 deaths each year. This is more than tornadoes and hurricanes combined.

Natalia clicks on a link that takes her to a Web page about severe weather safety. After skimming the contents of the page, she decides to click on the Lightning Safety link.

Clicking on the Lightning Safety link opens a new Web page on Natalia's computer screen. As the link indicates, the Web page contains information about lightning safety.

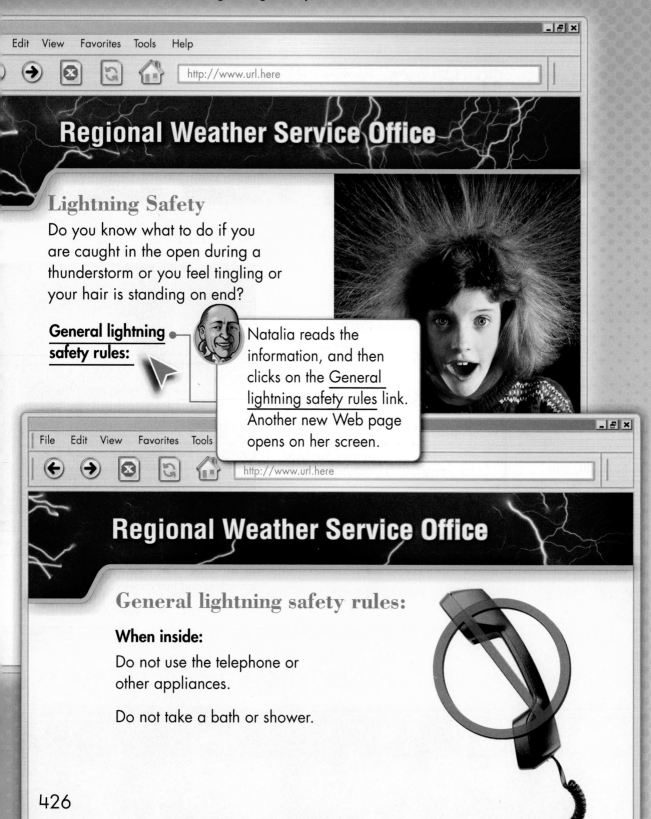

Edit   View   Favorites   Tools   Help

http://www.url.here

Regional Weather Service Office

Lightning Safety

Do you know what to do if you are caught in the open during a thunderstorm or you feel tingling or your hair is standing on end?

General lightning safety rules:

Natalia reads the information, and then clicks on the General lightning safety rules link. Another new Web page opens on her screen.

File   Edit   View   Favorites   Tools

http://www.url.here

Regional Weather Service Office

General lightning safety rules:

When inside:

Do not use the telephone or other appliances.

Do not take a bath or shower.

Regional Weather Service Office

When outside:

Go to a safe place right away, such as inside a strong building. A hard-top automobile with the windows up can also offer fair protection.

If you are boating or swimming, get out of the water right away and move to a safe place away from the water!

If you are in a wooded area, take cover under a thick growth of relatively small trees.

If you feel your hair standing on end, squat with your head between your knees. **Do not lie flat!**

Stay away from: isolated trees or other tall objects, bodies of water, sheds, fences, convertible automobiles, tractors, and motorcycles.

If you are outside and your hair stands on end, squat with your head between your knees.

427

Common Core State Standards

Language 4.b. Use common, grade-appropriate Greek and Latin affixes and roots as clues to the meaning of a word (e.g., *telegraph, photograph, autograph*). **Also Foundational Skills 4.b., Speaking/Listening 5.**

Let's **Learn** It!

READING STREET ONLINE
ONLINE STUDENT EDITION
www.ReadingStreet.com

Vocabulary

Root Words

Word Structure Many academic words in the English language contain roots, or word parts, from other languages. When you read a word whose meaning you are unsure of, look for a root word that can help you figure out the word's meaning.

Practice It! Find the word *fortress* on page 414 in *Eye of the Storm*. The root *fort* comes from the Middle English word meaning "strong." Use the root to help you figure out the meaning of *fortress*.

Fluency

Appropriate Phrasing

Partner Reading Using punctuation cues helps you know when to slow down, pause, or change the pitch of your voice as you read.

Practice It! With a partner, practice reading *Eye of the Storm*, pages 416–417. Slow down for commas. Stop for periods. When each of you has finished, offer suggestions on how to improve.

428

Media Literacy

When you give a presentation to a group, use proper grammar.

Weather Broadcast

In a weather broadcast, an announcer tells about the weather in an area and the expected weather for the next few days.

Practice It! Use information from *Eye of the Storm* to create a weather report for the day Hurricane Andrew struck land. Prepare by watching TV weather reports. Notice the informal language the reporter uses and the way he or she delivers the broadcast. Use maps when you make your report.

Tips

Listening ...

- Listen attentively to the speaker.
- Be ready to ask questions.

Speaking ...

- Use accurate information in your broadcast.
- Speak informally but clearly as you deliver your report from your written notes.

Teamwork ...

- Ask detailed questions.
- Answer questions with details and examples.

3 DAY FORECAST

TUE	WED	THU
80°	83°	8

Oral Vocabulary

Let's Talk About

Changes in Nature

- List ways the natural world can change its appearance.

- Offer examples of those changes.

- Speak loudly enough so everyone can hear your ideas.

READING STREET ONLINE
CONCEPT TALK VIDEO
www.ReadingStreet.com

Common Core State Standards
Literature 1. Refer to details and examples in a text when explaining what the text says explicitly and when drawing inferences from the text.

Envision It! | Skill Strategy

Skill

Strategy

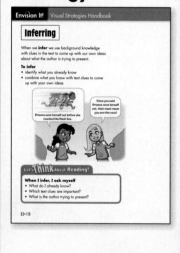

READING STREET ONLINE
ENVISION IT! ANIMATIONS
www.ReadingStreet.com

Comprehension Skill

🎯 Generalize

- A generalization is a broad statement based on several examples.

- A generalization can be valid (logical) or faulty (wrong) depending on the number of examples on which it is based and on how logical and careful the thinking is.

- When making a generalization, ask yourself if it is supported by facts. A faulty one is not.

- Use the graphic organizer below to help you identify generalizations as you read "Davy Crockett."

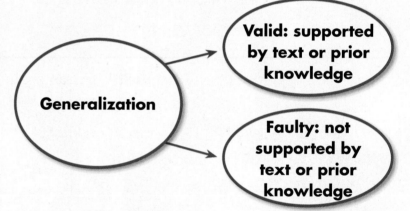

Comprehension Strategy

🎯 Inferring

When you infer, you combine your background knowledge with evidence from the text to come up with your own idea about what the author is trying to present. Active readers often infer the ideas, morals, lessons, and themes of a written work.

DAVY CROCKETT

David "Davy" Crockett was born on August 17, 1786, in Tennessee. As a young man, Crockett spent a lot of time hunting. Most of the food his family ate came from the animals he hunted. They ate the meat of deer, elk, turkeys, and bears. One year, Crockett said he shot more than fifty bears.

Skill What clue word signals a generalization? Can it be supported by facts?

When Crockett was twenty-eight, he fought against the British in the War of 1812. After the war, he explored the forests of Tennessee. In 1821, Davy was elected to the Tennessee congress. He was in office for four years. In 1827, he was elected to the U.S. House of Representatives. After losing in 1831, he ran again in 1833 and won. He stayed in office until 1835.

Strategy What can you infer about Davy Crockett's personality? Provide evidence to support your answer.

After leaving office, Davy traveled to Texas. He fought to make Texas independent from Mexico. Crockett was killed during the Battle of the Alamo in March of 1836.

Davy Crockett had the most exciting and interesting life of any frontiersman. He was a skilled rifleman and hunter. He fought in wars and was elected to public office several times.

Skill Which statement in this paragraph has a faulty generalization? Explain why.

Your Turn!

❚❚ Need a Review? See the *Envision It! Handbook* for help with generalizing and inferring.

▶ Ready to Try It? Use what you've learned about generalizing as you read *Paul Bunyan*.

Common Core State Standards
Language 4.b. Use common, grade-appropriate Greek and Latin affixes and roots as clues to the meaning of a word (e.g., *telegraph, photograph, autograph*).

Envision It! | Words to Know

harness

lumberjacks

thaw

announcement

feature

requirements

unnatural

untamed

Vocabulary Strategy for

🔄 Affixes: Suffixes

Word Structure A suffix is a word part that is added to the end of a word. When a suffix is added to a base word, it changes the meaning of the word. For example, the Middle English base word of *boldly* is *bold*, which means "fearless" or "courageous." The suffix *-ly* means "having the form or appearance of." So, *boldly* means "appearing courageous."

1. Look at the unknown word to see if it has a base word that you know.

2. Check to see if a suffix has been added to the base word.

3. Ask yourself how the suffix changes the meaning of the base word.

4. Try that meaning in the sentence to see if it makes sense.

Use what you know about suffixes to figure out the meanings of *announcement, requirements, unnatural,* and other unknown words as you read "Working with Babe."

Words to Write Reread "Working with Babe." Write a paragraph about a time when you worked hard. How did you feel when you finished? Use words from the *Words to Know* list in your writing.

Working with Babe

Back in the old days, lumberjacks used oxen to help move logs out of the woods. At first, when Paul Bunyan opened his own logging camp, Babe the Blue Ox did all the work himself. Paul's camp was so successful that Babe soon needed help. At the start of the spring thaw, he put up an announcement calling for oxen to help him.

Besides the obvious feature of being huge, Babe asked that the oxen that applied be

- strong enough to pull logs 300 feet in diameter
- wide enough to hold a 10-foot basket of food on their backs
- tame enough to care for a newborn lamb

Babe did not have time to deal with untamed oxen. He needed them to be able to go right to work. Hundreds of oxen showed up to work. Before being hired, the oxen boldly said they had some requirements of their own. They each wanted ten bags of oats a day. They each wanted a harness lined with the softest fur. And, even though it seemed unnatural, they wanted an endless supply of chocolate chips! It is a well-kept secret that oxen love sweets.

Your Turn!

Need a Review? For help with using suffixes to determine the meanings of unknown words, see *Words!*

Ready to Try It? Read *Paul Bunyan* on pp. 436–449.

435

Tall tales are humorous stories with characters who have superhuman abilities. As you read, think about how the exaggerated details help explain many of the natural features of the American frontier.

PAUL BUNYAN

BY MARY POPE OSBORNE

ILLUSTRATIONS BY HARVEY CHAN

Question of the Week

What causes changes in nature?

It seems an amazing baby was born in the state of Maine. When he was only two weeks old, he weighed more than a hundred pounds, and for breakfast every morning he ate five dozen eggs, ten sacks of potatoes, and a half barrel of mush made from a whole sack of cornmeal. But the baby's strangest feature was his big curly black beard. It was so big and bushy that every morning his poor mother had to comb it with a pine tree.

Except for that beard, the big baby wasn't much trouble to anybody until he was about nine months old. That was when he first started to crawl, and since he weighed over five hundred pounds, he caused an earthquake that shook the whole town.

When the neighbors complained, the baby's parents tried putting him in a giant floating cradle off the coast of Maine. But soon a delegation of citizens went to the baby's parents and said, "We're sorry, folks, but you have to take your son somewhere else. Every time he rolls over in his cradle, huge waves drown all the villages along the coast."

So his parents hauled the giant toddler to a cave in the Maine woods far away from civilization and said good-bye. "We'll think of you often, honey," his mother said, weeping. "But you can't come back home—you're just too big."

"Here, son," his father said. "I'm giving you my ax, my knife, my fishing pole, and some flint rocks. Good-bye and good luck."

After his parents left, the poor bearded baby cried for thirty days and thirty nights. He was so lonely, he cried a whole river of tears. He might have cried himself to death if one day he hadn't heard *flop, flop, flop.*

When the baby looked around, he saw fish jumping in his river of tears. He reached for his father's fishing pole and soon he was catching trout. He used his father's knife to clean and scale what he had caught and his father's ax to cut wood for a fire. He started the fire with his flint rocks and cooked his catch over the flames. Then he ate a big fish dinner and smiled for the first time in a month.

That's the story of how Paul Bunyan came to take care of himself in the Maine woods. And even though he lived alone for the next twenty years, he got along quite well. He hunted and fished. He cut down trees and made fires. He battled winter storms, spring floods, summer flies, and autumn gales.

Nothing, however, prepared Paul Bunyan for the wild weather that occurred on the morning of his twenty-first birthday. It was a cold December day, and when Paul woke up, he noticed gusts of snow blowing past the mouth of his cave. That was natural enough. What was unnatural was that the snow was blue.

"Why, that's beautiful!" Paul said. And he pulled on his red-and-black mackinaw coat, his corn-yellow scarf, and his snow boots. Then grinning from ear to ear, he set out across the blue hills.

The snow fell until the woods were covered with a thick blanket of blue. As Paul walked over huge drifts, bitter winds whistled through the trees and thunder rolled in the sky. But he soon began to hear another sound in the wind—"Maa-maa."

"Who's there?" Paul called.

"Maa-maa."

"Who's there?" said Paul again. His heart was starting to break, for the cries sounded as if they were coming from a baby crying for its mother and father.

"Maa-maa."

"Where are you, baby?" Suddenly Paul saw a tail sticking right up out of a blue snowdrift. When he pulled on the tail, out came the biggest baby ox on Earth. Except for its white horns, the creature was frozen deep blue, the same color as the snow.

"He-ey, babe!" Paul shouted.

"Maa-maa-maa."

"Hush, hush, hush, babe," Paul whispered as he carried the frozen ox back home.

"There now," he said, setting the blue creature gently down in front of his fire. "We'll get you warmed up all right."

Paul fell asleep with his arm around the giant baby ox. He didn't know if the frozen babe would live or not. But when the morning sun began shining on the blue snow outside the cave, Paul felt a soft, wet nose nuzzling his neck. As the rough tongue licked his cheeks and nose and eyelids, Paul's joyous laughter shook the earth. He had found a friend.

Paul Bunyan and Babe the Blue Ox were inseparable after that. Babe grew so fast that Paul liked to close his eyes for a minute, count to ten, then look to see how much Babe had grown. Sometimes the ox would be a whole foot taller. It's a known fact that Babe's full-grown height was finally measured to be forty-two ax handles, and he weighed more than the combined weight of all the fish that ever got away. Babe was so big that when he and Paul trekked through forests, Paul had to look through a telescope just to see what Babe's hind legs were doing.

In those times, huge sections of America were filled with dark green forests. And forests were filled with trees—oceans of trees—trees as far as the eye could see—trees so tall you had to look straight up to see if it was morning, and maybe if you were lucky, you'd catch a glimpse of blue sky.

It would be nice if those trees could have stayed tall and thick forever. But the pioneers needed them to build houses, churches, ships, wagons, bridges, and barns. So one day Paul Bunyan took a good look at all those trees and said, "Babe, stand back. I'm about to invent logging."

"Tim-ber!" he yelled, and he swung his bright steel ax in a wide circle. There was a terrible crash, and when Paul looked around he saw he'd felled ten white pines with a single swing.

Paul bundled up the trees and loaded them onto the ox's back. "All right, Babe," he said. "Let's haul 'em to the Big Onion and send 'em down to a sawmill."

Since both Babe and Paul could cover a whole mile in a single step, it only took about a week to travel from Maine to the Big Onion River in Minnesota.

"She's too crooked. Our logs will get jammed at her curves," Paul said to Babe as he peered through his telescope at the long, winding river. "Let's see what we can do about that." He tied one end of the rope to Babe's harness and the other around the end of the river. Then he shouted, "Pull! Pull!"

And Babe huffed and puffed until he pulled all the kinks out of that winding water.

"There! She's as straight as a gun barrel now," Paul said. "Let's send down these logs."

After that Paul and Babe traveled plenty fast through the untamed North Woods. They cut pine, spruce, and red willow in Minnesota, Michigan, and Wisconsin. They cleared cottonwoods out of Kansas so farmers could plant wheat. They cleared oaks out of Iowa so farmers could plant corn. It seems that the summer after the corn was planted in Iowa, there was a heat wave. It got so hot the corn started to pop. It popped until the whole state was covered with ten feet of popcorn. The wind blew the popcorn over to Kansas, where it fell like a blizzard. Unfortunately, the Kansas cows thought it *was* a blizzard and immediately froze to death.

When next heard of, Paul and Babe were headed to Arizona. Paul dragged his pickax behind him, not realizing he was leaving a big ditch in his tracks. Today that ditch is called the Grand Canyon.

When they got back from out west, Paul and Babe settled down on the Big Onion River. One night, after the two had spent the day rolling thousands of logs down the river, Paul was so tired he couldn't even see straight. As he lay under the stars, his giant body aching, he said, "Babe, it's time I started me a logging camp. I'm gonna hire a bunch of fellers to help me."

You might say this was a turning point for Paul Bunyan. Not for thirty years, since the day his parents had left him crying all alone in that Maine cave, had he asked a single human being for help. But the next day Paul and Babe hiked all over the northern timberlands, posting signs that said: LOGGERS NEEDED TO WORK FOR PAUL BUNYAN. IF INTERESTED, COME TO BIG ONION, MINNESOTA, TO APPLY.

Word spread fast. Since all the woodsmen had heard of Paul Bunyan, hundreds of thousands of them hurried to Big Onion, eager to be part of his crew.

Paul wanted the biggest and brawniest men for his camp, so he made an announcement to all the men who'd gathered to apply for the job. "There's only two requirements," he said. "All my loggers have to be over ten feet tall and able to pop six buttons off their shirts with one breath."

Well, about a thousand of the lumberjacks met those requirements, and Paul hired them all. Then he built a gigantic logging camp with bunkhouses a mile long and ten beds high. The camp's chow table was so long that it took a week to pass the salt and pepper from one end to the other. Paul and Babe dug a few ponds to provide drinking water for everyone. Today we call those ponds the Great Lakes.

But feeding that crew of giants was a bigger problem. One day Paul's cook, Sourdough Sam, said to Paul, "Boss, there's no way I can make enough flapjacks for these hungry fellers. Every morning the ones who don't get seconds threaten to kill me."

The next day Paul built Sam a flapjack griddle the size of an ice-skating rink. Then he lit a forest fire underneath that burned night and day.

"But how'm I supposed to grease this thing?" Sam asked.

"Every morning before dawn we'll get a hundred men to strap bacon fat to the bottoms of their shoes and skate around the griddle till you're ready to cook," Paul said.

Well, after Paul got the flapjack griddle all squared away, he figured he needed a bookkeeper to keep track of all the food bills. So he hired a man named Johnny Inkslinger. Johnny kept the payroll, and he took care of Babe's hay and grain bills, and about ten thousand and two other things. He used a fountain pen that was twenty feet long and connected by a giant hose to a lake filled with ink. It's said that Johnny figured out he could save over four hundred and twenty gallons of ink a year just by not crossing his *t*'s and dotting his *i*'s.

Everything at the Big Onion Lumber Company ran pretty smoothly until the year of the Hard Winter. That winter it was so cold that one day Shot Gunderson, Paul's foreman, rode up to Paul's shanty on his saddled bear with a whole list of problems.

"Boss, we've got trouble!" he said. "When the fellers go out to work, their feet are getting so frostbitten, they're starting to fall off."

"That's bad," Paul said, scratching his beard. "Well, tell the fellers to let their whiskers grow. Then when their beards get down to their feet, they can knit them into socks."

"Good thinkin'," said Shot.

"What else?" said Paul.

"The flames for all the lanterns are freezing!"

"Well, just take the frozen flames outside and store them somewhere," Paul said. "Then wait for them to melt in the spring."

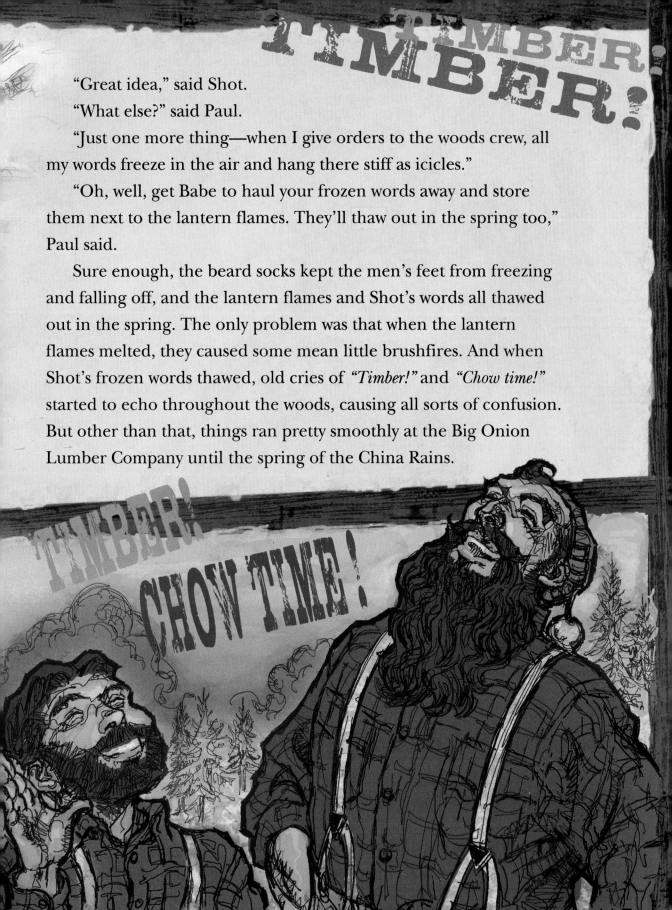

"Great idea," said Shot.

"What else?" said Paul.

"Just one more thing—when I give orders to the woods crew, all my words freeze in the air and hang there stiff as icicles."

"Oh, well, get Babe to haul your frozen words away and store them next to the lantern flames. They'll thaw out in the spring too," Paul said.

Sure enough, the beard socks kept the men's feet from freezing and falling off, and the lantern flames and Shot's words all thawed out in the spring. The only problem was that when the lantern flames melted, they caused some mean little brushfires. And when Shot's frozen words thawed, old cries of *"Timber!"* and *"Chow time!"* started to echo throughout the woods, causing all sorts of confusion. But other than that, things ran pretty smoothly at the Big Onion Lumber Company until the spring of the China Rains.

447

One day that spring, Shot Gunderson burst into Paul's shanty with his pant legs soaking wet. "Boss, we've got a problem! The rains are starting to come *up* from the ground instead of down from the sky."

"They must be coming from China," said Paul. "Order two thousand umbrellas. When they come, cut the handles off and replace them with snowshoe straps."

Shot did as Paul said, and soon all the loggers were wearing umbrellas on their shoes to keep the China Rains from shooting up their pant legs.

Unfortunately, the China Rains caused a crop of ten-foot mosquitoes to attack the camp. The men tried using chicken wire for mosquito nets. Then they started barricading the doors and windows of the bunkhouse with two-ton boulders to keep them out. Finally they had to vacate the bunkhouse altogether when the mosquitoes tore off the roof.

"Get some giant bumblebees," Paul ordered Shot. "They'll get rid of the mosquitoes."

Shot did as Paul said. The only problem was, the bees and the mosquitoes fell madly in love, and soon they were having children. Since the children had stingers on both ends, they caught the loggers both coming and going!

But Paul finally outsmarted the bee-squitoes.

"If there's one thing a bee-squito loves more than stinging, it's sweets," Paul said. So he got them to swarm to a Hawaiian sugar ship docked in Lake Superior. And when the whole bunch got too fat to move, he shipped them to a circus in Florida.

Well, there's stories and stories about Paul Bunyan, Babe the Blue Ox, and the Big Onion Lumber Company. For many years, old loggers sat around potbellied stoves and told about the good old times with Paul. They told how Paul and Babe logged all the trees in Minnesota, then moved on to Washington, Oregon, and Alaska. And when last heard of, the two were somewhere off the Arctic Circle.

The old loggers are all gone now, but many of their stories still hang frozen in the cold forest air of the North Woods, waiting to be told. Come spring, when they start to thaw, some of them might just start telling themselves. It's been known to happen.

Common Core State Standards

Literature 1. Refer to details and examples in a text when explaining what the text says explicitly and when drawing inferences from the text. **Also Writing 9.**

Envision It! | Retell

Think Critically

1. Tall tales are written with exaggeration that helps portray the story or the character as humorous. Have you ever told a story and exaggerated the details? Did it make the story funnier? How? **Text to Self**

2. A tall tale uses common speech and exaggerated details to tell a humorous story. What are some examples of common speech in the story? What expressions would you have used in the story? **Think Like an Author**

3. Use details from the story to support the generalization that Paul Bunyan and Babe the Blue Ox were inseparable. **Generalize**

4. Think about how Paul acts and what he does when he finds a baby blue ox in a snowdrift. What can you infer about Paul's personality from his actions? **Inferring**

5. **Look Back and Write** Look back at the question on page 437. How does this tall tale explain changes in nature? Provide evidence to support your answer.

   Key Ideas and Details • Text Evidence

Meet the Author

MARY POPE OSBORNE

Growing up, Mary Pope Osborne lived in many different places. Ms. Pope's father was in the military, and so her family traveled around a lot. Like Paul Bunyan, she traveled and lived in many different countries and states, but without the ax and a blue ox. As a young girl, she lived in Austria, Oklahoma, Florida, Virginia, and North Carolina. As a teenager, Ms. Pope found she enjoyed discovering new towns and cities.

In college, Ms. Pope realized she could also find adventure by staying in one place. She majored in religion and theater, and discovered that she satisfied her love of learning about faraway cultures. After college, Ms. Pope visited many of the countries she had read about. She lived in a cave in Greece and traveled in "rickety vans" across Asia and the Middle East.

Ms. Pope is the author of the popular *Magic Tree House* series. Her characters have adventures just like hers!

Use the *Reader's and Writer's Notebook* to record your independent reading.

Common Core State Standards

Writing 2.a. Introduce a topic clearly and group related information in paragraphs and sections; include formatting (e.g., headings), illustrations, and multimedia when useful to aiding comprehension. **Also Language 1., 1.f.**

Let's Write It!

Key Features of a Summary

- is a short retelling of a story or an article

- includes only key events or main ideas

- retold in the same sequence as the original

READING STREET ONLINE
GRAMMAR JAMMER
www.ReadingStreet.com

Narrative

Summary

A **summary** is a shortened retelling of a story or an article. A summary only provides the main points; minor details are not included. The student model on the next page is an example of a summary.

Writing Prompt Think about a story you know well. Now write a summary of the plot in the order in which the story's events occurred.

Writer's Checklist

Remember, you should . . .

✓ use your own words.

✓ include only the most important events and details.

✓ use the same order of events as the original story.

✓ use irregular verbs correctly.

✓ capitalize the titles of books, stories, and essays.

A Summary of <u>Cinderella</u>

Cinderella **was** a girl whose father remarried after her mother died. Soon after, her father died, and Cinderella had to live with her stepmother and stepsisters. They treated her terribly and forced her to do all the work.

Meanwhile, the king wanted his son to get married, so he decided to put on a ball and invite all the unmarried girls in the kingdom. Cinderella wanted to go but had nothing to wear except rags.

The night of the ball, Cinderella was visited by a fairy godmother who dressed her in a beautiful gown and **sent** her to the ball. But she had to leave by midnight. Cinderella **went** to the ball and danced with the prince, but she had to leave him when the clock **struck** midnight. She accidentally **left** her shoe behind.

The prince wanted to find her, so each woman in the kingdom was asked to try on the shoe to see if it fit. It didn't fit anyone. When Cinderella tried it on, though, it fit. The prince **found** his new princess!

Genre A **summary** includes only the most important information.

Writing Trait Sentence variety creates rhythm and style.

Irregular verbs are used correctly.

Conventions

Irregular Verbs

Remember Irregular verbs do not form the past and the past participle by adding -ed or -d to the present-tense form.

Common Core State Standards

Informational Text 2. Determine the main idea of a text and explain how it is supported by key details; summarize the text. **Also Informational Text 1., 5.**

Genre
Expository Text

- Expository text contains facts and information about a subject.

- Most expository text contains a main idea (what the topic is about) with details that support it.

- Expository text can also include comparisons or cause-and-effect relationships. This organization helps readers understand the ideas presented in the text.

- Read "A Very Grand Canyon." Look for elements that make this selection an expository text. What is the selection about? What details support this main idea?

A VERY GRAND CANYON

BY ANN GADZIKOWSKI

It is huge and deep and was formed millions of years ago. People who visit have trouble finding the words to describe it. Words like *impressive, incredible, fantastic,* and *awesome* are not enough. Just as surprising as its size are the various temperatures from top to bottom. What is it? It's the Grand Canyon!

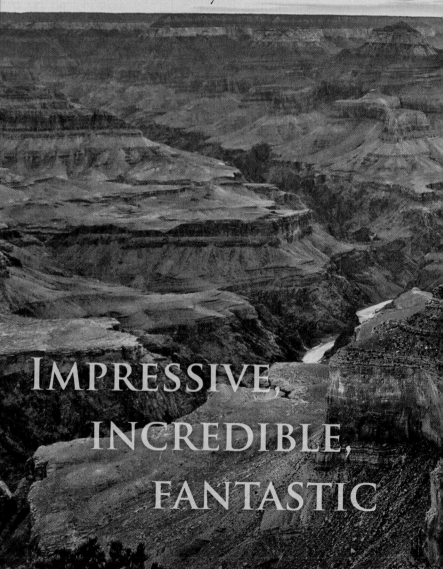

IMPRESSIVE, INCREDIBLE, FANTASTIC

454

The Grand Canyon, located in the state of Arizona, is 277 miles long as measured in river miles. That river is the Colorado River, which flows along the canyon floor. In some places, the canyon is more than a mile deep from rim to bottom and more than ten miles wide. Today most of the Grand Canyon and the area around it is called the Grand Canyon National Park.

Long ago, the Colorado River flowed over a flat plain. Like many other canyons, over the course of millions of years, the flow of water caused the dirt and rock to wear away. Little by little, the natural process of erosion formed the Grand Canyon.

Let's Think About...

Summarize what caused the Grand Canyon to form.
Expository Text

The Colorado River slices through the Grand Canyon.

Nearly five million people visit the Grand Canyon every year. Most visitors view the canyon from the top. Others make a trip all the way to the bottom. There are no roads, just trails. So unless you want to take a raft down the river, the only way to get to the bottom of the Grand Canyon is by hiking or riding a mule. Although it is a mile straight down from the rim to the bottom, it is a long, hard seven miles of winding trails to get there.

You may be surprised to know that the temperature at the top of the canyon is vastly different from the temperature below. For example, the weather at the South Rim is comfortable during the summer, but it can be chilly during the winter. The North Rim is also cool during the summer. However, it is closed during the winter months because it receives so much snow. In contrast, the temperature in the Inner Gorge, or the inside of the Grand Canyon, can be 20–25 degrees warmer than at the top. That is an extreme change in temperature.

So why is the top of the canyon so much cooler than the Inner Gorge? There are several reasons. First, the South Rim and North Rim are located around 7,500 feet above sea level. The Inner Gorge is located at 2,000 feet above sea level. The air is cooler at the higher elevation. Second, the Inner Gorge does not receive any shade from the hot sun. The rocks literally bake in the sun all day long. That is why the Inner Gorge is the hottest region of the Grand Canyon.

Let's Think About...

What does the author compare and contrast on this page?
Expository Text

Hikers need to be extra careful as they travel down to the bottom. Some experts suggest limiting hikes to the early morning or late afternoon. That is when the sun is at its lowest point in the sky. That way, hikers will not be moving in the sweltering heat. Also, hikers need to drink plenty of water so they don't become dehydrated. Dehydration can lead to heat stroke and exhaustion. Hikers also need to bring plenty of water with them. That's because there aren't many places to pick up water inside the Inner Gorge.

Some experts also warn hikers from traveling inside the Inner Gorge between the months of May and September. That's when the area is the hottest. For example, the average temperature inside the Inner Gorge between June and August is well over 100 degrees. During those months, inexperienced hikers should stick to the South and North Rims, where the temperature is much cooler.

The Grand Canyon is one of the most beautiful places in the world. Millions of people visit it every year. Would you like to hike down to the bottom?

Hikers need to be prepared when they hike the Inner Gorge.

Let's **Think** About...

Summarize the main idea of this text. Summarize what details support that idea. **Expository Text**

Let's **Think** About...

Reading Across Texts Both *Paul Bunyan* and "A Very Grand Canyon" include examples of extreme types of weather. Make a chart to compare and contrast these examples.

Writing Across Texts What if Paul Bunyan hiked the Grand Canyon today? Write a paragraph that describes his hiking adventures and the weather he might encounter.

Common Core State Standards

Language 4.b. Use common, grade-appropriate Greek and Latin affixes and roots as clues to the meaning of a word (e.g., *telegraph, photograph, autograph*). **Also Foundational Skills 4., 4.b., Speaking/Listening 4., 5.**

Let's Learn It!

READING STREET ONLINE
ONLINE STUDENT EDITION
www.ReadingStreet.com

Vocabulary

Affixes: Suffixes

Word Structure A suffix at the end of a word can help you figure out the word's meaning. The suffix *-al* means "relating to." For example, adding the suffix *-al* to the word *season* makes the word *seasonal. Financial* means "relating to finances."

Practice It! Look at page 438 in *Paul Bunyan* and find words that end with the suffix *-y*. Make a list of the words and write a definition for each.

Fluency

Appropriate Phrasing

Partner Reading Use punctuation cues to guide your voice as you read. Paying attention to punctuation marks will help you put words together as you read.

Practice It! With a partner, identify the punctuation marks on pages 440 and 441 of *Paul Bunyan.* Look for commas, periods, exclamation points, dashes, and quotation marks. Then take turns reading aloud.

Listening and Speaking

When you give a presentation to a group, look directly at your audience.

How-to

A how-to demonstration uses words and pictures to show how to make an item or do an activity. The purpose is to teach others how to perform a task.

Practice It! Design a demonstration explaining how to cook pancakes. Set out a list of ingredients and write up steps to follow. Consider showing pictures of equipment used when cooking pancakes. Present your how-to demonstration to the class.

Tips

Listening ...

- Listen attentively to the speaker.
- Ask relevant questions.

Speaking ...

- Express an opinion about the demonstration and support it with accurate information.
- Maintain eye contact with your audience as you speak.
- Use irregular verbs correctly.

Teamwork ...

- Restate any steps if necessary.
- If possible, follow the oral directions.

Common Core State Standards

Literature 5. Explain major differences between poems, drama, and prose, and refer to the structural elements of poems (e.g., verse, rhythm, meter) and drama (e.g., casts of characters, settings, descriptions, dialogue, stage directions) when writing or speaking about a text.
Also Literature 2., 10.

Poetry

- Poets often repeat words, phrases, or sentences. This repetition helps create the poem's **meter**.

- Lines of poetry can be grouped in **stanzas**. Lines in a stanza can break evenly or unevenly.

- The way a poem's lines break helps create meter as well.

- **Lyrical** poems **rhyme**. They have the form and quality of a song.

- Read "Autumn" and "Falling Snow." Look at how the poets have grouped the lines in their poems. Listen for sounds the poets repeat.

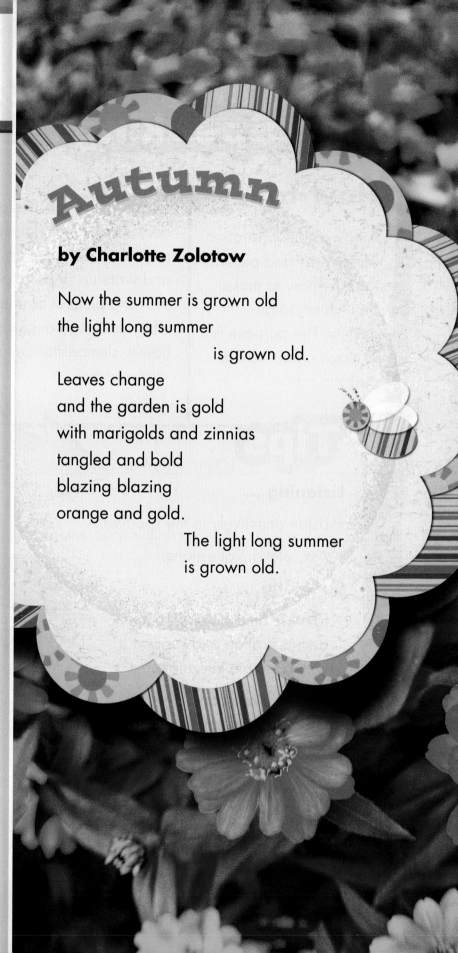

Autumn

by Charlotte Zolotow

Now the summer is grown old
the light long summer
                    is grown old.
Leaves change
and the garden is gold
with marigolds and zinnias
tangled and bold
blazing blazing
orange and gold.
                    The light long summer
                    is grown old.

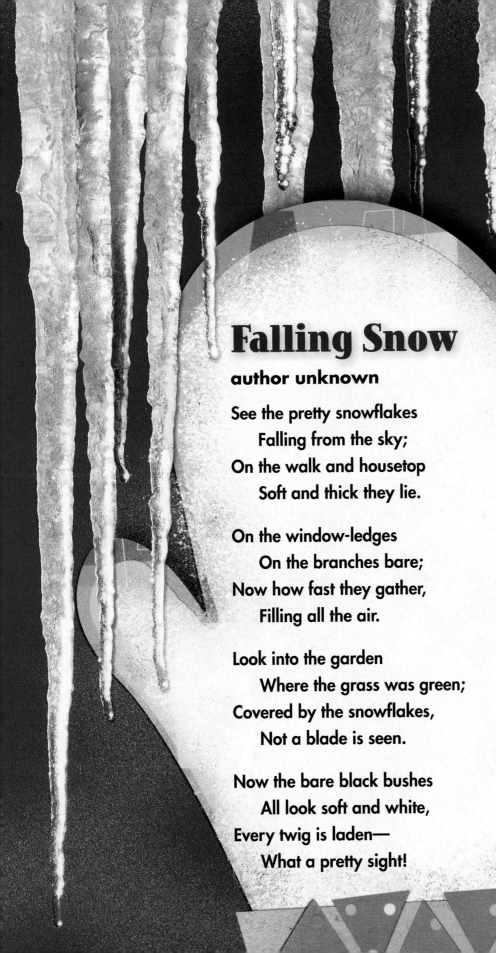

Falling Snow

author unknown

See the pretty snowflakes
    Falling from the sky;
On the walk and housetop
    Soft and thick they lie.

On the window-ledges
    On the branches bare;
Now how fast they gather,
    Filling all the air.

Look into the garden
    Where the grass was green;
Covered by the snowflakes,
    Not a blade is seen.

Now the bare black bushes
    All look soft and white,
Every twig is laden—
    What a pretty sight!

Let's **Think** About...

Reread "Autumn."
Can you hear
words and sounds
being repeated?
They create the
poem's **meter**.

Let's **Think** About...

The lines in this
poem all break in
the same place. Is
it easier to hear the
meter?

Let's **Think** About...

How do you know
this is a **lyrical**
poem?

461

Spring meadow
a child's bicycle
tied to a tree

by Yu Chang

462

Weather

by Eve Merriam

Dot a dot dot...dot a dot
Spotting the windowpane.
Spack a spack speck...flick a flack fleck
Freckling the windowpane.

A spatter a scatter...a wet cat a clatter
A splatter a rumble outside.
Umbrella umbrella umbrella umbrella
Bumbershoot barrel of rain.

Slosh a galosh . . .slosh a galosh
Slither and slather a glide
A puddle a jump a puddle a jump
A puddle a jump puddle splosh
A juddle a pump aluddle a dump a
Puddmuddle jump in and slide!

How to Use This Glossary

This glossary can help you understand and pronounce some of the words in this book. The entries in this glossary are in alphabetical order. There are guide words at the top of each page to show you the first and last words on the page. A pronunciation key is at the bottom of page 465. Remember, if you can't find the word you are looking for, ask for help or check a dictionary.

The entry word is in dark type. It shows how the word is spelled and how the word is divided into syllables.

The pronunciation is in parentheses. It also shows which syllables are stressed.

Part-of-speech labels show the function or functions of an entry word and any listed form of that word.

an·ces·tor (an′ses′tər), *NOUN.* person from whom you are descended, such as your great-grandparents: *Their ancestors had come to the United States in 1812.* ❏ PLURAL **an·ces·tors.**

Sometimes, irregular and other special forms will be shown to help you use the word correctly.

The definition and example sentence show you what the word means and how it is used.

464

Aa

ac·count (ə kount′), *NOUN.* statement telling in detail about an event or thing; explanation: *We gave them an account of everything that had happened.* ❏ PLURAL **ac·counts.**

ad·vice (ad vīs′), *NOUN.* opinion about what should be done; suggestion: *My advice is that you study more.*

a·maze (ə māz′), *VERB.* to surprise greatly; strike with sudden wonder; astound: *He was amazed at how different the strand of hair looked under a microscope.* ❏ VERB. **a·mazed, a·maz·ing.**

am·bi·tion (am bish′ən), *NOUN.* something for which you have a strong desire: *Her ambition is to be an oceanographer.*

an·nounce·ment (ə nouns′mənt), *NOUN.* a public or formal notice: *The announcement was published in the newspapers and posted on the bulletin board and the Internet.*

announcement

ap·pren·tice (ə pren′tis), **1.** *NOUN.* beginner; learner. **2.** *NOUN.* person learning a trade or art by working for a tradesman or artist for a certain length of time with little or no pay: *Joe was an apprentice before he became a licensed plumber.*

ar·gu·ment (är′gyə mənt), NOUN.
discussion by persons who disagree; dispute:
*She won the argument by producing facts to
prove her point.*

ar·range·ment (ə rānj′mənt), NOUN.
adjustment, settlement, or agreement: *No
arrangement of the dispute could possibly
please everybody.* ❑ PLURAL **ar·range·ments.**

as·sort·ment (ə sôrt′mənt), NOUN.
collection of various kinds: *These scarves
come in an assortment of colors.*

at·mo·sphere (at′mə sfir), **1.** NOUN. air
that surrounds the Earth: *Earth's atmosphere
is made up of gases.* **2.** NOUN. air in any given
place.

au·di·ence (ȯ′dē əns), NOUN. group of
people gathered to hear or see something:
The audience at the theater enjoyed the play.

au·di·tion (ȯ dish′ən), NOUN. act of hearing
to test the ability, quality, or performance of
a singer, actor, or other performer.

Bb

badg·er (baj′ər), **1.** NOUN. a hairy gray
mammal, larger than a weasel, that feeds at
night and digs holes in the ground to live
in. **2.** VERB. to keep on annoying or teasing;
bother or question persistently: *Please stop
badgering me about it!* ❑ VERB. **badg·ered,
badg·er·ing.**

bank¹ (bangk), **1.** NOUN. ground bordering
a river, lake, etc.; shore: *We fished from
the bank.* **2.** NOUN. a shallow place in a
body of water; shoal: *the fishing banks of
Newfoundland.*

bank² (bangk), **1.** NOUN. place of business
for keeping, lending, exchanging, and
issuing money. **2.** VERB. to keep or put
money in a bank: *I bank the money I earn
baby-sitting.*

bar·gain (bär′gən), NOUN. agreement to
trade or exchange; deal: *You can't back out
on our bargain.*

bawl (bȯl), VERB. to shout or cry out in a
noisy way: *a lost calf bawling for its mother.* ❑
VERB. **bawled, bawl·ing.**

be·wil·der (bi wil′dėr), VERB. to confuse
completely; puzzle: *bewildered by
the confusing instructions.* ❑ VERB.
be·wil·dered, be·wil·der·ing.

bi·ol·o·gist (bī ol′ə jist), NOUN. a scientist
who studies living things, including
their origins, structures, activities, and
distribution.

a	in *hat*	ėr	in *term*	ô	in *order*	ch	in *child*	ə	= a in *about*
ā	in *age*	i	in *it*	oi	in *oil*	ng	in *long*	ə	= e in *taken*
â	in *care*	ī	in *ice*	ou	in *out*	sh	in *she*	ə	= i in *pencil*
ä	in *far*	o	in *hot*	u	in *cup*	th	in *thin*	ə	= o in *lemon*
e	in *let*	ō	in *open*	ú	in *put*	ŦH	in *then*	ə	= u in *circus*
ē	in *equal*	ȯ	in *all*	ü	in *rule*	zh	in *measure*		

bluff • descendant

bluff¹ (bluf), *NOUN.* a high, steep slope or cliff.

bluff² (bluf), *VERB.* to fool or mislead, especially by pretending confidence: *She bluffed the robbers by convincing them that the police were on the way.* ❑ *VERB.* **bluffed, bluffing.**

bluff (Definition 1)

bril·liant (bril′yənt), *ADJECTIVE.* shining brightly; sparkling: *a brilliant diamond.*

bris·tle (bris′əl), **1.** *NOUN.* one of the short, stiff hairs of some animals or plants, often used to make brushes. **2.** *VERB.* to make fur stand up straight: *The kitten bristled when it saw the dog.* ❑ *VERB.* **bris·tled, bris·tling.**

Cc

chem·i·cal (kem′ə kəl), **1.** *NOUN.* of, about, or in chemistry. **2.** *ADJECTIVE.* working, operated, or used in chemistry: *a chemical fire extinguisher.*

cho·rus (kôr′əs), *NOUN.* anything spoken or sung all at the same time: *The children greeted the teacher with a chorus of "Good morning."*

club (klub), **1.** *NOUN.* a group of people joined together for some special purpose. **2.** *NOUN.* a wooden or metal stick with a long handle, used in some games to hit a ball: *golf clubs.* **3.** *VERB.* to hit with a club or something similar.

Con·sti·tu·tion (kon′stə tü′shən), *NOUN.* the written set of fundamental principles by which the United States is governed.

con·trac·tor (kon′trak tər), *NOUN.* someone who agrees to supply materials or to do work for a certain price: *My family hired a contractor to build our new house.*

cow·ard (kou′ərd), *NOUN.* person who lacks courage or is easily made afraid; person who runs from danger, trouble, etc.

coy·o·te (kī ō′tē *or* kī′ōt), *NOUN.* a small, wild, wolflike mammal living in many parts of North America that is known for its sad-sounding howling at night.

coyote

Dd

de·scend·ant (di sen′dənt), **1.** *NOUN.* person born of a certain family or group: *a descendant of the Pilgrims.* **2.** *NOUN.* offspring; child, grandchild, great-grandchild, and so on: *You are a direct descendant of your parents, grandparents, and earlier ancestors.*

de·struc·tion (di struk′shən), *NOUN.* great damage; ruin: *The storm left destruction behind it.*

dis·hon·est (dis on′ist), *ADJECTIVE.* not honest; tending to cheat or lie: *A person who lies or steals is dishonest.*

dis·tinc·tion (dis tingk′shən), *NOUN.* something that makes one especially worthy or well known; honor: *He has the distinction of being the best chess player in his school.*

dock (dok), *NOUN.* platform built on the shore or out from the shore; wharf; pier: *Ships load and unload beside a dock.*

draft (draft), **1.** *NOUN.* current of air: *I felt a cold draft by the window.* **2.** *NOUN.* an early, rough copy of writing: *She made two drafts of her book report before she handed in the final form.*

dude (düd), **1.** *NOUN.* in the western parts of the United States and Canada, a person raised in the city, especially an Easterner who vacations on a ranch. **2.** *NOUN.* a guy; fellow (slang).

Ee

em·ploy·ment (em ploi′mənt), *NOUN.* work; job: *She had no difficulty finding employment.*

es·say (es′ā), *NOUN.* a short written composition that makes a point about something: *I wrote an essay about why school should go all year.*

etch (ech), **1.** *VERB.* to engrave a drawing or design on a metal plate, glass, etc. **2.** *VERB.* to impress deeply: *Her face was etched in my memory.* ❏ *VERB.* **etched, etch·ing.**

etch (Definition 1)

ex·pect (ek spekt′), *VERB.* to think something will probably happen: *They expected the hurricane to change directions.* ❏ *VERB.* **ex·pect·ed, ex·pect·ing.**

Ff

fas·ci·nate (fas′n āt), *VERB.* to interest greatly; attract very strongly; charm: *She was fascinated by the designs and colors in African art.* ❏ *VERB.* **fas·ci·nat·ed, fas·ci·nat·ing.**

fa·vor (fā′vər), *NOUN.* act of kindness: *Will you please do me a favor?*

fea·ture (fē′chər), **1.** *NOUN.* part of the face: *Your eyes, nose, mouth, chin, and forehead are your features.* **2.** *NOUN.* thing that stands out and attracts attention: *Your plan has many good features.*

fore·cast (fôr′kast′), *NOUN.* statement of what is coming; prediction: *What is the weather forecast for today?* ❏ *PLURAL* **fore·casts.**

foul (foul), *VERB.* to make an unfair play against. ❏ *VERB.* **fouled, foul·ing.**

467

frost • infest

frost (frôst), **1.** *NOUN.* a freezing condition; temperature below the point at which water freezes: *Frost came early last winter.* **2.** *NOUN.* moisture frozen on or in a surface; feathery crystals of ice formed when water vapor in the air condenses at a temperature below freezing: *There was frost on the windows this morning.*

Gg

gla·cier (glā′shər), *NOUN.* a great mass of ice moving very slowly down a mountain, along a valley, or over a land area. Glaciers are formed from snow on high ground wherever winter snowfall exceeds summer melting for many years.

gleam (glēm), *VERB.* to flash or beam with light: *The car's headlights gleamed through the rain.* ❑ *VERB.* **gleamed, gleam·ing.**

grand (grand), *ADJECTIVE.* excellent; very good: *We had a grand time at the party last night.*

Hh

hard·ware (härd′wâr′), *NOUN.* articles made from metal: *Locks, hinges, nails, and screws are hardware.*

har·ness (här′nis), **1.** *NOUN.* the leather straps, bands, and other pieces used to hitch a horse or other animal to a carriage, wagon, plow, etc. **2.** *NOUN.* any similar arrangement of straps, bands, etc., especially a combination of straps by which a parachute is attached to someone.

harness (Definition 1)

home·land (hōm′land′), *NOUN.* country that is your home; your native land.

hoop (hu̇p or hüp), *NOUN.* ring; round, flat band: *a hoop for embroidery; a basketball hoop.*

howl·ing (hou′ling), *ADJECTIVE.* very great: *a howling success.*

hum·ble (hum′bəl), *ADJECTIVE.* not proud; modest: *to be humble in spite of success.*

Ii

im·pres·sive (im pres′iv), *ADJECTIVE.* able to have a strong effect on the mind or feelings; able to influence deeply.

in·fest (in fest′), *VERB.* to spread in great numbers throughout an area and cause harm: *Mosquitoes infest swamps.* ❑ *VERB.* **in·fest·ed, in·fest·ing.**

in·land (in′lənd), *ADVERB.* in or toward the interior: *He traveled inland from New York to Chicago.*

in·sult (in sult′), *VERB.* to say or do something very scornful, rude, or harsh: *She insulted me by calling me a liar.* ❏ *VERB.* **in·sult·ed, in·sult·ing.**

Jj

jer·sey (jėr′zē), *NOUN.* shirt made of soft, knitted cloth that is pulled over the head: *Members of the hockey team wear red jerseys.*

joint·ed (join′tid), *ADJECTIVE.* having a joint (the place at which two bones or other parts are joined together) or joints: *Lobsters have jointed legs.*

Ll

la·goon (lə gün′), *NOUN.* pond or small lake, especially one connected with a larger body of water.

land·slide (land′slīd′), *NOUN.* mass of earth or rock that slides down a steep slope.

landslide

las·so (la′sō), *VERB.* to catch with a long rope with a loop on one end. ❏ *VERB.* **las·soed, las·so·ing.**

long (lông), **1.** *ADJECTIVE.* measuring a great distance from end to end: *A year is a long time.* **2.** *VERB.* to wish very much; desire greatly: *long to see a good friend.* ❏ *VERB.* **longed, long·ing.**

lum·ber·jack (lum′bər jak′), *NOUN.* person whose work is cutting down trees and sending the logs to the sawmill; woodsman; logger. ❏ *PLURAL* **lum·ber·jacks.**

lumberjack

Mm

man·u·fac·ture (man′yə fak′chər), **1.** *VERB.* to make by hand or by machine, often by many people doing specific parts of the work. **2.** *NOUN.* process of making articles by hand or by machine, especially in large quantities. ❏ *NOUN.* **man·u·fac·tur·ing.** ❏ *VERB.* **man·u·fac·tured, man·u·fac·tur·ing.**

mar·vel (mär′vəl), *VERB.* to be filled with wonder; be astonished: *She marveled at the beautiful sunset.* ❏ *VERB.* **mar·veled, mar·vel·ing.**

mas·sive (mas′iv), *ADJECTIVE.* big and heavy; bulky: *a massive boulder.*

me·mor·i·al (me môr′ē əl), *ADJECTIVE.* helping people to remember some person, thing, or event: *a memorial service.*

migrate • quicksand

mi·grate (mī′grāt), *VERB.* to go from one region to another with the change in the seasons: *Most birds migrate to warmer climates in the winter.* ❏ *VERB.* **mi·grat·ed, mi·grat·ing.**

mood·y (mü′dē), *ADJECTIVE.* sunk in sadness; gloomy; sullen: *They sat in moody silence.*

Nn

nat·ur·al·ist (nach′ər ə list), *NOUN.* person who makes a study of living things.

Oo

of·fend (ə fend′), *VERB.* to hurt the feelings of someone; make angry; displease; pain: *My sad friend was offended by my laughter.* ❏ *VERB.* **of·fend·ed, of·fend·ing.**

Pp

par·lor (pär′lər), **1.** *NOUN.* formerly, a room for receiving or entertaining guests; sitting room. **2.** *NOUN.* room or set of rooms used for various business purposes; shop: *a beauty parlor, an ice cream parlor.*

patch (pach), **1.** *VERB.* make by joining patches or pieces together: *patch a quilt.* **2.** *VERB.* piece together; mend: *patch the worn-through elbow on a jacket.* ❏ *VERB.* **patched, patch·ing.**

pe·cul·iar (pi kyü′lyər), *ADJECTIVE.* strange; odd; unusual: *It was peculiar that the fish market had no fish last Friday.*

pol·i·tics (pol′ə tiks), *NOUN SINGULAR OR PLURAL.* the work of government; management of public business: *Our senior senator has been engaged in politics for many years.*

pos·i·tive (poz′ə tiv), *ADJECTIVE.* permitting no question; without doubt; sure: *We have positive evidence that the Earth moves around the sun.*

prair·ie (prâr′ē), **1.** *NOUN.* a large area of level or rolling land with grass but few or no trees, especially such an area making up much of central North America. **2.** *NOUN.* (regional) a wide, open space.

prairie (Definition 1)

praise (prāz), *VERB.* to say that a thing or person is good. ❏ *VERB.* **praised, prais·ing.**

pre·serve (pri zėrv′), *VERB.* to keep from harm or change; keep safe; protect: *Good nutrition helps preserve your health.* ❏ *VERB.* **pre·served, pre·serv·ing.**

pres·sure (presh′er) *NOUN.* the continued action of a weight or other force: *The small box was flattened by the pressure of the heavy book on it.*

pride·ful (prīd′fəl), *ADJECTIVE.* haughty; having too high an opinion of oneself; egotistical.

Qq

quick·sand (kwik′sand′), *NOUN.* a very deep, soft, wet sand that will not hold up a person's weight: *Quicksand may swallow up people and animals.*

Rr

re·call (ri kȯl′), *VERB.* to call back to mind; remember: *I can recall stories told to me when I was a small child.* ❑ *VERB.* **re·called, re·call·ing.**

re·hears·al (ri hėr′səl), *NOUN.* the act of rehearsing; process of preparing for a public performance: *The rehearsal for the show was a disaster, but opening night was great.*

re·quire·ment (ri kwīr′mənt), *NOUN.* a demand; thing demanded: *That school has a requirement that students wear uniforms.* ❑ *PLURAL* **re·quire·ments.**

re·sist·ance (ri zis′təns), *NOUN.* thing or act that resists; opposing force; opposition: *Air resistance makes a feather fall more slowly than a pin.*

re·spon·si·bil·i·ty (ri spon′sə bil′ə tē), *NOUN.* the act or fact of taking care of someone or something; obligation: *We agreed to share responsibility for planning the party.*

rick·et·y (rik′ə tē), *ADJECTIVE.* likely to fall or break down; shaky; weak: *a rickety old chair.*

rim (rim), *NOUN.* an edge, border, or margin on or around anything: *the rim of a wheel, the rim of a glass.*

riv·er·bed (riv′ər bed′), *NOUN.* channel in which a river flows or used to flow.

riverbed

roam (rōm), *VERB.* to go about with no special plan or aim; wander: *roam through the fields.* ❑ *VERB.* **roamed, roam·ing.**

round·up (round′up′), *NOUN.* act of driving or bringing cattle together from long distances.

ruf·fled (ruf′əld), **1.** *ADJECTIVE.* gathered into a ruffle to trim a garment. **2.** *VERB.* to make rough or uneven: *A breeze ruffled the lake. The chicken ruffled its feathers when the dog barked.* ❑ *VERB.* **ruf·fling.**

rum·ble (rum′bəl), *VERB.* to make a deep, heavy, continuous sound: *Thunder was rumbling in the distance.* ❑ *VERB.* **rum·bled, rum·bling.**

rush (rush), **1.** *NOUN.* a grasslike plant with a hollow stem that grows in wet soil or marshy places. **2.** *VERB.* to move with speed or force: *We rushed to the station.* ❑ *PLURAL OR VERB.* **rush·es.**

Ss

scales (skāls), *NOUN.* thin, flat, hard plates that form the outer covering of some fishes, snakes, and lizards: *The fish's scales glistened silver in the sunlight.*

scan (skan), *VERB.* to glance at; look over hastily. ❑ *VERB.* **scanned, scan·ning.**

scent (sent), *NOUN.* a smell, often pleasant: *The scent of roses filled the air.*

script (skript), *NOUN.* manuscript of a play, movie, or radio or TV show.

Glossary

sculpture • swat

sculp·ture (skulp′chər), **1.** *NOUN.* the art of making figures by carving, modeling, casting, etc. Sculpture includes the cutting of statues from blocks of marble, stone, or wood; casting in bronze; and modeling in clay or wax. **2.** *NOUN.* sculptured work; piece of such work. ❑ *PLURAL* **sculp·tures.**

sculpture (Definition 2)

se·lect (sə lekt′), *VERB.* to pick out; choose: *Select the book you want.* ❑ *VERB.* **se·lect·ed, se·lect·ing.**

shat·ter (shat′ər), *VERB.* to break into pieces suddenly: *A rock shattered the window.* ❑ *VERB.* **shat·tered, shat·ter·ing.**

shim·mer (shim′ər), *VERB.* to gleam or shine faintly: *Both the sea and the sand shimmered in the moonlight.* ❑ *VERB.* **shim·mered, shim·mer·ing.** ❑ *ADJECTIVE.* **shim·mer·y.**

shriek (shrēk), *VERB.* to make a loud, sharp, shrill sound: *People sometimes shriek because of terror, anger, pain, or amusement.* ❑ *VERB.* **shrieked, shriek·ing.**

slope (slōp), *NOUN.* any line, surface, land, etc., that goes up or down at an angle: *If you roll a ball up a slope, it will roll down again.*

snag (snag), *NOUN.* a hidden or unexpected obstacle: *Our plans hit a snag.*

sol·emn·ly (sol′əm lē), *ADVERB.* seriously; earnestly; with dignity: *The children solemnly listened to their great-grandfather.*

spe·cies (spē′shēz), *NOUN.* a set of related living things that all have certain characteristics: *Spearmint is a species of mint.*

speech·less (spēch′ləs), *ADJECTIVE.* not able to talk: *He was speechless with wonder.*

spur (spėr), *NOUN.* a metal point or pointed wheel worn on a rider's boot heel and used to urge a horse on. ❑ *PLURAL* **spurs.**

spur

stern (stėrn), *ADJECTIVE.* harshly firm; hard; strict: *a stern parent.*

still (stil), **1.** *ADJECTIVE.* staying in the same position or at rest; without motion; motionless: *to stand or lie still. The lake is still today.* **2.** *VERB.* to make or become calm or quiet: *The father stilled the crying baby.* ❑ *VERB.* **stilled, stil·ling.**

surge (sėrj), *NOUN.* a swelling motion; sweep or rush, especially of waves: *Our boat was upset by a surge.*

swat (swät), *VERB.* to hit sharply or violently: *swat a fly.* ❑ *VERB.* **swat·ted, swat·ting.**

sym·pa·thet·ic (sim′pə thet′ik), *ADJECTIVE.* having or showing kind feelings toward others; sympathizing: *She is a sympathetic friend.*

Tt

ter·ror (ter′ər), *NOUN.* great fear: *The dog has a terror of thunder.*

thaw (thȯ), *VERB.* to make or become less cold: *After shoveling snow, I thawed my hands and feet in front of the fire.*

tim·id (tim′id), *ADJECTIVE.* easily frightened; shy: *The timid child was afraid of the dark.*

tow·er·ing (tou′ər ing), **1.** *ADJECTIVE.* very high: *a towering mountain peak.* **2.** *ADJECTIVE.* very great: *Developing a polio vaccine was a towering achievement.*

trop·i·cal (trop′ə kəl), *ADJECTIVE.* of or like the regions near the equator, where the sun is the brightest and the temperature is the hottest: *tropical heat.*

Uu

un·be·liev·a·ble (un′bi lē′və bəl), *ADJECTIVE.* incredible; hard to think of as true or real: *an unbelievable reason for being late.*

un·com·fort·a·ble (un kum′fər tə bəl), *ADJECTIVE.* uneasy; not comfortable: *I felt uncomfortable when they stared at me.*

un·nat·ur·al (un nach′ər əl), *ADJECTIVE.* not natural; not normal.

un·tamed (un tāmd′), *ADJECTIVE.* wild; not domesticated: *Untamed animals are wary of people.*

Vv

vain (vān), *ADJECTIVE.* having too much pride in one's looks, ability, etc.: *a good-looking but vain person.*

vast (vast), *ADJECTIVE.* very great; immense: *Texas and Alaska cover vast territories.*

Ww

wage (wāj), *NOUN.* the money paid for work done, especially work paid for by the hour: *His wages average $450 a week.*
❏ *PLURAL* **wages.**

wharf (wôrf), *NOUN.* platform built on the shore or out from the shore beside which ships can load and unload.

wil·der·ness (wil′dər nəs), *NOUN.* a wild, uncultivated region with few or no people living in it.

wilderness

Yy

yearn (yėrn), *VERB.* to feel a longing or desire; desire earnestly: *I yearned for home.*
❏ *VERB.* **yearned, yearn·ing.**

Word List English/Spanish

Unit 1

Because of Winn-Dixie
grand / estupendo
memorial / conmemorativa
*peculiar / peculiar
positive / segura
prideful / orgullosa
recalls / recuerda
rehearsal / ensayo
*selecting / seleccionando

Lewis and Clark and Me
docks / muelles
migrating / emigrando
scan / escudriñar
scent / aroma
wharf / embarcadero
yearned / anhelaba

On the Banks of Plum Creek
badger / tejón
bank / orilla
bristled / de punta
jointed / articulados
patched / remendados
ruffled / erizados
rushes / juncos

The Horned Toad Prince
bargain / pacto
*favors / favores
lassoed / enlazó
*offended / ofendida
prairie / pradera
riverbed / lecho
shrieked / chilló

Letters Home from Yosemite
*glacier / glaciar
*impressive / impresionante
*naturalist / naturalista
*preserve / preservar
slopes / laderas
*species / especies
wilderness / zona silvestre

Unit 2

What Jo Did
fouled / hizo una falta
hoop / aro
jersey / camiseta
*marveled / se maravillaban
rim / canasta
speechless / estupefactos
swatted / le dio
unbelievable / increíble

Coyote School News
bawling / berreando
*coyote / coyote
dudes / dandis
roundup / rodeo
spurs / espuelas

* English/Spanish cognate: A **cognate** is a word that is similar in two languages and has the same meaning in both languages.

Acknowledgments

Text

Grateful acknowledgment is made to the following for copyrighted material:

Albert Whitman & Company

"The Man Who Named the Clouds" by Joan Holub and Julie Hannah. Text copyright © 2006 by Julie Hannah and Joan Holub. Illustrations copyright © 2006 by Paige Billin-Frye. First published in 2006. "My Weather Journal" From *The Man Who Named The Clouds* by Joan Holub and Julie Hannah. Text copyright © 2006 by Julie Hannah and Joan Holub. Illustrations copyright © 2006 by Paige Billin-Frye. First published in 2006. Rights granted by Albert Whitman & Company.

Alfred A. Knopf a div of Random House

"Paul Bunyan, the Mightiest Logger of Them All" from *American Tall Tales by Mary Pope Osborne,* copyright © 1991 by Mary Pope Osborne. Illustrations copyright © 1991 by Michael McCurdy. Used by permission of Alfred A. Knopf, an imprint of Random House Children's Books, a division of Random House, Inc.

Alfred A. Knopf a div of Random House & Harold Ober Associates

"We're All in the Telephone Book" from *The Collected Poems Of Langston Hughes* by Langston Hughes edited by Arnold Rampersand with David Roessel, Associate Editor, copyright © 1994 by The Estate of Langston Hughes. Used by permission of Alfred A. Knopf Inc., a division of Random House and also reprinted with the permission of Harold Ober Associates Incorporated.

Atheneum Books for Young Readers an imprint of Simon & Schuster Children's Publishing Division

Reprinted with the permission of Atheneum Books for Young Readers, an imprint of Simon & Schuster Children's Publishing Division from *Here's What You Do When You Can't Find Your Shoe* by Andrea Perry. Text copyright © 2003 Andrea Perry.

Candlewick Press

From *Because of Winn-Dixie* by Kate DiCamillo. Copyright © 2000 by Kate DiCamillo. Used by permission of the publisher, Candlewick Press, Somerville, MA.

Curtis Brown, Ltd

"City I Love", Copyright © 2002 by Lee Bennett Hopkins. First appeared in *Home to Me: Poems Across America*, published by Orchard Books. Reprinted by permission of Curtis Brown, Ltd.

David Higham Associates

"Homework" from *Egg Thoughts And Other Frances Songs* by Russell Hoban. Copyright © 1964, Copyright © 1972 by Russell Hoban. Reprinted by permission of David Higham Associates.

Dial Books for Young Readers a div of Penguin Group (USA) & Curtis Brown, Ltd

"His Hands" from *My Man Blue* by Nikki Grimes. Text copyright © 1999 by Nikki Grimes. Used by permission.

Dorling Kindersley Ltd a div of Penguin Books, Ltd

"Horse Heroes" by Kate Petty. Approximately 950 words (pp. 4-10) from *Dk Readers Level 4 Horse Heroes* by Kate Petty (Dorling Kindersely 1999). Text copyright © Kate Petty, 1999. Copyright © Dorling Kindersley, 1999. Reproduced by permission of Penguin Books Ltd.

Dorling Kindersly & Lelooska Foundation

"The Ant and the Bear" from *Spirit of the Cedar People: More Stories and Paintings of Chief Lelooska* edited by Christine Normandin. A DK Inc. Book, 1998. Estate of Don Lelooska Smith, Lelooska Foundation.

Dutton Children's Books a div of Penguin Group (USA)

"What Jo Did", from *Tall Tales: Six Amazing Basketball Dreams* Charles R. Smith, Jr., copyright © 2000 by Charles R. Smith, Jr. Used by permission of Dutton Children's Books, A Division of Penguin Young Readers Group, A Member of Penguin Group (USA) Inc., 345 Hudson Street, New York, NY 10014. All rights reserved.

Dutton Children's Books a div of Penguin Group (USA) & The Gersh Agency

From *Adelina's Whales* by Richard Sobol, copyright © 2003 by Richard Sobol. Originally published by Dutton Children's Books, a division of Penguin Putnam books for young Readers. Used by permission.

Goodman & Associates

"How Night Came from the Sea" by Mary-Joan Gerson. Illustrations by Carla Gelombe. Text copyright © 1994 by Mary-Joan Gerson. Illustrations copyright © 1994 by Carlas Golembe. Used by permission of Goodman Associates and by Carla Gelombe.

G.P. Putnam's Sons a div of Penguin Group (USA)

From *Eye Of The Storm* by Stephen Kramer, copyright © 1997 by Stephen Kramer, text. Used by permission of G.P. Putnam's Sons, A Division

HarperCollins Publishers

"On the Banks of Plum Creek" by Laura Ingalls Wilder. Text copyright © 1937, 1965 Little House Heritage Trust. Used by permission of HarperCollins Publishers.

Henry Holt & Company, LLC

Text and illustrations from *Lewis and Clark and Me, A Dog's Tale* by Laurie Myers, illustrated by Michael Dooling. Text copyright © 2002 by Laurie Myers, illustrations copyright © 2002 by Michael Dooling. Text and illustrations from *Coyote School News* by Joan Sandin. Copyright © 2003 by Joan Sandin. Used by permission of Henry Holt and Company, LLC.

Lisa Halvorsen

"Letters Home from Yosemite" by Lisa Halvorsen. Copyright © 2002. Used by permission of Lisa Halvorsen.

Margaret K. McElderry Books an imprint of Simon & Schuster Children's Publishing Div & Janet S. Wong

"Speak Up" from *Good Luck Gold And Other Poems* by Janet S. Wong. Copyright © 1994 Janet S. Wong. Reprinted by permission.

Marian Reiner Literary Agent

"Weather" from *Catch a Little Rhyme* by Eve Merriam. Copyright © 1966 by Eve Merriam. Copyright renewed 1994 by Dee Michel and Guy Michel. Used by permission of Marian Reiner.

Missouri Ruralist

Excerpt from an Interview given by Laura Ingalls Wilder to the Missouri Ruralist in 1918. From *Missouri Ruralist 1918*. Reprinted by permission.

Peachtree Publishers

"The Horned Toad Prince," Text © 2000 by Jackie Mims Hopkins. Illustrations © 2000 by Michael Austin. Reprinted by permission of Peachtree Publishers.

Philomel Books a div of Penguin Group (USA) & Curtis Brown, Ltd

"So You Want to be President?" by Judith St. George, illustrated by David Small. Copyright © 2000 by Judith St. George. Used by permission.

Saturday Evening Post Society

"Midwest Town" by Ruth De Long Peterson. Reprinted from *The Saturday Evening Post* magazine, © 1954. Saturday Evening Post Society.

Scott Treimel

"Autumn" by Charlotte Zolotow from *River Winding*. Copyright © 1970 by Charlotte Zolotow. Used by permission of Scott Treimel NY.

Yu Chang

'From *Spring Meadow* by Yu Chang. Reprinted by permission of Yu Chang.

Note: Every effort has been made to locate the copyright owner of material reproduced on this component. Omissions brought to our attention will be corrected in subsequent editions.

Cover: (T, B) Shutterstock, (C) Image Source

Illustrations

EI2–EI13 Bill McGuire; EI16–EI25 Kenny Kiernan; 86–98 Susan Swan; 134 Amanda Hall; 165–168 Patrick Corrigan; 224 Sachiko Yoshikawa; 234–246 Jimmy Holder; 252 Shelly Hehenberger; 307, 352 Peter Bollinger; 310–312 Lee White; 436–448 Harvey Chan; W2–W15 Leslie Harrington

Acknowledgments

Photographs

Every effort has been made to secure permission and provide appropriate credit for photographic material. The publisher deeply regrets any omission and pledges to correct errors called to its attention in subsequent editions.

Unless otherwise acknowledged, all photographs are the property of Pearson Education, Inc.

Photo locators denoted as follows: Top (T), Center (C), Bottom (B), Left (L), Right (R), Background (Bkgd)

CVR (Wall) Image Source; **CVR** (Pavement) Shutterstock; **CVR** (Palm trees) Shutterstock; **18** (B) Raul Touzon/Getty Images; **20** (B) Brand X Pictures/Punchstock Royalty Free; **20** (B) Food Pix/Jupiter Images; **20** (CC) Monkey Business/ Fotolia; **24** (C) GoGo Images/Alamy; **24** (B) Flint/Corbis/Jupiter Royalty Free; **24** (T) Purestock/Photolibrary Royalty Free; **26** Everett Collection, Inc. **27** (CL) Getty Images; **27** (R) 20th Century Fox/Suzanne Tenner/Art Resource; **28** (C) Everett Collection; **29** (BR) Everett Collection; **30** (BR) Everett Collection; **31** (TR) Getty Images; **32** (CR) Getty Images; **34** (B) Twentieth Century Fox Film Corp/ Photofest; **35** (T) Dave King/DK Images; **36** (TL) 20th Century Fox/Suzanne Tenner/Art Resource; **37** (B) Everett Collection; **42** (B) Everett Collection; **43** (TR), (TL) Everett Collection; **46** (BC) Nick Hanna/Alamy; **46** (B) Corbis; **47** Old Visuals Everett Collection/ Jupiter Royalty Free; **50** (T) R Rusak/ Shutterstock; **50** (C) Jim Zuckerman/Corbis/ Jupiter Royalty Free; **50** (B) Nick Clements/ Getty Images; **54** (T) Getty Images; **56** (B) Getty Images; **72** (C) Mark M. Lawrence/Corbis; **73** (TL) NASA; **74** (C) JSC/NASA; **74** (T) Mark M. Lawrence/Corbis; **78** (B) Jan Butchofsky-Houser/Corbis; **78** (BL) Michael DeYoung/ Corbis; **79** (TR) Randy Faris/Corbis; **81** (TR) Bettmann/Corbis; **82** (B) Bilderbuch/Alamy; **82** (C) Eyecandy Images/Photos to Go; **82** (T) Joe McDonald/Corbis; **101** (B) AP Images; **101** (T) Granger Collection; **105** (C) Bettmann/ Corbis; **107** (TL) Laura Ingalls Wilder Memorial Society; **107** (CC), (CR) Granger Collection; **109** (TR) Age fotostock/Superstock; **110** (B) ImageState/Alamy; **111** (CC) Russ Bishop/ Alamy; **114** (T) Horizon International Images Limited/Alamy; **114** (B) INTERFOTO Pressebildagentur/Alamy; **114** (C) Robert Destefano/Alamy; **136** (B) Douglas Peebles/ Corbis; **139** (BC) Douglas Peebles/Corbis; **139** (CR) Harvey Lloyd/Getty Images; **141** Gary Crabbe/Alamy; **142** (T) Images&Stories/Alamy; **142** (C) Peter Barritt/Alamy; **142** (B) Randy Faris/Jupiter Royalty Free; **143** (TL), (TR) Corbis; **143** (B) Getty Images; **144** (TR) Getty Images/Punchstock; **144** (C) Scott Bufkin/ Fotolia; **144** (CR), (TL) Getty Images; **145** (CR) Getty Images; **146** (BR) Corbis; **146** (Background) Getty Images; **147** (BC) Corel/Fotosearch Com, LLC; **147** (CR) Getty Images; **147** (TR) Corbis; **148** (T) (B) Corel; **149** (TR) Corbis; **149** (BR) Corel; **150** (C) Harvey Lloyd/Getty Images; **151**(CR) Corbis; **151** (BR) Corel/Fotosearch Com, LLC; **151** (TC) Corel; **152** (TL) donyanedomam/Fotolia; **152** (CR) Don Mason/ Corbis; **153** (C) (BL) Getty Images; **154** (C) Corbis; **155** (CR) Phil Schermeister/Corbis; **155** (TC) Corel; **155** (TR) Getty; **160** (C) Dr. Edward J. Allen; **161** (CL) Western History Collections/Western History Collections, University of Oklahoma Library; **161** (TL), **162** (CL) Sascha Burkard/Shutterstock; **162** (T) Danielle Marks; **163** (B) Rob McCorkle/Texas Parks & Wildlife; **165** (T) James Hager/Robert Harding World Imagery/Getty Images; **170** (C) Paul King/Getty Images; **172** (TR) Getty; **172** (BR) Image Source; **173** (Background) Jeremy Horner/Corbis; **175** (TR) Getty; **176** (B) Getty; **176** (T) (C) Jupiter Royalty Free; **177** (T) Corbis; **192** (CR) Blend Images/Superstock; **193** (BR) Blend Images/Superstock; **173** (TR) Jupiter; **195** (T) Jeff Greenberg/Alamy; **196** (B) Getty; **196** (BL) Jupiter; **197** (BR) Corbis/ Jupiter; **199** (T) Yann Arthus-Bertrand/Corbis; **200** (B) Bill Miles/Corbis; **200** (C) Grady Harrison/Alamy; **200** (T) Paul Edmonton/ Getty; **201** (R) Macduff Everton/Corbis; **227** (BR) Nicholas Prior/Getty Images; **228** (Background) Blend Images/Jupiter; **228** (TC) Brand X Pictures/Punchstock; **231** (TR) Gabriel Bouys/AFP/Getty Images; **231** (BR) Jamie & Judy Wild/Danita Delimont; **232** (C) Richard Melloul/Sygma/Corbis; **232** (T) Getty; **232** (B) Jupiter; **233** (TR) Bettmann/Corbis; **256** (Background) Isabelle Vayron/Sygma/Corbis; **257** (B) Corbis/Jupiter; **257** (CC) Corbis; **259** (TR) Getty; **260** (B) David Stoecklein/ Corbis; **260** (C) Paul A. Souders/Corbis; **260** (T) Reuters/Corbis; **261** (BR) ©Tan Kian Khoon/ Fotolia, LLC; **261** (T) Image Source; **261** (T) Jupiter; **262** Bob Langrish/Animals Animals/ Earth Scenes; **264** (BR) Private Collection, Peter Newark American Pictures/Bridgeman Art Library; **264** (BC) Private Collection, Peter Newark American Pictures/Bridgeman Art Library; **265** (BR) Private Collection, Peter

Antonyms

An antonym is a word that has the opposite meaning
of another word. *Day* is an antonym for *night*.

Day

Night

Antonym = Opposite

Strategy for Antonyms

1. Identify the word for which you want to
   find an antonym.
2. Think of other words or phrases that have
   the opposite meaning.
3. Use a thesaurus to help you find
   antonyms.
4. Use a dictionary to check the antonyms'
   meanings so that you use the word that
   best communicates your ideas.

Synonyms

A synonym is a word that has almost the same meaning as another word. *Hot* is a synonym for *scorching*.

Hot

Scorching

Synonym = Same

Strategy for Synonyms

1. Identify the word for which you want to find a synonym.
2. Think of other words or phrases that have the same, or almost the same, meaning.
3. Use a thesaurus to help you find more synonyms, and make a list.
4. Use a dictionary to find the word that best communicates your ideas.

Base Words

A base word is a word that can't be broken into smaller words. *Friend* is the base word in *friendly* and *friendship*.

Earth

Unearthly

Earth is the base word.

Strategy for Base Words

1. Look for a base word in the unknown word.
2. Determine the meaning of the base word.
3. Guess the meaning of the unfamiliar word. Does it make sense in the sentence?
4. Check the meaning in a dictionary.

Prefixes

A prefix is a word part added to the beginning of a base word to form a new word.

Wrap

Unwrap

Common Prefixes and Their Meanings

un–	not
re–	again, back
in–	not
dis–	not, opposite of
pre–	before

Strategy for Prefixes

1. Look at the unknown word and identify the prefix.
2. What does the base word mean? If you're not sure, check a dictionary.
3. Use what you know about the base word and the prefix to figure out the meaning of the unknown word.
4. Use a dictionary to check your guess.

Suffixes

A suffix is a word part added to the end of a base word to form a new word.

Shoeless

Shoe

Common Suffixes and Their Meanings

-ly	characteristic of
-tion	act, process
-able	can be done
-ment	action or process
-less	without

Strategy for Suffixes

1. Look at the unknown word and identify the suffix.
2. What does the base word mean? If you're not sure, check a dictionary.
3. Use what you know about the base word and the suffix to figure out the meaning of the unknown word.
4. Use a dictionary to check your guess.

Context Clues

Context clues are the words and sentences found around an unknown word that can help you understand the word's meaning. Use context clues to figure out what a fireworm is.

I can't decide whether to write my underwater-creature report on a starfish, dolphin, fireworm, or octopus.

Strategy for Context Clues

1. Look for clues in the words and phrases around the unknown word.
2. Take a guess at the word's meaning. Does it make sense in the sentence?
3. Use a dictionary to check your guess.

Related Words

Related words all have the same base word.

Cycle

Bicycle

Cyclist

Strategy for Related Words

1. Find the base word in your unknown word.
2. Identify the meaning of the base word.
3. Guess the meaning of the unfamiliar word. Does it make sense in the sentence?
4. Use a dictionary to check your guess.

Word Origins: Roots

Many English words contain Greek and Latin roots.

Telephone

Dentures

Tractor

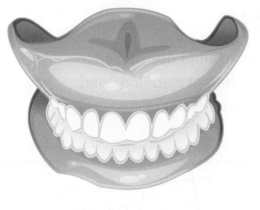

Latin Roots

dent	tooth
dict	to say; to speak
scrib	to write
sub	under; below
tract	to pull
vis	to see

Greek Roots

auto	self
bio	life
micro	very small
ology	the study of
phon	sound; voice
scope	see
tele	far

Strategy for Roots

1. Use what you know about Greek and Latin roots to guess the meaning of the unknown word.
2. Does your guess make sense in the sentence?
3. Use a dictionary to check your guess.

Multiple-Meaning Words

Multiple-meaning words are words that have different meanings depending on how they are used. Homonyms, homographs, and homophones are all multiple-meaning words.

Homographs

Homographs are words that are spelled the same but have different meanings and sometimes different pronunciations.

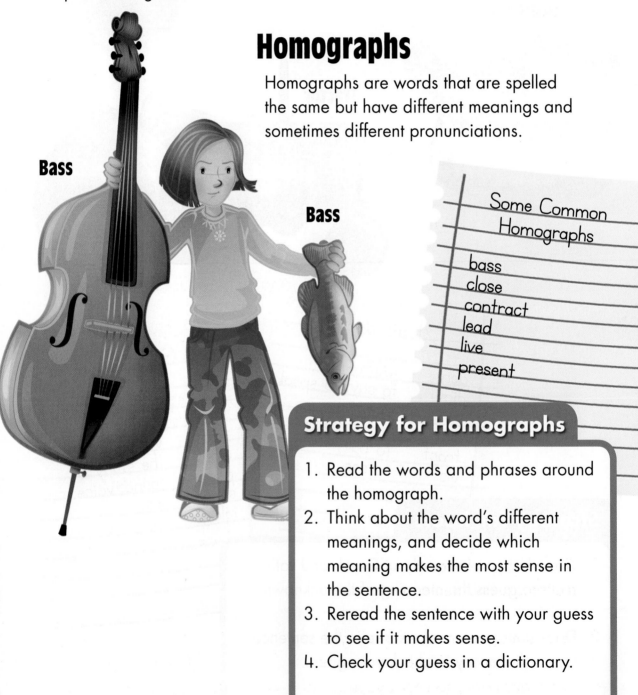

Bass

Bass

Some Common Homographs

bass
close
contract
lead
live
present

Strategy for Homographs

1. Read the words and phrases around the homograph.
2. Think about the word's different meanings, and decide which meaning makes the most sense in the sentence.
3. Reread the sentence with your guess to see if it makes sense.
4. Check your guess in a dictionary.

Homonyms

Homonyms are words that are pronounced the same and have the same spelling, but their meanings are different.

Squash

Squash

Some Common Homonyms

pen
duck
ear
bank
bark

Strategy for Homonyms

1. Read the words and phrases near the homonym.
2. Think about the word's different meanings, and decide which one makes the most sense.
3. Reread the sentence with your guess to see if it makes sense.
4. Use a dictionary to check your guess.

Homophones

Homophones are words that are pronounced the same way but have different spellings and different meanings.

Ball

Bawl

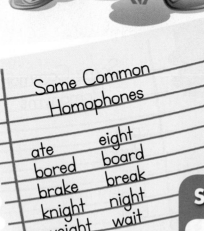

Some Common Homophones

ate	eight
bored	board
brake	break
knight	night
weight	wait

Strategy for Homophones

1. Think about the different spellings and meanings of the homophones.
2. Check a dictionary for definitions of the words.
3. Use the word that best fits your writing.

This chart can help you remember the differences between homonyms, homographs, and homophones.

Understanding Homographs, Homonyms, and Homophones

	Pronunciation	Spelling	Meaning
Homographs	may be the same or different	same	different
Homonyms	same	same	different
Homophones	same	different	different

Homograph

present

present

bark

Homonym

bark

Homophone

aisle

isle

Dictionary

A dictionary is a reference book that lists words alphabetically. It can be used to look up definitions, parts of speech, spelling, and other forms of words.

punc•tu•al ❶ (pungk′ chü əl), ❷ *ADJECTIVE.* ❸ prompt; exactly on time: ❹ *He is always punctual.* ❺ ✳ *ADVERB* **punc′tu•al•ly.**

❶ Pronunciation

❷ Part of speech

❸ Definitions

❹ Example sentence

❺ Other form of the word and its part of speech

Strategy for Dictionary

1. Identify the unknown word.
2. Look up the word in a dictionary. Entries are listed alphabetically.
3. Find the part of the entry that has the information you are looking for.
4. Use the diagram above as a guide to help you locate the information you want.

Thesaurus

A thesaurus is a book of synonyms. Sometimes it will also contain antonyms. Look through the synonyms to find one with the best meaning by using a dictionary.

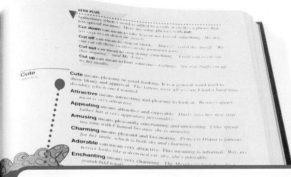

cute

adjective

attractive, appealing, amusing, charming, adorable, enchanting.

ANTONYMS: ugly, dull, unappealing

Strategy for Thesaurus

1. Look up the word in a thesaurus. Entries are listed alphabetically.
2. Locate the synonyms for your word.
3. Find the word with the exact meaning you want.